# Making The Business Case

**James A. Cannon** specialises in organisation development and has consulted with organisations in the United Kingdom, North America, Europe and Asia. He runs an extensive range of training courses for the Chartered Institute of Personnel and Development (CIPD) as well as other organisations. His career has included director appointments in Charterhouse, Black & Decker and Thorn EMI in organisation development, human resources, information technology and general management, including founding Solutions Electronic Services. In 1989 he started his own consultancy as well as co-founding Cavendish Partners, now merged with Right Coutts, a firm specialising in career counselling and coaching.

e-mail: cannassoc@msn.com

www.cannassoc.com

The Chartered Institute of Personnel and Development is the leading publisher of books and reports for personnel and training professionals, students and all those concerned with the effective management and development of people at work. For details of all our titles, please contact the publishing department:

*tel*: 020 8612 6204

*e-mail* publish@cipd.co.uk

The catalogue of all CIPD titles can be viewed on the CIPD website:

www.cipd.co.uk/bookstore

# Making The Business Case

## How to create, write and implement a successful business plan

James A. Cannon

Chartered Institute of Personnel and Development

Published by the Chartered Institute of Personnel and Development
151 The Broadway, London, SW19 1JQ

First published 2006

Typeset by Curran Publishing Services, Norwich, Norfolk

Printed in Great Britain by
The Cromwell Press, Trowbridge, Wiltshire

British Library Cataloguing in Publication data

A catalogue of this publication is available from the British Library

ISBN 1-8439-8135-1

Chartered Institute of Personnel and Development, 151 The Broadway, London, SW19 1JQ

Tel: 020 8612 6200

E-mail: cipd@cipd.co.uk   Website: www.cipd.co.uk

Incorporated by Royal Charter. Registered Charity No. 1079797

*To Robert and Clare*

# Contents

# CONTENTS

# CONTENTS

# CONTENTS

# Figures

# Tables

# TABLES

# Acknowledgements

Many people have contributed, often unwittingly, to the development of the ideas in this book. My thanks are due to Rita McGee and Roger Niven for many helpful comments on the manuscript, to Ron Howard with whom I have collaborated on human resource planning, and to Richard Coates, Neil Johnston and Tim Harding for helpful insights. I am indebted particularly to students on the CIPD courses Developing the Strategic Manager and Human Resource Planning for their challenging questions, which have sharpened my own thinking. I have had the privilege of working with many clients and organisations over the years and I am grateful to them for the opportunity of learning as well as contributing. Many of the examples in the book come from these experiences. I am grateful to Clare Cannon ACA for checking the financials and finally, my thanks are due to my wife, Sue for her careful reading of the manuscript. However, what deficiencies there may be are all mine.

James A. Cannon
Hedgerley, June 2005

# Preface

*'Boss, why don't we provide coaching to our top team?'*

*'Sounds a good idea; what is the business case?'*

*'Ugh ...'*

Every day in every organisation in the world people are making decisions – about how they spend their time, their money and their effort. How they make those decisions and the basis for their judgements determines whether the enterprise survives or fails in whatever sector of the economy they happen to be. At the heart of a sound decision in any organisation is a business case: how the organisation should decide where to place its resources and effort. A business case examines the options in any decision, marshals evidence to show why a course of action is preferable, and identifies the resources required and the benefits that might accrue.

The human resources (HR) function, like any other activity in the enterprise, is continually examining options, such as whether to invest in training or recruit people who are already trained, whether to put money into base pay or more into other benefits, or whether to invest or not in an employment assistance programme. Whereas when manufacturing is evaluating alternative options in purchasing machinery the outcomes and benefits are more easily measured, evaluating intangibles in HR is more difficult. Nevertheless HR still needs to attempt the exercise and use the methods that are available, if approval is to be won.

A business case by itself, however, does not translate an idea into action. A business plan draws together the elements into a coherent whole. It includes a number of ingredients such as an analysis of the situation, identification of future goals, possible strategies to achieve the goals, resources required to accomplish the plan, consideration of the sensitivity of the outcome to different factors that might intervene and what is required to deliver implementation with demonstrable benefits to the enterprise.

When the enterprise as a whole sets out to develop a business plan all too often HR is left to the end to pick up the pieces of plans that failed to fully take account of the human dimension. Contributing at the outset to the formation of the enterprise business plan should be the goal of all HR professionals. In many organisations the role and function of HR has changed in recent years from being the 'guardian of the rules' towards being the business partner facilitating, advising and supporting line managers running their part of the firm. In this new world HR has no divine right to rule but has to market itself internally if it is to continue to justify its position at the top table.

A key role for HR lies in facilitating the planning process. Skilled at drawing people together and building consensus, a facilitator steers the process to achieve outcomes with maximum commitment. In addition, when HR plays the role of facilitator it gives representatives of the function access to the business meetings where strategy is determined, allowing an understanding of the issues. HR plans can then be better informed and more closely aligned with the business realities.

The revised accounting standards now incorporate the requirement for an operational and financial review. While a comprehensive list of HR information to be included has still to emerge at the time of writing, directors and especially HR professionals will need to fully understand what human resource information is relevant to assessing the future performance of their business. They need to include information if, in their view, it will assist investors to assess the potential of the company. Information must include a statement of the strategies and descriptions of the company's resources and its principal risks. What auditable information will be needed to satisfy these requirements is still an open question, but it is likely that investors and analysts will surely take more note where organisations can show how their human resource policies improve the productive capacity of the organisation.

This book then, sets out to show how HR can present the options in the form of a business case, develop a sound business plan for the function and contribute effectively to the business plan for the organisation. In this way the effectiveness of decision-making is enhanced and HR can demonstrate that it truly is a business partner.

Chapter 1 sets out the components of a business plan, identifies what is meant by a business case and identifies the ingredients in an HR strategy. I consider the factors driving the world economy and organisational strategy as well as looking at turning a business case into a business plan. The chapter finishes with introducing the case of Persco which shows an example of how a business case is developed.

Chapter 2 describes how to facilitate the process of business planning and explores different approaches to get commitment to the resulting plan.

Chapter 3 identifies the information required – both internal and external – to establish a business case. Types of data, how to gather it and some of the pitfalls faced when gathering costs and benefits of alternative courses of action are the areas of focus. Our starting point is a situation analysis and we consider what is required to prepare a business case. How we find a defensible position for our proposed action is covered as well as the second stage of the Persco case.

Chapter 4 gets to grips with the numbers and examines how to prepare the basic financial tables.

Chapter 5 shows a template for writing a business plan together with points to remember when presenting a plan.

Chapter 6 examines how to make decisions, how to deal with problem areas and how to avoid possible traps, both in individual and group decision-making.

Finally, in Chapter 7 we conclude with a chapter on how to work the plan to achieve effective implementation, approaches to recover the situation if things go wrong and two case studies highlighting some of the factors that help or hinder achieving a successful outcome.

The Appendix lists a range of tools and techniques for analysing and presenting information in a form that is persuasive and facilitates arguing the business case. Where these tools are mentioned in the text, they are shown in ***bold italics*** eg ***SWOT***.

All chapter notes are collected at the end of the book under the header 'Notes'.

# 1

# Business planning – developing a plan for the future

*If you don't take charge of your destiny, someone else will.*

*Jack Welch, General Electric*

## WHY YOU NEED TO READ THIS BOOK

I am writing these words, sitting in the guesthouse of an oil refinery in the Gulf, after a senior manager has told me a story:

> *so he just said to me that he needed to spend thousands of dollars on this new 'coaching' programme. There was no justification, no expected return – in fact no business case at all! He is living in cloud cuckoo land! How can I trust a manager like that? I don't see him as a long-term prospect.*

The harsh facts of life indicate that this is not a peculiar requirement of oil refineries. Whether you work in the public, private or voluntary sectors in the United Kingdom or anywhere else, and you have any aspirations to command the future fortunes of your organisation, knowing how to devise and present a business case is essential for survival. Turning that case into a practical plan may then make the difference between survival and prosperity.

'But,' you protest, 'Business plans are done by accountants and you need to be an ACA to write one.' I beg to differ, and in this book I hope to show you how it can be done. Whether you are in HR, marketing or any other function, mastering the basics of business planning is an essential skill for organisational survival and one without which your future career is limited.

Join me on the journey – and it might even be fun!

# INTRODUCTION

The continuing growth in individual, corporate and national prosperity comes primarily from our ability year by year to do more with less. Business planning, whether done systematically as we shall describe in this book, or more informally, lies at the heart of deciding how to allocate scarce time and effort to achieve our goals in the most efficient manner.

In this first chapter, I set out to explore the concept of a business case, the ingredients in a business plan, show some examples and describe how a business case can be turned into a practical plan.

After some definitions we start by identifying the roots of a business plan, namely the vision, mission and strategy of the business. The first step in developing a business case is to identify the issues faced by the organisation. These issues might arise as a result of the organisation lagging behind competitors, or where new technologies could be exploited. The formulation of a strategy to deal with the issues identified and the process of identifying and articulating different choices of approach is discussed here. In addition, I examine the first stage of a case study, Persco, which we shall follow through the book. Persco is not a real organisation, but the case study is what journalists might call a 'composite' – it is based on the experiences of real organisations, in both public and private sector that I have been involved with over the years, both as an employee and a consultant. It is a case of an HR department that has to change its ways of working to save money and improve effectiveness.

# TOOLS FOR ANALYSIS

Before architects can design a new building they need to measure the size and shape of the land on which it is to stand, the availability and position of the services like water, sewage, gas and electricity, whether the soil is likely to subside, whether there is a possibility of flooding and so on. To make their task easier they will use a variety of tools to help them do this, ranging from a simple tape measure to sophisticated computer modelling software. Likewise, before we can start to plan a business case we need to analyse the situation that our organisation is in and the environment in which it operates.

Fortunately there are a variety of tools and models that can help us. In the Appendix I have described a selection of some of the more useful tools for business planning. Where they are referenced in the text they are shown in italics, eg *SWOT*. If you are unfamiliar with one of these tools when you come across it in the text, do take the time to read the note in the Appendix and think about how the tool could be used in your organisation.

The tools in the Appendix are:

- Balanced scorecard
- Benchmarking
- Bottlenecking
- Contingency diagram
- Core competencies
- Cost analysis tools
- Cost–benefit analysis
- Critical incident
- Critical path analysis
- Critical success factors
- Customer–supplier relationships
- Decision tree
- Fishbone analysis
- Gantt/milestone chart
- Human resource planning template
- Interest mapping
- Lifetime cost analysis
- Methods of forecasting
    - correlation and regression
    - time series and trends analysis
    - scenario planning and forecasting tools
    - validity and reliability of forecasts and estimates
    - dealing with uncertainty
- Measuring change
- Milestone chart
- Modelling
- 'Niciling'
- Problem-solving process
- Risk analysis
- Root cause analysis

- Sensitivity analysis
- Stakeholder analysis
  - force field analysis
- SWOT analysis
- Timelines
- Value chain analysis

## WHAT IS A BUSINESS CASE?

A business case is the presentation of an argument for a considered course of action in terms of its impact on the success of the enterprise. In the private sector this will almost invariably involve ascertaining the implications for costs and/or revenues; in the public sector it will probably be costs and/or service levels. The argument is usually designed to show why a particular course of action is better than the present or other alternatives. There may, however, be other impacts that the business case should consider.

> A charity presented a business case to its funders showing the costs of delivering better services to clients and the benefits in terms of client satisfaction.

> A local authority presented to a government department the implications of a proposed policy to change the traffic system. The effect was to increase the acceptance by other authorities of the need to undertake other changes in its traffic management.

So, to return to the dialogue in the Preface (pxix), the HR manager might have replied to the challenge from the MD about the value of coaching by saying:

*The business case for coaching rests on several possible tangible benefits and a number of intangibles.*

*Coaching aims to improve performance by helping people think through problems and issues for themselves. The result should be* better quality work.

*I can present research evidence that shows that coaching helps people to do their jobs better, increases their satisfaction and so contributes to* retention. *If we retain one person as a result of this initiative, the saving in the executive search fee would cover the cost of coaching.*

*We have agreed as a company to spend about 2 per cent of payroll cost on development for each broad group of staff. We made this decision by comparison to best practice in our industry. Amongst senior managers, this proposal to spend about £6,000 per person on five managers represents about 1 per cent of the pay bill of the group. It is within our existing* policy and budget.

*Given our commitment to development, the* alternatives *for the same investment, might be a management course or some other general training initiative. However, this initiative is targeted at each person's needs and so is likely to be more effective. Indeed, where in the past we have used coaching, feedback has invariably shown this to be so. This result has been especially true in cases where changed behaviour is required, or the need to think through how to apply knowledge and experience already gained to novel situations.*

*Coaching, because it can be fitted in round tight schedules and is done in short sessions, is more time efficient for busy executives.* Time saved *expressed in payroll costs compared with other development options we estimate at about £1,000 per person. The* opportunity cost *though of that time spent is much greater. If that time could be translated into one extra customer, the whole investment is justified.*

Critical incident analysis *in other organisations has shown three possible benefit areas:*

- *difficult staff situations where there is conflict and which rely on the seniors' influencing and interpersonal skills*

- *being accessible (as opposed to being away on, say, a residential management course) to deal with crisis situations as they arise*

- *greater confidence in their leadership to deal with novel and challenging problems.*

*Our* competitors *are offering this opportunity to a wider group than we are, and recent recruits have talked positively about it.*

*In our last* benchmarking *exercise of ourselves against best in class, we identified 60 per cent of other organisations offering coaching to key executives.*

'OK,' said the boss. 'You have made the case, but I want to see evidence after the first year that we have gained benefit.'

This dialogue illustrates some of the ways a case can be argued, but the sting in the tail at the end points to a crucial component in good business plans. It is easy to spend the money on the investment, coaching in this example, but it is harder to ensure benefits are gained. One way we obtain benefits is to plan how to do it at the outset. This is where we turn to a business plan.

## WHAT IS A BUSINESS PLAN?

A business plan is based on a business case, and turns those sometimes-theoretical costs and benefits into a practical plan of implementation. It is based on several ingredients derived from the answers to the following questions:

- What do the customers (internal and external) want? In writing a plan, market intelligence will need to be gathered on customers' needs and competitor offerings. We need to be careful about the quality of data and search for hard data wherever we can.

- Over what period of time are we looking? Is this a short-term action plan involving activity over perhaps no more than a year, and focused on a limited project or issue, or is it more connected to the overall strategic direction of the business, with a more fundamental implication for the direction taken in the future? Of course, even limited short-term business plans need to connect to the longer term.

- How well does this proposal fit with the strategic aims of the organisation? Does it support and integrate with initiatives currently under way? Clearly if it does not, the case will need to be that much stronger.

- What are the options and the pros and cons of the alternative courses of action?

- What changes might be required to our current mode of operation? Is it practicable and feasible to bring this about? Many a plan has failed because the changes proposed were not practicable. Conversely, a too narrow view of what is possible might ignore the more radical and innovative solutions, which all organisations periodically need in order to prosper. The plan needs to recognise not only the longer-term strategic changes but also the shorter-term practical aspects. Who is going to do what tomorrow?

- What is the financial cost–benefit of the proposal? Financial advisors and other financially interested parties such as banks will want to see the impact of the proposals on the profit and loss statement of the business and the implications for cash flow. Even if it appears an attractive proposition, is it affordable within the resources available and is it the best use of what resources are available? There is always an opportunity cost of pursuing a course of action in the short term, ie something has to be foregone.

- What risks are involved?

- What are the critical success factors that will make the difference between success and failure?

- Are we confident that we have the necessary competence to turn a theoretical plan on paper into a practical reality that delivers what is promised?

- How can we best judge whether we are on track and whether the plan is working and delivering the benefits we had hoped for?

A business plan has a number of advantages:

- It gives a clear yardstick by which to measure the performance of individuals, groups and the organisation.

- It forces an appraisal of the present situation, the options going forward and a road map to get to a desired future. The debate surrounding such an appraisal creates a common understanding amongst business leaders of the issues and dilemmas they face and allows faulty thinking to be corrected on paper rather than in the business.

- It is a useful tool for communicating to the organisation the direction of the organisation and rationale for the choices that have been made.

- It provides, when linked with the functional plans from other parts of the enterprise a plan for the whole organisation. Functional plans for operations might include how to improve productivity, utilisation and reduction of work in progress and waste. IT might include plans to build a resilient architecture to improve up-time when the business demands 24/7 working.

- It gives confidence to the financial community (shareholders, owners, bankers, the Treasury) that this is a sound financial operation that has a future and therefore is worthy of continuing support and investment.

## An example of a business planning process

### The training and conference centre

A company had a training and conference centre which came to the attention of the CEO, who in his drive for cost reductions asked the director responsible to show why it was cost-effective not to close it. The director set out the following plan.

He first examined the current situation. He did a **SWOT analysis** and identified the costs associated with the physical assets – largely fixed costs, the semi-variable costs such as staff, and the variable costs related to each delegate such as course materials and food.

He then explored the different options. He looked at closing it and conducting the activities – meetings and training – outside. He also looked at the impact of stopping training. He also explored the reverse option of investing further and attracting new business.

He examined the demand for services from customers and looked to see whether there was untapped demand that might be capitalised, or duplicate services being offered.

He facilitated several debates across the company about these options, until one seemed to be the most cost-effective solution in terms of delivering costs savings overall, while continuing to provide services in a more focused way for key customers.

He then set about working with a team of interested parties to plan a course of action to get from the current position to the intended goal.

Finally he put in place a financial plan with suitable milestones showing the expected impacts on the bottom line month by month of implementation.

A year later, when he reviewed performance of the department with the CEO, the centre had been closed and a partnership agreement reached with another centre nearby. Training continued to be provided with little disruption, but at a significantly reduced cost.

## IS BUSINESS PLANNING POSSIBLE IN A FAST-CHANGING WORLD?

'No battle plan ever survived the first shot.' So said General Eisenhower. In a world where each day brings fresh change, one might be forgiven for thinking that planning is impossible. Indeed military history is full of tales of failed plans. In the First World War, General Von Schlieffen developed a plan that took the German army to Paris where a review would then take place. They never reached Paris and there was no opportunity for earlier revisions to this flawed plan.

However, plans should not be confused with prediction. Prediction seeks to identify what *will* happen, whereas planning seeks to ensure that something *does* happen. Business plans identify and anticipate: possibilities that might enhance performance of the organisation, opportunities that may lie unexploited, and threats where defences need to be developed. They also show the costs that will occur and the benefits that will arise if the plan is fulfilled. The major value, though, lies in planning, rather than the plans. It is the process of thinking through the issues, getting ready to take action, that places the organisation in a better position to respond more flexibly to a changing world.

Plans might therefore change in the light of changed circumstances. John Maynard Keynes, the famous economist, was criticised once for changing his economic prescriptions. 'If I didn't,' he is alleged to have remarked, 'I would be like a parrot who can only squawk, "It is going to be fine today."'

As an example, the benefits of HR planning are shown in Table 1.1.

Table 1.1 / **Benefits of planning for HR**

| Activity | Benefit | Value |
|---|---|---|
| Demand planning | better utilisation | lower labour costs |
| Recruitment planning | vacancies filled more quickly | lower costs of overtime / temps |
| Wastage analysis | fewer surprises control labour t/over | lower costs of recruitment / training |
| Career planning | management retention better morale improved performance | less recruitment fewer mistakes |

## 'START WITH THE END IN MIND'

Where does one start in developing a business plan? A traveller once asked the way to London, to which he was told, 'Well, if I was going to London, I would not start from here.' So, a good start is to recognise where you are and then to identify where you want to get to. Whether we like it or not, we can only start from where we are, however much we may wish we were starting from another position. A good business plan is in tune with the vision and mission of the organisation, and works with a credible strategy that is linked to other parts of the business. Think therefore where the plan will eventually lead. Try to imagine the business when your ideas are implemented. Some key questions are:

- What will the organisation be like when the plan is implemented?

- What do our different senses tell us? What does the organisation look like, sound like, feel like and smell like?

- What will be the impact on people involved?

- What will they say in the newspapers and professional press about the changes that have come about?

- What might be said if it goes wrong?

Getting a clear picture of the end point helps to keep the plan focused.

Before proceeding further, some explanation of these commonly used words might be in order:

## Vision

The ancient prophet said, 'Without a vision the people perish.'

Vision gives us a view of what we would like to be. It sums up our potential of what can be done – it identifies what we have to be in order to survive. For some it is a distant peak in the mountain range – it lifts heads and energises. "I have a dream," said Martin Luther King, and his vision galvanised a people. It has as much to do with the heart as the head. Vision helps to determine what we preserve and what we change. But vision does not help with deciding what we are focusing on at present. Mission does that.

## Mission

Mission defines what our organisation currently does. It is driven by the vision. It is the reason for our existence. It defines what we are here to do. It is the overarching goal and the enduring purpose of the organisation. It is the benchmark against which we can compare the activities with which the organisation is currently engaged. The best are usually short, memorable, and understandable to anyone anywhere – and are focused on what really matters. 'Overnight' was the mission statement of one parcel carrier. Everyone in the business knew what mattered – getting the parcel there tomorrow. But the mission is usually too encompassing. It does not define what we must do to deliver that mission or our preferred route. Strategy, goals and objectives do that.

## Strategy

Strategy is the route map for delivering our mission. It defines the choices of approach, the options for moving from where we are to where we want to be. There may be many different options for achieving the current mission, let alone a future vision. All may be possible, but the mark of a successful strategy is that it gets us to achieving our current mission and along the way to our vision more quickly, using resources (for example, people, money and facilities) more effectively, with less pain than the alternatives. Good strategic thinking always entails probing to see if there is a better way to accomplish the mission and seeking a better use for the limited resources we have at our disposal. Strategy looks at what core competence the organisation has built and what differentiates it today from others.

Spotting unexploited opportunities is the stuff of new strategy development. A hospital supply company once was very upset with customers who mistook it for another company when ordering materials. But it soon realised it could keep the customer happier by passing these orders on to the competitor, and in the process get to know its customers' needs better. In due course it offered a better product than its competitors.

In the final analysis, a strategy's success is determined by how well the business achieves a sustainable competitive advantage over time. But strategy must be implemented if it is to yield results. Goals help to do this.

## Goals

Goals translate strategy into specific action and thus define how we are to deliver the mission. They give us tools to define the scope of our organisation's activities. They can help in clarifying organisation priorities or where resource and emphasis must be placed. They allow us to describe what success looks like. They answer the question, 'What do we have to achieve to be successful?' But goals do not define what you have to do. Objectives do that.

## Objectives

If the organisation is to be effective, each person in it must understand what part he or she plays in delivering the goals. The connection between the individual and organisational goals lies in a cascade of objectives that move down from those goals to divisional, departmental, and finally individual objectives. If all the individual objectives are fulfilled, the organisational goals should be as well. If they are not, it probably indicates that some objectives have not been assigned and so are unlikely to be accomplished. Objectives should answer the question, 'What do you expect of me?' Performance appraisal in due course should answer the question, 'How am I doing against those objectives?'

## Values

Values are the glue holding us together – they define the commonly shared view of how we do things around here. They are a mixture of what we are and what we would like to be. All organisations have values – the things we hold to be important in our behaviour and beliefs – but sometimes they are not made clear. Values clarify guiding principles in how we should act, as we seek to deliver our goals. Many value statements sound good – in theory. 'We place out customers first.' 'We deliver good value to our customers and profits to our shareholders.' None of these are wrong, but they often leave people at the front line confused as to what to do. Indeed, it is the dilemmas people face and how they resolve them that are important rather than the words. It was the French philosopher Jean-Paul Sartre who said, 'We know our values by the choices we make.' Wrestling with ambiguity is part of a manager's job. However, the greater the ambiguity, the more likely there is to be variability in the way people act, and the less likely there is to be a sense of what is right to do in any situation.

We can see how these can be applied by looking at an example.

An example: I have a *vision* of a pleasant evening – a film, a meal, some friends, and so on. I crystallise this into a *mission* to see a film in the city with a friend and eat afterwards. My strategy is to ask him to book the tickets because he works next door to the cinema, and for me to drive up and pick him up (as opposed to all the other choices of route, method of travel, and ways of obtaining tickets). My *goal* is to pick him up on time. His goal is to get the tickets. My resulting *objectives* are to ensure sufficient petrol is in the car and that I have calculated when to set off. I know I have to be on time as to do otherwise would create stress for my friend and jeopardise our evening. My *values* are such that I recognise this as an undesirable behaviour.

# WHAT IS DRIVING YOUR ORGANISATION?

The formulation of a strategy lies at the heart of developing a sound business case. Yet the vision and desires of those in command, as well as the myriad of forces shaping the world about us, will in part determine that strategy. Fundamentally, there are five dominant forces shaping our world at the beginning of the twenty-first century, indicated in the box.

## Five forces shaping our world

- The Internet – the acceleration in the application of information technology and communications.

- The emergence of large trading blocks, eg EU, NAFTA, ASEAN.

- Globalisation of business – WTO.

- Break up of existing power blocks (eg communism, several dictatorships). Power to supra national bodies (UN, EU, OAU) and to local regions.

- Knowledge industries as the driver of the new world economy.

Let us explore these five forces in more detail:

- The convergence of ever more powerful computing and telecommunications technologies has given rise to the rapid emergence of the Internet. The Internet will increasingly shape any organisation, of whatever type, whether in the way it interacts with customers, clients or voters, the provision of information to employees and stakeholders of all kinds, or the way its own knowledge of the world is gathered.

- The emergence of large trading blocks has implications for where facilities are sited, for which nationalities work permits are easy or hard to obtain, and for the costs of doing business due to differing regulations.

- The globalisation of business creates the opportunities for huge market dominance on the one hand by multinationals, and the emergence of niche players that can operate globally on the other. The organisations in the middle are being squeezed.

- The break up of old power blocs, such as the Soviet Union, has changed the shape of Europe in recent decades, and the reverberations are still being felt in the rest of the world.

- Knowledge industries are having a growing effect on the economy, and challenge HR to find and retain talent. In Figure 1.1 we see that traditionally, reward has tended to correlate with skills in organisations in a linear relationship. Now, the curve has changed towards one where the best of any kind command higher and higher rewards while the rewards for marginal differences in skill are not recognised. If your organisation produces nothing other than knowledge in the form of advice, information or expertise, then survival is dependent on having the best. Like any other scarce commodity, the price is rising.

The net effect of these drivers is to affect the very survival of our organisations, and ultimately the people we employ. In determining the numbers of people we need, therefore we need to consider what drives the demand for different types of people and how some of the factors above are changing the traditional equations. For example, consider technology's impact on the skill sets of many jobs, or how globalisation has changed the structure

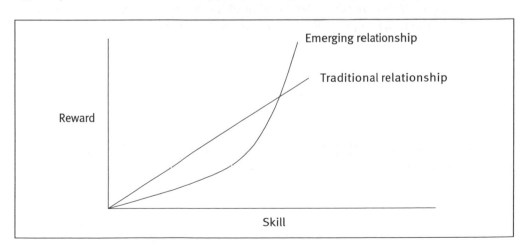

*Figure 1.1 / **Relationship between reward and skills***

of outsourcing. Figure 1.2 suggests a matrix of key drivers and job categories, the combination of which will determine the numbers of staff required. For example, the number of customer service staff will be determined by the number of customers who are dealing with the company directly, rather than using other channels of distribution. The number of staff will change if the method of sale changes to be via distributors.

| | Staff categories | | |
|---|---|---|---|
| Key drivers | Customer service staff | HR | Accounts |
| eg no of direct customers | Yes | No (could be yes if other categories of staff increase and so total number of staff increases) | Yes |

Figure 1.2 / **What are the drivers of staff numbers in your business?**

An organisation employed a number of telephone ordering personnel to take orders from catalogue customers. To determine the numbers it needed for budgeting purposes, it used a ratio of telephone personnel to numbers of customers which had been a good guide for a number of years. The advent of Internet ordering dramatically changed the ratio, which the organisation had failed to anticipate. With a better understanding of the Internet it might have reduced staff by natural wastage at little cost. In the event it embarked on a major redundancy programme.

The starting point for developing a plan has to be therefore the formulation of a strategy.

# HUMAN RESOURCE STRATEGY: WHAT IS IT AND WHY DO YOU NEED ONE?

## Some definitions

An organisational strategy has been defined as 'a road map to the future', and as such, seeks to answer two fundamental questions: where do we want to go and how do we want to get there?

A human resource strategy (HRS) aims to underpin the organisation's strategy and show how the different activities associated with managing people can enable the organisation's strategy to be delivered more effectively.

Planning comes from strategy, not the other way round. 'Planning helps to translate intended strategies into realised ones, by taking the first step that can lead to effective implementation' (Mintzberg 1993). Sometimes strategy lies hidden. A chief executive once said, 'I don't have a strategy, I respond quickly to the market place.' He had a strategy, but he didn't describe it as such. His strategy was to maintain a highly flexible organisation that could respond faster than his competitors to market demands, and it gave him competitive advantage. Planning sometimes has the role and benefit of forcing strategy to be more clearly articulated.

A typical HRS will address issues surrounding resourcing (planning, recruitment, internal promotions and transfers), development (training, career management), performance management (productivity improvement), reward (pay and benefits, job evaluation), employee relations (consultation, communication, discipline and grievance), culture (organisation development), and the efficiency of the HR function in delivering timely cost-effective services. A consequence of many HRSs is that the HR function has to realign itself with the needs of the business. In an electrical retailer, a division of Thorn, HR had to shift from being 'guardians of the rules' to 'facilitators of change' in order to deliver the performance improvement the business strategy demanded.

David Ulrich, an academic, classifies HR activity into transactional and transformational (Figure 1.3). His research (Ulrich 1996) indicates that a shift is occurring in many organisations away from transactional towards more transformational work, because of the need for HR function to add more value.

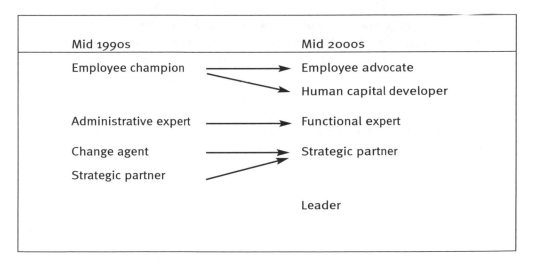

*Figure 1.3 / HR roles*
Source: Ulrich, D. and Brockbank, W. (2005) Role call, *People Management*, 16 June.

To accomplish this change, the HRS must chart a difficult course as the reduction in transactional work usually arises from work simplification, automation, outsourcing, or getting staff and line management to do more of the basic work themselves. This is often unpopular. It is, however, increasingly demanding issues like these that highlight the importance in an HRS of addressing how change, implied by the strategy, is to be accomplished.

## The benefits

The benefits to be gained from an HRS lie in a coherent approach to managing people, which reinforces the behaviour desired to accomplish goals. A motoring organisation, for example, set out to improve customer service and identified the need to improve telephone contact with members. The HRS identified that the best approach was to break down the hierarchical control structure, giving greater freedom and discretion to staff on the front line, and through enhanced skills in dealing with customer queries, satisfy more queries faster. Merely training without greater freedom, or greater discretion without the training, would not have resulted in the benefits.

In another company, however, HR set about a programme of reform and revitalisation and focused its efforts on developing a competency framework. Its belief was that by adopting good HR practice in each area, the business would be helped to make better recruitment and training decisions. However the business strategy required HR to be focused on employee relations in achieving more job flexibility through negotiation with the trade unions. This mismatch in priorities and strategic alignment caused the business to fail in achieving its targets through a lack of work flexibility, and incidentally, HR to feel frustrated that the business was not interested in adopting best HR practice.

An airline launched a management programme some years ago to encourage faster operational decision-making through greater empowerment of first-line supervisors. However, soon after the end of the training a newly empowered manager made a mistake in all innocence and came up against the old style disciplinary process. Others who saw this realised that it was safer to 'keep your head below the parapet', despite the freedoms they now enjoyed. An HRS in this instance would have identified the need to realign the disciplinary process to ensure that mistakes were used for positive learning.

## Choices

Strategy makes explicit what is often only implicit. Strategy brings to the surface critical choices, and these will be different for each organisation. In an international aviation organisation, the HR department spent a long time ensuring that its advice was the very best, but it resulted in frustration for its customers at the long delays in getting a decision. Its strategy then changed towards a bias for action, at the expense of sometimes having to revisit issues.

An insurance company, however, identified that its control of many activities had left managers disempowered and dependent. Its strategy was to move a number of HR transactions such as holidays, sickness recording and information queries on to an Intranet, available to line managers, and move the HR teams' time and attention to giving advice and problem resolution. A vital ingredient in the implementation of the strategy was to equip HR staff with the consulting and facilitation skills to make this a reality. This story illustrates a perennial dilemma of organisations, which strategy has to constantly wrestle with: what to tightly control, usually through centrally determined policy, versus what to give freedom to local management to decide.

Employee relations is an area of multiple choice. Vertex, a services company born out of the merger of North West Water with NORWEB (North West Electricity), 'has moved from traditional collective bargaining to de-recognition to a non-union employee consultation model and back to collective bargaining based on partnership and consultation.'[1] Its strategy was to look for a new way of working and experiment boldly until it found it.

In Wallace and Tiernan, a pump manufacturer with English and German subsidiaries, two different strategies emerged reflecting different philosophies, market conditions and choices. The English company paid high wages and sought to recruit skilled people who could be productive from day one. The German subsidiary recruited less skilled personnel at lower cost but invested heavily in training. A time of skill shortage in the United Kingdom resulted in a switch of strategy towards the German model. Strategy therefore helps to identify choices and the consequences of each. No strategy, though, lasts forever.

## Performance

The imperative of every organisation is to perform sufficiently to survive and prosper, and increasingly to improve that performance year on year. Performance invariably improves only marginally when the emphasis is solely on getting staff to work harder. Significant improvements only come through changes in the way people work, and in the choices of what they do. Identifying the levers of performance and choosing what and how to pull them is an output of strategy. The BBC used the Burke–Litwin model of performance (Figure 1.4) and set about specific change and development activities to enhance each element of the model. It identified as a priority the need to create a common vision and set of skills amongst the leadership, in order to deliver enhanced performance. Its HRS therefore focused on this area to start with.

Organisations that have a high proportion of their work concentrated on repetitive activities often seek performance improvement by routinisation. The results of many

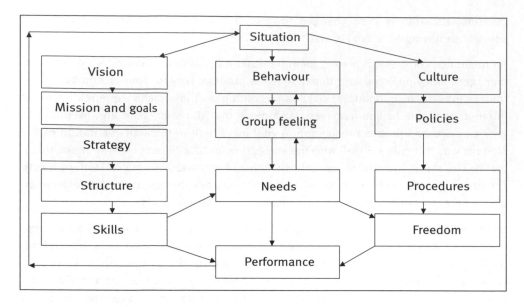

*Figure 1.4 / How do we get people to perform?*
Based upon: Burke, W. and Litwin, G.H. (1992)

organisations' efforts through process re-engineering are impressive. For example *Yellow Pages* achieved a four times improvement in cost per transaction through process redesign. However, the corollary of this approach is that repetition can reduce the capacity and willingness of the organisation to continually look for improvements. In such organisations the HRS will find ways of continually challenging the organisation. North West Water after privatisation wanted to challenge existing thinking, and so sent managers and key opinion formers to look at water treatment round the world. They came back brimming with ideas and often from countries that previously they would have dismissed as places from which there was nothing to learn.

Process re-engineering has in some instances 'dehumanised' work because of an excessive emphasis on systems. An effective HRS balances the competing demands in an organisation and helps to create a more integrated approach. David Guest, professor of organisational psychology at London University, who surveyed organisations that appeared to be using strategic human resource management, highlighted this need for balance. He concluded that four goals appeared to be the underlying principles: strategic integration of personnel and business strategies, building high-commitment workforces, a focus on quality, and flexibility.

## Balancing continuity and change

An HRS identifies what should be kept and cherished in the current ways of working, what needs to be enhanced, and what needs to be abandoned. The Richard Rogers

Partnership, an architectural practice, has grown in size due to its worldwide success. Its HRS recognised the need to retain its strong informal teamworking ethos, yet establish modern procedures in recruitment and appraisal and reward to ensure efficiency and equity. Mars, the manufacturer of food and confectionery, has had a long history of leading-edge practices in HR management. Its HRS identified the need to retain its excellent employee relations as well as developing improved productivity through better human resource planning. A critical strategy then for the HR function was to equip itself with the latest tools and techniques for planning and productivity improvement. It wanted to ensure that it took every opportunity for helping the organisation improve its performance whenever it arose. This enabling strategy illustrates the need for HR functions to be well trained and nimble in their approach, and thus be able to seize every opportunity to help the organisation move forward.

A critical question for any HRS is when to start a change process. In Figure 1.5, a graph is shown of performance of a company/work unit relative to competition, assuming a rate of change less than competition. The question that the graph raises is when to change (and that assumes that you have knowledge of where you are on this graph).

If you change at point A when the necessity is apparent, you have little time and few options other than to cut costs. If you change at point B – the optimum – you don't know this is optimum until you have reached A. If you change at point C, you are potentially diverting resources from improving current performance in order to achieve future (at that point unknown) gains.

Point C is the best long-term strategic solution, but it takes brave and farsighted management to do it. The reality is that most companies change at point A.

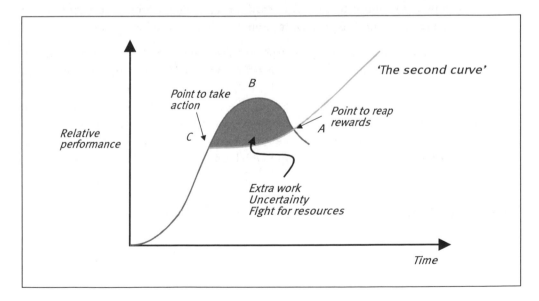

Figure 1.5 / *The challenges of change*

## Turning choices into action

If strategy is about making choices, what helps to make them? HRS will deploy a range of tools to help. A good starting point is to identify the *critical success factors* (see p214): identifying what the organisation needs to concentrate on in order to be successful. For Riverside, a housing association in Liverpool, it was reacting quickly to tenants' concerns. Its HRS identified that a call centre with pleasant and knowledgeable staff was going to be critical to delivering that outcome. It has taken time and investment to achieve a satisfactory level of service, but it is unique among housing associations, and thus will give competitive advantage as they compete for tenants and funds. It also entailed the development of a sophisticated computer system, and highlighted the necessity for the HRS and the business strategy to be closely integrated. Peter Drucker once said that success in organisational life is indivisible; all the parts have to work, and work together.

An HRS sees implementation of strategy and dealing with resistance as an intrinsic part of the strategy itself. When IATA decided that its HRS involved changing the culture of the organisation (less bureaucratic, more commercial and customer focused), it set about designing a process over several years that engaged the whole organisation, sought to reinforce positive behaviours with a reward system in line with the new culture, and helped managers to 'walk the talk'. Riverside Housing's approach to improving customer care was not only to increase the training in basic skills, but also to do it via a series of facilitated workshops that involved everyone, and encouraged a more positive view of the organisation. It reasoned that staff who felt good about the organisation and would exhibit that enthusiasm to customers were critical to success. This would only come about by involving staff more, dealing with their objections and criticisms face to face, and thus motivate them to release more discretionary effort.

In summary, a human resource strategy (HRS) is designed to enable the organisation to accomplish its organisational strategy. It presents the choices the organisation has to face to achieve its goals, and focuses effort in those areas where there is the best return. A good strategy identifies what should be preserved and what should change, and it helps to integrate the different aspects of the organisation's activities into a more coherent pattern of working that makes sense to all the stakeholders. Finally, a successful HRS is a spur to action, without which any strategy is of little value.

# WHAT DOES A BUSINESS-DRIVEN HR STRATEGY LOOK LIKE?

One word sums up the answer to this question: alignment. This alignment comes about where HR policies and processes are aligned with the business strategy to produce an organisation specifically crafted to deliver the vision, mission and goals of the enterprise. It comes from understanding how the organisation adds value and how in turn HR can add value to this value chain.

*We discovered that an employee's ability to see the connection between his or her work and the company's strategic objectives was a driver of positive behaviour. We were also able to establish fairly precise statistical relationships. We began to see exactly how a change in training or business literacy affected revenues.*

*Rucci* et al *1998*

Understanding the *critical success factors* of the business, translating those into key behaviours that deliver the additional value, and then finding measures that demonstrate or otherwise, satisfactory performance, is at the heart of the exercise. The box points to some strategic questions that link the two.

---

## Strategic questions

| *Business planning* | *HR planning* |
|---|---|
| What business are we in? | What sort of people do we need? |
| Where are we going? | What implications on structure or resourcing? |
| SWOT analysis of business | How does this relate to our HR capability? |
| What are the main strategic issues facing the business? | How do these affect the structure, strategy or resourcing? |

Adapted from Armstrong (1992).

---

The difference that such a process makes should lie in the performance of the organisation. Paradoxically, the majority of HR activity will continue as before. What changes are the mental map that underpins those activities, the measures of success by which they are judged, and the balance of time and attention focused on those activities that significantly add value.

---

Prior to Christopher Columbus setting sail, he no doubt ensured that his sailors were competent. No doubt he did it in a medieval way, but there were features that we would recognise today — training in core skills, setting standards, feedback on performance, praise and criticism. As they sailed across the Atlantic, the application of the sailors' skills was little different from their inshore sailing; the difference lay in the internal mental map of Columbus. He had a vision of where he wanted to take his people beyond the frontiers of their experience.

Becker *et al* (2001) suggest a seven-step model for identifying how to align HR strategy with business strategy and so implementing HR's strategic role.

---

## Transforming the HR architecture into a strategic asset

- Clearly define the business strategy.

- Build a business case for HR as a strategic asset.

- Create a strategy map:

  - leading and lagging indicators
  - tangible and intangibles.

- Identify HR deliverables.

- Align the HR architecture with HR deliverables:

  - HR function – HR system – strategic employee behaviours.

- Design the strategic management system.

- Develop the HR scorecard (leading, lagging, costs control and value creation measures).

- Measure HR tangibles and intangibles to show performance relationships.

- Implement management by measurement.

Source: Becker, Huselid and Ulrich (2001).

---

Once the performance drivers are more clearly understood, the HR strategy becomes clearer and a number of questions need to be asked:

- What competences do we need to recruit/develop to have the minimum capability and capacity to deliver required performance?

- What are behavioural characteristics of the culture required that underpin this performance? In Table 1.2, an example is shown of a water company that deliberately defined the attitudes, beliefs and behaviours that it wished to continue, reinforce or abandon.

- What policies will ensure we retain and build maximum commitment of our key staff?

- What are the assumptions about staff utilisation and productivity upon which the business plan is based? Are they realistic?

- Is our performance management system aligned with the organisational strategy in terms of both the deliverable objectives and the behaviours required, as well as done in a way that reinforces the cultural values to which we aspire?

- Is there sufficient resilience in our employee relations that we can cope with change, and are we communicating in a way that leads others to trust us?

- Are staffs rewarded for actions that help the achievement of objectives?

---

In one company, staff were rewarded for loyalty to their boss and length of service. Company strategy called for greater flexibility and more lateral movement of staff to spread best practice more quickly and to break down departmental silos. There was considerable resistance until the reward system was changed to place greater emphasis on responding to new challenges and acquiring new skills.

---

Table 1.2 / **Beliefs, attitudes and behaviours at a water company**

| Action | Beliefs | Attitudes | Behaviours |
|---|---|---|---|
| Continue | Current staff are competent. Top management in agreement with strategy. Customer service is key. Technical expertise is important. Work hard and play hard. | Pride and enthusiasm. Commitment. | Open communications. Discretionary effort. Commitment demonstrated by top management. Team working. |
| Reinforce | Openness and trust. Continuous improvement. Fair treatment of all staff. | Learn from mistakes. 'Can do' philosophy. Personal responsibility for training and development. | Develop our people. Listen to people. Performance focused on objectives. Pushing for higher achievement. |
| Abandon | Demarcation is best. 'Threat of sack is the only motivator.' | 'We know best.' 'It's not my job.' 'Pass the blame to others'. | Negative criticism. No interest outside their job. Long hours for the sake of it. |

Despite these simple and eminently logical questions, finding practical answers can be difficult. The potential complexity of it all can easily deflect business planning. There is no reason that business planning should not start with key problems at the opposite end from broad strategy. One maxim of organisation life is to 'scratch where you itch', or focus on the issues of the day, and the bottlenecks you face.

## If it all seems too much – refine the problem

Table 1.3 / *Refining the problem*

| If the problem: | Then: |
| --- | --- |
| Is stated in terms of studying, analysing and recommending. | Suggest a small-scale and results-driven pilot to test new ideas. |
| Involves resources and/or authority outside your control. | Identify a smaller part of the problem that you could tackle. Determine whether an additional or different sponsor or team membership would be appropriate. |
| Is too large and/or long-term. | Identify sub-goals or milestones.Work in a single geographic area.Work with a subset of customers.Work on one part of a production system. |
| Is in an area where people are not ready to give it a go. | Start in an area or with a problem where they are. Make sure you find a sponsor who powerfully and convincingly presents the problem or issue to others. Keep the sponsor heavily involved during the course of the project. |
| Is so specific it pre-empts your ability to get to the route of the issue or decide its aim. | Ask the sponsor to broaden it and/or allow the team to set specific measures and dates for accomplishment. |
| Is in a department where larger changes are under way. | Consider delaying the project or working on an issue not directly affected. |
| Involves hidden agendas. | Gently point out the ramifications of selecting this problem or issue. Work to minimise potentially harmful impacts. |

## MAKING THE BUSINESS CASE – RATIONAL DECISION-MAKING ABOUT SCARCE RESOURCES

Let us turn now to clarifying more specifically what is in a business case. Below is a checklist of questions to consider before developing one. In Chapter 2, we will look in more detail how to facilitate the development of a business case and in Chapters 3 and 4, we look at the information required.

- Have we identified a benefit for the organisation? If so:

    - Does the proposal lower costs or increase profitable revenue?
    - Does it have intangible benefits that are valued by key stakeholders (such as share holders and customers)?
    - Does it support the longer-term strategic direction of the organisation?

- Is there a good reason to change from our current way of operating? What is driving the necessity for change?

- What options have we considered, including:

    - Doing nothing and maintaining the status quo.
    - Stopping the activity.
    - More radical options such as partnerships and outsourcing.
    - More limited scope of the project. Where do we get the maximum return for our effort? It is worth considering Pareto's law (sometimes called the 80:20 rule) where 80 percent of the benefit can come from 20 percent of the investment.

- Have we examined the full range of costs and benefits – both tangible and intangible?

- Have we factored in to the financial case the commercial terms, such as contractual restraints, time delays for third parties to be contracted, and availability of investment funding, costs and benefits through the whole life of the project?

- Who are the stakeholders and how will their interests be affected by this proposal? (*Interest mapping*).

- Is this project feasible given the constraints of time and budget? These aspects of project management will need to be addressed in some detail in the business plan.

- Have we identified the assumptions on which the case is based and shown why they are valid?

- Final test: If it were your organisation, would you accept the proposal?

The Office of Government Commerce (www.ogc.gov.uk) publishes material on developing a business case, and suggests a more detailed template, shown in Chapter 5. In Chapter 6 we explore further the issue surrounding making decisions.

# TURNING A BUSINESS CASE INTO A BUSINESS PLAN

Once a business case is clearly articulated and is of benefit to at least the important stakeholders, the next step is to turn it into a plan. To do this requires a number of activities that we shall be exploring in more detail later in Chapters 2 and 5. In brief, they are:

- Investigating your current operations and analysing them to produce a situation analysis. You might start with a *SWOT analysis* and then carry out further in-depth analysis on key areas. The task is to understand what is happening to the organisation in terms of money, people, markets, customers, competition and operations.

- Articulating the way forward to give a clear direction and sense of purpose. You might start with clarifying the vision and mission, and go on to clarify more precisely the goals for the next period. Goals are not wish lists. They must be seen to be attainable.

> In one company, the chief executive announced that the goal for the next year was a 20 per cent increase in sales and income before tax. However the market was shrinking by 5 per cent, a new product required investment in R&D which would be unlikely to yield benefit before year two and there was the wrong calibre of staff in sales and marketing to achieve the target. No one believed that the figures were achievable, and the authority and credibility of the board were lost.

- Developing a strategy for achieving the goals. A strategy should help us to identify where we are, where we should go, the alternative routes we can take and the decisions we need to take to find the best way forward.

- Analysing the risks and the ways they might be controlled or mitigated. It was Harold Macmillan, a former prime minister, who when asked what he feared, said 'Events.' No matter how detailed the plan, events can overtake it. Having in place contingencies if things go wrong helps to keep a sober perspective and avoid being overcome by enthusiasm. (See Appendix for a *Contingency diagram*.)

- Turning a plan into reality comes down to assigning tasks to individuals and reordering priorities. Doing this in a way that gets enthusiastic support is one of the most critical activities in any business plan – and one that is all too easily given little attention.

- Creating a financial plan that accurately identifies all the likely costs to be incurred and shows the impact of different revenue assumptions.

- Finally, creating documentation that answers people's questions, gives sufficient information to allow decision-makers to make decisions, can be used to monitor progress and gives people confidence that this is a feasible plan.

## PERSCO – A CASE STUDY

Persco is a service company in the media world employing about 1,000 people. A conventional HR department was under pressure to reduce costs. The initial reaction was negative as no one could see how the company could reduce costs. 'We could cut the stationery budget, or not recruit or train, but where does that leave us?' said one disgruntled member of the seven-person team. 'Nevertheless', said the HR director, 'we need to find a way to deliver core services at a lower cost. We need to develop a business case for a radical change of our way of working and then work it up into a practical business plan.'

The team began to think that their strategy needed to change towards creating a much more compelling reason that people should join and stay, and this came down to the culture of the firm and specifically how people were managed. They believed therefore that they needed to put more emphasis on developing line managers to adopt a more motivational style of management, in tune with the kinds of professionals the company sought to employ. This meant that they also had to encourage line managers to do more people management for themselves, suitably equipped with training and IT. HR's role would become a business partner, providing advice and guidance for managers, with only a limited shared service function providing administration.

The MD responded to this suggestion by saying, 'Sounds like a good strategy, but what will you need by way of investment? Will your customers buy it? And what is the evidence that this change has worked elsewhere?'

## SUMMARY OF THE KEY POINTS FROM THIS CHAPTER

In this chapter we have explored the concept of a business case and a business plan. I have tried to show the necessity for good planning in making sound decisions about scarce resources. In formulating a plan, I have shown the relevance of a set of statements about vision, mission, strategy, goals, objectives, and values to place the plan on a firm foundation.

In determining where we start, I suggested that one approach was to look at what drives your organisation. Global changes such as technology and terrorism, while they may appear to be remote, affect all our lives with increasing rapidity. Understanding these drivers helps us to start developing an HR business-driven strategy. Aligning HR with the needs of the business, now and in the future, lies at the heart of a good plan. For some, this will be a counsel of perfection, and a simpler approach is suggested for those by refining the problem to more specific issues of the moment.

A question we shall consider after every chapter is, 'So what do I do now?' Good plans start with asking questions, and a checklist of questions to consider in developing a business case is included. In the next chapter we shall consider the process we might adopt, but in the meantime, we need to investigate our current situation, identify the options for the future and develop a strategy for how we can proceed. This will provide the basis for turning a business case into a plan.

# 2

# Facilitating the business planning process – engaging others and building the critical mass of support

*T'ain't what you do, it's the way that you do it.*

T'ain't What You Do, *Sy Oliver and Trummy Young, 1939*

## INTRODUCTION

This chapter sets out to describe a step-by-step process for developing a business plan. In Chapter 1 we discussed the hierarchy of strategies and plans. A corporate plan informs a subsequent cascade of functional plans. They in turn provide the feedstock to future plans, about the practical experience of implementation – what has worked and what has not. Where the approach offered here differs from some writers is in the focus on facilitating commitment to the plan, in addition to the deployment of various tools for analysis described in the Appendix. In times past, books on business planning would recommend that 'Senior managers will present the strategy to departmental managers who will cascade it down through the organisation' (Friend and Zehle 2004). Current thinking points to a more circular, iterative process involving top-down and bottom-up information flows.

To summarise the steps in the business planning process:

- Clarify the vision, mission, goals and values of the organisation.

- Analyse the environment and the position of the organisations in it.

- Carry out a situation analysis:

    - history
    - issues and challenges
    - stakeholder analysis
    - market place and competition
    - customers

- – financials
- – people and organisation
- – operations
- – technology.

- Develop an outline business strategy and a human resource strategy to support it.

- Gather data.

- Adjust the proposed strategy in the light of analyses.

- Develop a business case for the proposal.

- Test the business case by modelling different scenarios and assessing sensitivity to key risks.

- Develop an implementation plan.

- Present the plan and gain approval.

- Implement and adjust according to the practical difficulties encountered.

Such a plan requires time, effort, resource and commitment if a thorough job is to be done. In Chapter 5 we examine how to write a plan, but for now, we are interested in gaining support as we work through the process.

The Chinese General Lao Tsu wrote (according to some translations) that a 'leader is one, who at the end of the day, his followers say, they did it themselves'. It is wise advice for any business planner. Why? Well, business plans invariably imply change of some kind and as we shall explore in Chapter 7, when focusing on implementation, change invariably invokes resistance amongst some interested groups. (See *interest mapping* for a tool to identify winners and losers.)

A strategy to gain support is therefore essential to try and get stakeholders involved and to understand the logic of the case as early as possible. Gathering stakeholders together in planning events and meetings is therefore an essential part of the planning process. Any project needs to have someone ultimately responsible. Many people may be involved but the buck needs to stop somewhere. 'Bacon and eggs,' some wit once remarked, 'shows the difference between involvement and commitment. The chicken was involved but the pig was committed.'

## THE PROCESS OF PLANNING

In a changing world, where the ink on the business plan is hardly dry before it is out of date, it is easy to consider the process of planning to be a waste of time. However, as we suggested in Chapter 1 the plan is less important than the planning process. Tom

Peters (1991) has remarked that there are no good plans, but there are good planning processes. It is the activities associated with gathering and sifting information in a structured way, of deliberating with colleagues and surfacing hidden assumptions, that create a shared understanding of the issues and the best choices going forward. The time horizon of any plan will to some extent be dictated by some of the key investment decisions. If you are developing a new aero engine, then the planning horizon is determined by the development lead times of new technology and its eventual application in an airplane. The lead times also may be dictated by some of the functional strategies such as the time taken to recruit and train aero engineers.

One of the values of business planning lies in its encouragement of a common understanding of the business, by virtue of the interaction that has to go on between all those involved. It helps in the process of 'sense making' (Weick 1995) – that state of shared understanding of the world about us. Indeed, the business planning process is a good vehicle for organisation development, by getting 'into the room' those who have a stake in the success of the project or business. It increases the sense of shared ownership and responsibility, as well as limiting the effect of 'armchair' critics.

A common mistake is to see business planning as essentially a writing activity, but this is only the last part of the process. The major effort is in engaging the relevant people in determining the right strategy, researching to get the facts, deliberating with those affected about the right course of action and building a consensus on the route forward.

Another mistake is to see business planning as only the province of top management. Success in any venture relies on people at the sharp end to make it happen. Checking into a hotel recently, I saw a card advertising a new business service (24-hour business centre support). I enquired about it, only to be told, 'It's just come from head office. I don't know anything, you will have to ask the manager tomorrow.' No doubt someone at head office was mystified as to why there was so little take-up of the new service!

While there may be commercial sensitivities, the more those who are likely to be involved in implementation participate in planning, the more they can contribute and indeed feel part of the venture. Invariably those closer to the customers have a better understanding of the real issues and, if empowered to do so, can often fine-tune the plan in action.

Furthermore, when there is broad involvement and change to the plan is necessary, it is easier to bring it about, as there is already a hinterland of shared experience and knowledge.

The process of developing the plan requires several questions to be answered:

- What is the scope of the plan and its terms of reference?

- Who is leading and taking responsibility for pulling the plan together?

- Who are the people who will be involved in decision-making? There are the decision-makers, who need to be involved at the heart of the business plan. It is on their work and judgements that many will rely. The decision-takers are those, often senior managers, who need to finally sign off any plans. Third, there are the influencers, those who are listened to by decision-takers and need to be positive towards the plan.

- How will information be gathered and the plan be written?

- What is the timetable?

- Who are the stakeholders who need to be involved or consulted? A RASI chart can sometimes help to identify who is responsible for what. (See Figure 2.1.)

- How are the people involved to be co-ordinated? Does there need to be a project structure with defined roles and meeting plan or is it more informal?

Involvement also provides the opportunity for stimulating creativity through synergy. The Head of Sony Corporation once remarked that instead of believing there were better people outside the organisation, if they were to only harness the intelligence they already had within, they could do so much more and indeed solve most of the problems they faced. The Dutch have an old saying, 'The windows to the mind open from the inside.' So some of the ways we can stimulate creativity are by challenging the inhibitors to creativity. In A *whack on the side of the head*, Roger von Oech (1992) identifies a number of factors identified in the box, which inhibit our capacity for original thought.

---

**Responsibility chart (RASI)**
*The different roles participants may play*

**R** – *Responsibility for delivering what is required*
**A** – *Approval (with right to veto?)*
**S** – *Support (able to put resources against)*
**I** – *Inform (to be kept informed)*

| | Participants | | | | | |
|---|---|---|---|---|---|---|
| Decisions | | | | | | |
| | | | | | | |
| | | | | | | |
| | | | | | | |
| | | | | | | |
| | | | | | | |

*Here is an example:*

| Decisions | Participants | | | | | |
|---|---|---|---|---|---|---|
|  | A | B | C | D | E | F |
| 1 | R |  | A | S |  | I |
| 2 | S | R | I | A | I | I |
| 3 | I | R | S | A | I | S |
| 4 |  |  |  |  |  |  |
| 5 |  |  |  |  |  |  |

*For decision 1, A is responsible for delivering, C has the power of approval, D is willing to give support and F needs to be kept informed. For decision 2, C, E and F need to be kept informed, so a more time consuming task for B. Participant B has two actions to their name (2 and 3) and so may be under some pressure.*

*Figure 2.1 / **Responsibility chart (RASI)***

## Mental locks – inhibitors to creative thinking

- The right answer

  *– Gutenberg 'forgot' that wine presses can only be used for wine*

- That's not logical

  *– the use of metaphors to think differently*

- Follow the rules

  *– Picasso: every act of creation is first of all an act of destruction*

- Be practical

  *– Balance the artist and the judge – what if and the creative no*

- Play is frivolous

  *– What then is the right way of living? Life must be lived as a play – Plato.*

- Don't be foolish

  – *The role of the fool in the courts of Kings – to defeat 'groupthink'*

- Avoid ambiguity?

  – *'How wonderful that we have met with a paradox. Now we have a hope of making some progress' – Niels Bohr*

- To err is wrong

  – *'if you hit every time, the goal is too near or too big' – Tom Hirshfield*

- I'm not creative

  – *No one has the monopoly of good ideas*

# A FACILITATED PROCESS

To overcome these inhibitors, a typical facilitated process might look something like this:

1. The senior team meet to review current progress, identify **SWOTs** and build a common vision of where they want to be going. The aim is to *clarify the vision, mission, goals and values of the organisation*. This process might also drive parallel activities of communicating that vision to build a broad-based understanding and support throughout the organisation.

2. To develop consensus of the broad strategy, facilitated events are organised of key people accompanied by the presentation of significant data (market trends, benchmarked performance, customer perceptions). The aim is to *analyse the environment and the organisation's position in it*. Consideration might need to be given as to what business they are in. Parker, the pen company, thought they made writing implements, but realised that they really made gifts. Black & Decker similarly thought they were an engineering company, until they too realised that many of their products were given as gifts (often by women to men). The output of this stage is a *situation analysis*.

3. An individual is assigned to lead the development of a business plan. The initial aim should be to *develop an outline business strategy and a human resource strategy to support it*.

4. The individual identifies major stakeholders and establishes a timetable of activities and meetings. The aim is to *gather data*.

5. As each component of the plan emerges, debates and discussion are facilitated to reach a broad consensus and *adjust the proposed strategy in the light of analyses*.

6. The next stage is to *develop a business case, test the business case by modelling different scenarios and assessing risks, and develop an implementation plan.* The plan needs to be checked and critiqued.

7. Finally, *present the plan and gain approval.*

8. Implementation action launched, including individual objective-setting.

9. Progress is reviewed against objectives and corrective action taken.

A point worth remembering when designing any process is to first identify the purpose of the process. What is it trying to achieve? Second, consider the outcomes. What do you want people to walk away with? Finally design the process to deliver these aims.

Figure 2.2 also shows the importance of follow-through after any event.

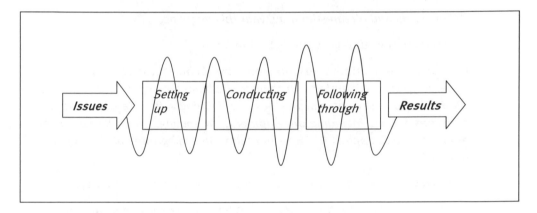

*Figure 2.2 / Core meeting process*

Let us now work through the steps and determine what processes might be most useful in each.

## Clarify the vision, mission, goals and values of the organisation

In recent years, developing vision and mission statements has become common, almost fashionable. In its train has come a certain cynicism that so much time and effort is spent on crafting a few words. The words that emerge are in fact less important than the process of discussion and debate to arrive at them.

In essence, sessions spent discussing these topics help senior managers gain a common understanding and increase the chances of working to common assumptions. In building consensus amongst the key individuals responsible for the direction of the organisation, there is a greater likelihood of shared ownership of the outcome.

Here is an example of a workshop designed to clarify the future direction of a business. In the box you will see an outline of the session with a section beneath it in italics that describes the process you might adopt.

---

1. Overview of historical trends and challenges including company, customer and product growth for the same timeframe.

   *Data pack available covering analyses of customers, products, markets, industry trends, organisation performance, competitive positioning and PESTEL (see Chapter 3). Brief presentation on key points, summary discussion on where we are now using a **SWOT analysis**.*

2. What is our vision for the future of our team?

   *Using words and pictures identify what this might be.*

3. So what are the strategic options for the future?

   *Use scenario planning or Johnson and Scholes (2001) approach to generating strategic options: Determine the basis for competitive advantage (Porter 1980 – see later in the box 'Developing a flexible organisation'), generate options including development, do nothing, exit and then review alternative approaches to implementation including internal development or acquisition.*

4. So what would we have to do to accomplish this vision and strategy?

   *Clarify what has to be achieved. What is the core mission of this organisation? What are the key activities? What assists us in its smooth running? Summarise with a **force field analysis** on helpers and hinderers.*

5. Identify financial targets and company strategic objectives

   *List **critical success factors** for each objective and key drivers.*

6. Assign responsibility for development of the business plan

   *Use **stakeholder analysis and interest mapping** to identify who should be involved to ensure buy in and subsequent smooth implementation.*

---

## Analyse the environment and the organisation's position in it

Carrying out a review of the organisation's performance relative to the market place and world at large (use PESTEL) to identify both the internal and external factors is a useful exercise to be done with multidisciplinary teams. Such an exercise can be beneficial for organisation development in that it increases individual's awareness of the issues that others across the organisation might face and the contributions they are making. While such exercises are good at identifying the headlines, they need to be supported with more rigorous analysis based on facts and data. Identify before the exercise whether appropriate resource is available to support the work.

Other tools might be deployed as well, such as *core competence* and *value chain analysis*.

## Carry out a situation analysis

*History, issues and challenges, stakeholder analysis, market place and competition, customers, financials, people and organisation, operations, technology*

This phase of gaining a clear understanding of the current situation has to integrate two perspectives: from the function associated with each area, for example, technology by the IT department, and a critical, dispassionate analysis to ensure realism. This poses dilemmas. Ignoring internal views and relying on an external view from say a consultant runs the risk of alienating the internal departmental support; whereas if only an internal view is sought, the harsh realities might be glossed over. A process to deal with this might be:

- Describe the overall process to all stakeholders.

- Ensure understanding of the need for a cool factual analytic review, and give assurances about how data will be used in a developmental way.

- Encourage a norm of best practice to benchmark all activities.

- Encourage a departmental *SWOT* analysis as a contribution to the analysis.

- Carry out a peer review to see what has been missed and whether there is consensus about the analysis.

- Maybe invite an external person (non-executive director? consultant?) to review the final work.

## Develop an outline business strategy and a human resource strategy to support it

There are two schools of thought about the process of developing strategy, the 'defined process' or 'prescriptive', and the 'emergent'. The former approach emphasises laying down a step-by-step process, whereas the latter argues from a more experiential viewpoint and suggests that strategy development is a more organic process. Strategy emerges as a result of continuously reviewing where you are against where you want to go, and weighing up possibilities and alternatives. While the latter approach probably reflects the reality in a lot of cases, it is difficult to keep track of where one is, and it poses problems of how to keep everyone informed.

Regardless of how it is done, it is helpful to have a framework in mind. Michael Porter (1980) identified three generic strategies: first, cost leadership, where the aim is to have a lower cost base than your competitors; second, differentiation, where you seek to be different in some way, in the eyes of your customers; and third, focus, where your advantage comes from doing a few things much better than your competitors.

A process needs to be established to identify which strategic option will give you competitive advantage. This might include:

- *Benchmarking* against competitors to identify whether you are already or have the potential to be a lower-cost provider.

- **Customer surveys** to identify unexploited need where your competences might be used to differentiate you from others.

- **Market surveys** to identify whether you have the ingredients to command and defend a niche in the market (a narrow target competitive scope in Porter's model) or whether you are sufficiently dominant to go for a broad target.

The next step might typically be to decide how to achieve the desired market position, either through internal development/acquisition of products and processes, leave things as they are, or leave that market altogether. Strategies of this major importance for the business are rarely taken in one meeting. They emerge from an iterative process of data analysis and discussion. Facilitating this process requires the proper provision of data and the capacity to rework it quickly to produce different scenarios. Keeping key executives in the process when there may be many conversations going on is a difficulty, especially when existing views of the business are being radically challenged and participants' thinking may proceed at different paces.

Bringing about change in the human organisation can take longer than changes to products or technologies. Where swift change in staff numbers is required, heavy cost penalties are often paid in the form of redundancies or recruitment campaigns. HR can easily be seen as 'blockers' or unable to contain staff costs. A key strategy, therefore, for HR to examine in organisations that are likely to undergo dramatic change is to increase the flexibility of the workforce.

The boxes 'Developing a flexible organisation' and 'Encouraging a climate of flexibility' provide a checklist of some of the approaches to consider.

## Developing a flexible organisation

- Build early warning systems.

- Multiskilling.

- Restructure work round core and non core.

- Outsource.

- Develop a network of portfolio workers who may have higher flexibility.

- Develop the alumni.

- The use of standby shifts.

- Change in contractual terms.

- Encourage a climate of flexibility.

## Encouraging a climate of flexibility

- Flexible working patterns.

- Process re-engineering.

- Empowerment/natural work teams.

- Cross-functional teams.

- De-layering (lean management).

- Customer focus ('who is my customer?').

- Re-training and development.

- Performance management.

- Competences and broad banding.

- Open communications.

## Gather data

The best strategy in the world is useless unless it can be turned into practical action. It is worth reviewing therefore how well we have been able to execute our last strategy. How well did we use the resources available? What did we fail to anticipate?

Some data will be gathered and analysed by an individual going through company and external data, maybe through a benchmarking club. Ensuring that meetings are well informed with timely and accurate data can help reduce the 'top of the head' assertion that intuitively may seem right but on cold analysis is wrong.

Some data is best gathered by getting a group together. This is especially true when you want to get synergistic thinking, that is, the kind that makes 2 plus 2 equal 5.

## Adjust the proposed strategy in the light of analyses

This stage is likely to be an iterative process as each analysis throws up new questions and debates. The ideal is to get the relevant people together with all the data. That is a counsel of perfection: a more likely scenario has the business planner producing multiple drafts as things change, and then seeking buy-in on an individual or small-group basis. The danger of this scenario is twofold – first, losing control of document sequence and who has agreed to do what, and second, getting caught in the cross-fire debate between parties who blame you for disagreements. The business planner should be seen as a neutral broker between the parties.

Finally, ensure that the plan still has integrity and it does not end up as a camel (a horse designed by a committee!).

## Develop a business case

Invariably gathering data to develop a case can be a solitary activity aided by those who know the precise data required. For example, use financial analysts for costs, marketing for data on the market and competition, and HR for information on the organisation.

## Test the business case by modelling different scenarios and assessing risks

In the same way that demanding consumers test products, get your critics and sceptics to explore the impact of their assumptions on the net benefit of the business case. If you leave the modelling to the technical expert, you may not explore all the possible set of circumstances, and you miss the opportunity of getting sceptics on side.

## Develop an implementation plan

In Chapter 7 we will explore implementation more fully. At the stage of developing the business plan it is all too easy to dismiss implementation with a phrase (which was seen in one business plan) such as 'Implement and adjust according to the practical difficulties encountered.' While this is true it does not go far enough in seeking to anticipate reactions to the proposal and the hurdles that might need to be overcome.

One way of finding out the problems of big systems or process changes is to embark on a simulation. Some years ago the BBC set about changing the way money flowed through the organisation by giving a budget to producers to buy resources. This process of 'producer choice' was a radical departure from previous practice, and many were sceptical. Deeply entrenched interests were also adversely affected. One weekend the Corporation undertook a large simulation of the new arrangements in a hall to test its feasibility and the problems there might be on implementation. The results were extremely helpful in understanding what staff were likely to face in the months ahead.

## Present the plan and gain approval

In Chapter 5 we will deal with the writing and presentation of the plan. Recognise that while business logic should be the basis for decision-making, we are always dealing with fallible people who are swayed by likes and dislikes, prejudices and emotional responses. Try to identify the sensitivities surrounding who should see what document first and work through people in the correct order to gain approval. Be careful to observe any particular rules, policies or formats to be followed.

Take any opportunity to discuss early drafts with key opinion formers. They are more likely to be positive if you have incorporated their points.

# FACILITATION

Facilitation is required at several stages of a business planning process and involves 12 tasks (Figure 2.3). Below are checklists of questions under each heading to ask of the group we are facilitating, or ourselves, to keep people on track.

## 1. Planning an event

Planning is designed to ensure that the purpose and product or outcomes of the event have been identified and the necessary resources prepared. The best way to start to plan an event is to work backwards from what needs to be accomplished. Then you can determine what actions need to be taken now and in the future to maximise the chances

## The 12 tasks of facilitation

1. Planning an event.

2. Agreeing objectives.

3. Creating the climate for success.

4. Managing the process.

5. Maintaining direction.

6. Monitoring progress.

7. Dealing with fears.

8. Managing conflict.

9. Developing action plans.

10. Summarising and reviewing outcomes.

11. Giving and receiving feedback.

12. Managing the wider organisation.

Figure 2.3 / **The 12 tasks of facilitation**

of their accomplishment. The major activity involves designing the process in order to reduce risks and minimise crises by preventing problems that can be anticipated.

### Core meeting process

In designing any event there will be stages, which are common to all events (see Figure 2.2).

Background materials (eg briefing documents, surveys of opinions, expert reports) may need to be gathered and disseminated before the meeting.

Consider the location. Is it to be in the organisation's own offices or offsite, some nice country house hotel, or on the factory floor? Location can set the context and style of the discussion. Be careful to set the room layout to maximise contribution (Figure 2.4).

Before you begin, establish a set of ground rules. These might include:

- mobiles off
- plain speaking and generous listening
- build on ideas

- keep focused on the topic

- keep to time

- no distractions (eg no access to e-mails or phone messages from the office except in an emergency).

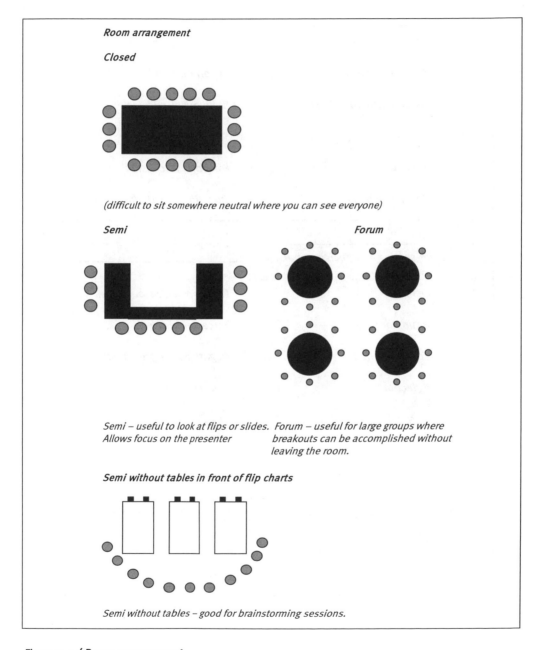

Figure 2.4 / **Room arrangement**

In designing the processes consider how best to engage the audience.

**Processes**

**Information gathering and receiving**

| | | | |
|---|---|---|---|
| ☐ | Plenary discussion | ☐ | Report out only |
| ☐ | Lecture with questions | ☐ | Breakout discussion |
| ☐ | Presentation | ☐ | Structured discussion |
| ☐ | Activity | ☐ | Free form discussion |
| ☐ | Check feelings | ☐ | Questionnaire during meeting |

**Problem-solving and decision-making**

| | | | |
|---|---|---|---|
| ☐ | Fishbone | ☐ | Listing probable outcomes |
| ☐ | Brainstorming | ☐ | Force field analysis |
| ☐ | Cost–benefit analysis | ☐ | Negative voting/eliminating |
| ☐ | Selection grid | ☐ | Flow charting |
| ☐ | Definitions | ☐ | Time line |
| ☐ | Charts | ☐ | Impact analysis |

**Setting the context/climate**

| | | | |
|---|---|---|---|
| ☐ | Icebreaker | ☐ | Stories |
| ☐ | Jokes | ☐ | Testimonials |

Figure 2.5 / **Processes**

### Some questions to keep in mind when planning an event

- What are we planning to do and why?
- What, who, when and where will I facilitate?
- How will my success as a facilitator be measured?
- What planning/preparation time do I need?
- What physical resources will I require and where will I get them?
- What specific group/individual dynamics may I need to take into account?
- What visual aids may I need to use?
- What materials will be needed for group members?
- How will I manage the time?
- What about breaks and handling of interruptions?
- What can I do to communicate and structure expectations before the event?
- What communication and follow through will be required after the event?

## 2. Agreeing objectives

Clarifying and agreeing objectives provide a starting point and establishes a common purpose for the group. Furthermore it helps to keep people focused on results and provides a useful prop to the facilitator when participants go off track. A common trap is to assume that everyone has similar expectations of the event and a common desire to achieve the same objectives. Clarifying objectives at the outset helps to surface those differences and deal with them. It can become more difficult to reconcile differences later in the event, especially if participants' investment in time and emotional energy results in intransigence.

### Sample questions used in agreeing objectives

- What is our purpose as a group?
- What is it that we want to achieve today?
- What are participants' personal needs from this meeting?
- To what extent are these individual needs compatible with our group's goals?
- How will we know if we've achieved our objective?
- By when must we have achieved this objective?
- What could make this a really effective use of our time?

## 3. Creating the climate for success

As facilitators we have a responsibility to create a positive climate. We therefore need to establish activities designed to ensure that all group participants are willing and able to fully contribute. We do this by asking the group to identify what would work for them, and surfacing any fears or concerns that might inhibit contributions. It can be helpful for facilitators to show that they are neutral, though identifying with the group's objectives, and that they are optimistic about the outcome. This is best done by demonstrating enthusiasm for the task at hand. When the facilitator models openness by disclosing any concerns he or she may have, the group realises that their own concerns are not unique and so can relax. Don't overdo it, otherwise the purpose of the event might become diverted towards therapy! Occasional humour (provided it is appropriate for the audience) can help to relax people.

### Sample questions for use in creating the climate for success

- How can we work together most effectively as a group?
- What could get in the way of us achieving our goals?
- What concerns/issues do you have at this time?
- How could we adversely affect this meeting?
- What will we do about the issue of confidentiality?
- What would need to happen in this group for you to be willing to express yourself fully and without reservation?

## 4. Managing the process

Facilitation has been likened to conducting, where the aim is to ensure that each person at the event plays their part, is able to make a useful contribution, and the group reaches the end of the event on time, with the intended outcome achieved. In order to do this, the facilitator designs, describes and follows a process that enables a group to achieve its objectives as effectively as possible. The defined process provides a route map that will enable the group to check where they are, and allows the facilitator to share the responsibilities for managing the group towards goal achievement.

### Questions to consider when deciding how to manage the process

- What structure or process can help us achieve our goals?
- What kind of boundaries do we need to establish in deciding how to proceed?
- To what extent is it appropriate to share the responsibility for deciding the process we will use?

- How independent is this group in terms of the task it is being required to perform?

- How frequently will we need to monitor progress?

- What may take us off course?

- What means will we use to give feedback and evaluate?

- Who else will be interested in the outcomes we reach?

- How will we share the task of managing ourselves?

## 5. Maintaining direction

When sailors set forth to cross an ocean, they consult charts and determine a compass bearing for their course. However much they have planned, the wind and tide in practice will be constantly pulling and pushing the boat off course. An analogous deflection will occur with any event, as the changing dynamics of the group affect how they grapple with the subject in hand. The facilitator's task is to ensure that participants stay on track and objectives are achieved, and that the group's efforts are aligned with organisational goals. Where there is not a unity of purpose and agreed objectives, there is always the likelihood of hijacking, and the facilitator's aim is ensure that such tactics do not deflect the group from their agreed objectives.

### Sample questions to use when maintaining direction

- Are we still focused on our original goal?

- Is what we are proposing to do here going to help us achieve our objectives?

- How well are we keeping to the course we originally set?

- Will the changes we have agreed help us keep on track?

- What is getting in the way of our staying clearly focused on the task?

- Is there a better way to help us achieve our plans than the way that we are currently going?

- What would we need to do to stay more focused and still enjoy the process of getting there?

- What can we learn from this intervention to help us avoid getting sidetracked again?

- How will we decide between what is sidetracking and what is important to explore even if not on the original agenda?

## 6. Monitoring progress

However much the process has been planned and agreed at the outset, perspectives will change as the event progresses. It is important therefore to check how the group is doing towards achieving its objectives and achieving the expected rate of progress. Such a review provides the opportunity to reassess the viability of the original objectives, to realign individual and group objectives, and provides data which will enable any corrective action to be taken. Furthermore, it shows responsiveness to the group's needs, and this can help to re-engage members who are losing interest or who have other priorities.

### *Sample questions to use when monitoring progress*

- How are we doing towards achieving our goals?
- What is working well/what needs to change?
- How far is this living up to individual expectations?
- On a scale of 1 to 10, how are we doing towards achieving the things we set ourselves?
- How well are we sticking to our ground rules?
- If you could change one thing in the way we are currently working, what would it be?
- What could we do to make even greater progress?
- Do we need to make any changes to our original objectives?

## 7. Dealing with fears

To be fearful or anxious is to be human! Fears and concerns exist, whether they are openly acknowledged or not. Fears may be as simple as whether the event will finish in time to catch a bus, or more complex, such as whether a participant might be exposed as less than competent. Fears are more likely to be manageable if they are brought out into the open rather than suppressed. Typically, the earlier a concern can be expressed, the easier it will be to address it, and the more energy there will be available to devote to problem-solving to address the concern. Many concerns resolve themselves through being named, acknowledged and legitimised. People's concerns can be voiced but not always resolved within a particular forum. Facilitators can play a key role in supporting individuals and groups to resolve their concerns and issues through interfacing with others in the organisation. In facing and naming our fears, rather than trying to sweep them under the carpet, it is possible to clear a difficult atmosphere and even to transform ourselves and our situations towards a more tightly knit and productive group.

The more facilitators are able to access and acknowledge their own fears and concerns to themselves, the more they will be comfortable in dealing with the fears of others. The extent to which a group can address and deal with their fears and concerns is directly related to a facilitator's willingness and ability to allow them to do so. It is the role of the facilitator to enable people to acknowledge and address their concerns. It is rarely the role of the facilitator to solve people's problems for them.

## Steps for addressing people's fears

1. *Ask people for their reservations, concerns or fears.* If this is done early in a facilitated process, it signals that this is an environment where emotions can be discussed openly. People may respond cautiously at first, particularly in a group situation. But asking for concerns helps to create the climate in which concerns can be addressed.

2. *Probe for clarification* if you are not certain about what is being expressed. Ensure that your voice tone is open and inviting rather than inquisitorial!

3. *Respond with empathy*: 'You feel ... because ...', remembering to describe the feelings (in your own words) and to describe the underlying experiences and/or behaviours associated with the feelings.

4. *Legitimise the concern.* One effective way in which a facilitator can do this is by recording the concern on a flipchart. Another is to check how many other people are sharing the concern.

5. Where appropriate, *allow time to elapse* between naming the concern and seeking to address it. This is because, first, people are often in a heightened state of nervousness at the beginning of a session, and second, many concerns do actually resolve themselves when allowed to surface.

6. When addressing the concern, *invite the ideas of the whole group* as to how it might be resolved. (Sometimes you may need to check that the person is comfortable for everyone to be discussing his or her issue.)

7. Try to ensure that *the person/people who own the fear also own its resolution.* Do check with people to ensure that concerns have been resolved.

8. If the fear cannot be resolved by those present, *offer your support to the person concerned* to help him or her take the issue up elsewhere in the organisation.

9. *Humour can be a balm* for tension and hurt feelings. Try to ensure that any humour is:

    – expressed with rather than against people
    – not used to smooth over issues that do need to be raised
    – appropriate for the audience.

---

### A typical dialogue

F   Now I have described the process and timetable for today, does anyone have any concerns?

P   The session on current performance.

F   What particularly worries you about the session on current performance?

P   We might get into conflict over who did what.

F   So, you feel that it might generate too much finger-pointing, because we might blame each other for past mistakes?

P   Yes.

F   Do other people feel this way?

Ps  Yes we do.

F   So how should we deal with this?

P   Let's try and if it gets sticky, stop.

F   Does everyone see this as a good way of proceeding?

Ps  Yes.

F   OK, so I will try to keep us on an even keel and make sure no one gets too battered in the process!

---

## 8. Managing conflict

A founding principle of western thinking is the idea of debate. A proposal is made, an alternative view is suggested and out of the debate comes a synthesis of new ideas.[2] Yet when debate turns to conflict the reverse occurs, as attitudes harden and protagonists' only concern becomes one of defending their position. Our task therefore as facilitators is to maintain healthy debate without the conversation descending into conflict. One commentator in describing an argument with his wife, said that he knew it was getting serious when she no longer listened to him, but rather 'gathered ammunition to support her view'. We must at all times try to keep people listening to each other.

We manage conflict by identifying and acknowledging conflicts when they occur. Some conflicts, where they are not impeding progress, are best left alone, as to deal with them would deflect the group from the real task.

## *Thoughts to bear in mind when managing conflict*

1. Differences are inevitable and can be highly productive.

2. The energy of unproductive conflict (hostility) can often be transformed into action.

3. Facilitators cannot be effective if they use win–lose conflict resolution techniques, because it will destroy the openness and trust which is essential to group functioning. This means that trying to manage conflict by overpowering it will not work for you as a facilitator. You may win a battle but you will certainly lose a war.

4. Be willing to operate within your personal limits of tolerance for conflict – accept that there may be benefit/value for the group if they see you, as their facilitator, operating within these limits.

5. Learn to be willing to work on increasing your limits of tolerance for conflict. This may be the most useful and helpful work that you undertake as a facilitator in terms of personal, group and organisation development.

6. Try to notice what things 'hook' you into internal conflict when you are facilitating. (It can help, for example, to consider the insights offered by psychometric questionnaires such as your MBTI/FIRO-B type.[3]) What causes you personal stress? What are the patterns that occur around conflict in your life? Are you willing to share these observations with the group, and invite them to help you manage your own personal conflicts? You have a right and a need to be human too, and sharing responsibility will increase their powers of observation and diagnosis as well as encouraging them to be open about their own conflict areas!

7. Learn to trust any feelings of conflict you are experiencing when you facilitate. They can often be clues to the unspoken conflicts that exist within the group.

8. Useful techniques when handling conflict:

    - allow people to vent
    - show empathy
    - clarify
    - acknowledge and accept different views
    - focus on behaviours
    - try to correct misinformation but don't argue the point
    - deal with conflict in the here and now.

9. Common unhelpful patterns when handling conflict:

    - denying that it exists
    - suppressing or smoothing over
    - withdrawing
    - ignoring

- responding defensively
- minimising or denying another point of view as valid
- compromising what is important to you
- taking sides.

10. Use a process like *NICILING*.

## 9. Developing action plans

Ultimately, the talking about business plans has to stop and action must be taken to implement them. It is at this stage that a facilitator has the difficult job of gaining commitments from individuals to take action. The task is to ensure that future actions after the event have been clarified, roles and responsibilities agreed, time frames established, resource needs identified and plans for monitoring progress confirmed. In order to generate as much commitment to action as possible, facilitators use questions to elicit volunteers, rather than tell people what to do and encourage behaviourally committed speaking. For example:

---

F  Who is going to take forward this action item?

P  OK, I will.

F  Thank you. So tell us what you will do.

P  Well, I will contact the supplier and obtain a quote and circulate to everyone.

F  And when can this be done by?

P  Before our next meeting.

F  Do you need any help from anyone?

P  No.

F  Can I check with the rest of the group; does this action and timescale fit with our other plans and actions?

G  Yes.

---

### Example questions for use in developing action plans

- What needs to happen next?
- How does it need to happen?
- Who will do it?

- By when will it need to be done?
- What resources will be required?
- How will we know if it's been done successfully?
- What follow through will be used?

## 10. Summarising and reviewing outcomes

If after a meeting you ask participants to describe what went on, you will invariably have different answers. We each make sense of our experience in different ways. So a facilitator has to work hard to ensure that there is shared understanding about what has taken place during the session.

In addition, reviewing the process helps to build a greater awareness amongst the group and helps them become more self-facilitative in the future. It helps future events to build on success and identify future areas for improvement.

### *Sample questions for use in summarising and reviewing outcomes*

- What has happened?
- What have we achieved?
- How well have we achieved our objectives?
- What's been most useful/valuable for you personally? Least useful/valuable?
- What changes would we make if we were to do the job again?
- What suggestions do you have for further improvement?

## 11. Giving and receiving feedback

The literature on high-performing organisations is vast, but one feature appears to be a consistent and enduring theme: high-performing teams and organisations have high-feedback environments. Yet feedback is difficult to do well if defensiveness is to be avoided. The aim of feedback is to develop awareness of the effect we have upon others and they upon us, and to recognise and encourage more effective behaviours.

### *Questions to consider when giving feedback*

- How can we create an environment in which it is easy to give and receive feedback?
- How can we be open in giving and receiving feedback?

- What are the ways to assess a person's readiness to receive feedback?

- How immediately can we give and receive feedback?

- What are the specific, concrete things upon which we can agree?

- How are these things affecting me? Are they affecting others differently?

- How much am I/others really willing to change?

- When can it be useful not to be open to feedback?

A summary is given in Table 2.1 of an approach:

*Table 2.1 / DASR feedback*

| | Do | Don't |
|---|---|---|
| **Describe** | Describe the other person's behaviour objectively. Use concrete examples. Describe the action not the motive. | Criticise the person. Use generalised or vague terms. Guess motives or play psychologist. |
| **Acknowledge** | Acknowledge your feelings. Express them calmly. Be positive about goals. Direct yourself to the specific problem behaviour. | Deny your feelings. Unleash emotional outbursts. Be negative or assume an offence has been committed. Attack the entire character of the person. |
| **Specify** | Ask for a change in behaviour. Specify the actions you want stopped or performed. Specify (if appropriate) what you are willing to change to make the agreement. | Merely imply you'd like a change. Ask for too much. Consider that only the other person must change. |
| **Reaffirm** | Reaffirm the other person's ability to make the change. End on a positive note. | Tell him or her your doubts as to his/her ability to change. Send him or her away concentrating on how you handled the interview, what he/she did wrong, or feeling depressed. |

## 12. Managing the wider organisation

Groups, if facilitated well, can develop an identity and purpose that encourages action with enthusiasm. The facilitator's task is to ensure that the group's efforts and activities are aligned with the context and goals of the organisation. Change inevitably brings conflict (see Chapter 7), and as we have discussed above, the facilitator's responsibility is to regulate this conflict to ensure it does not become unproductive. There will inevitably be the need to identify and remove obstacles to the implementation of new ideas in the wider organisation, and to ensure that organisational communication channels are clear.

### Questions to consider when managing the wider organisation

- What is the business mission and strategy and how does our work fit within this?
- What are the expectations of different groups:

    senior management?
    peers?
    my boss?
    my workgroup?
    groups I facilitate?

- What options do I have for shaping those expectations?
- What barriers are likely to arise?
- What is being communicated to whom about what?
- What further communication needs to take place?
- What could get in the way of my being effective in my role?

## EVALUATING THE OUTCOME

A good principle to adopt after any meeting is to evaluate what was achieved. On training courses, evaluations are often required, but rarely with other kinds of meetings. In Chapter 7 we explore more fully project reviews, but in the meantime facilitators need to check that action plans are realistic and robust to withstand the pressures that participants will experience. The pressures of their normal job and the routines of everyday life invariably reduce people's ability to implement new things after they step out of the event.

### Checklist for evaluating action plans

- Specificity of the plans.
- Realism.
- Thoroughness.
- Integration of action steps with regular routine.
- Anticipation of obstacles.
- Provisions for obtaining help.

- Provisions for obtaining commitment.
- Commitment of supervisor to success of plan.
- Provisions for tracking progress and follow-up.
- Measurability of results.
- Provisions for reward and recognition.

## PERSCO

Taking the team away for a day, the HR director laid out a process to help them begin to think about a new HR strategy. They started to clarify their vision by exploring what they each wanted to be part of in the future. They looked at what it would be like for their 'customers' as they sought HR services. They articulated this vision, as to be excellent in everything they did to reflect the high standards of the company as a whole. They wanted to positively model one of the core values – excellence. They believed, therefore, that they should continue to do well whatever they could – a preference for quality rather than quantity.

The team moved on to examine their mission. What was their enduring purpose in their desire to support an increasing effectiveness of the organisation? If the company was going to survive as a global media services company, it had to create an environment that attracted and retained the best global players. The team recognised that the days of seeing HR as something separate from the business were over, and that they played a vital role not only in improving the cost-effectiveness of delivery, but also in shaping their activities to enhance the productive capacity of the organisation.

The day finished with clarifying the next steps in developing the detail of the business plan and who would do what.

## SUMMARY OF THE KEY POINTS FROM THIS CHAPTER

In this chapter we have explored the steps in the business planning process and shown how HR professionals could play a role in facilitating the events that might occur. It is the process of planning that is as important as the plan itself, as it ensures, if done well, that there is a common understanding and consensus about the way forward. Facilitation is a skill that can greatly enhance the productive capacity of a group and the 12 tasks that have been described provide a framework. The chapter has shown some examples of how these steps are to be accomplished.

So what next? The challenges this chapter sets are first, to gain agreement to a process of planning and second, to identify and equip a facilitator to steer the process through to successful conclusion.

# 3

# Identifying, gathering and interpreting information for business planning

*When we first planned Apollo's trajectory to the moon, we realised that we were not aiming at a fixed target – it was moving. Only about 10 per cent of the rocket's journey was aimed at the moon. We were planning a rendezvous with the future.*

*NASA engineer*

## INTRODUCTION

This chapter sets out to identify the information required to develop a business case and examines the issues surrounding the process of gathering, analysing and presenting data in a way that will effectively argue the case. We will explore the sources of data, the types of data – financial and otherwise, how we evaluate costs and benefits and examine the application of these methods in the next stage of Persco.

However, before we investigate the practical issues of gathering the information required for business planning, we need to be aware of issues that affect the way we view that information.

## WHAT IS REALITY?

No data you gather will be perfect; information is rarely objectively, totally 'true'; facts are not often black and white. Furthermore you, and others involved in the planning process, will not often be able to see every side of every piece of information – your perspective will inevitably be skewed by past experience and expectation. Most of the time, most of us see what we expect to see.

To make things more complicated, before we even see the information it has already been distorted by the way it was collected: by the questions that were asked and by the questions that were not asked; by the assumptions that the people collating the data made about the answers they were given; and by the assumptions the people providing the data made about the questions they were asked.

All of this raises some interesting philosophical questions about the nature of reality. Those of you interested in exploring a rare opportunity afforded by your everyday work to consider philosophy can read the box. Those who want to cut to the chase simply need to know that the key methodological question for us concerns how we go about finding valid data. The sections that follow in this chapter and the Appendix set out some tools to help. Using multiple methods – triangulation[4] – can sometimes help to check our findings. However, you should:

- recognise the differing assumptions that a reader of a business case might make about the data presented

- remember that facts that may appear true to you, may not appear so to others

- be aware that perceptions, such as attitudes towards the company, may be treated by some as hard data, independent of the questioner; while to others they may be treated as figments of the questioner's imagination.

---

## Some philosophical questions

Gathering information for the purposes of drawing conclusions and making judgements about the world about us poses several fundamental philosophical questions surrounding data. They concern the form and nature of reality, the relationship between the analyst and the subject, and what methodologies are valid to find out what can be known.

### Form and nature of reality

From the nineteenth-century debate about whether the social sciences could be investigated in the same way as the natural sciences, two perspectives emerged: the positivist and the idealist. The positivist view holds that there is a reality independent of the observer's process of coming to know it. The goal of enquiry is to describe facts that are 'true', regardless of the observer.

The idealist tradition starts from a belief that knowing something cannot be separated from knowing oneself. The goal then of social enquiry is descriptive, as each interaction between researcher and subject is unique. This view focuses attention on the meaning of words and actions in a context, and suggests that reality is a construction of the mind. This construction will differ depending on the meanings ascribed to experience and actions emanating from the interpretation of those meanings.

These two traditions result in very different views of what is valid (Bakan 1966). Where idealists see the strength of qualitative research as lying in its fidelity of representation (because reality is socially constructed), the inextricable involvement by the researcher, with all the biases that that brings, is seen by positivists as the key weakness. This difference has led to a view that these different paradigms cannot be integrated. Guba and Lincoln (1994) provide a fuller account of these philosophical issues. Suffice to say for our purposes, care has to be taken in the assumptions we make about what is true. Much depends on your perspective. There is an ancient story told of three men watching the sun come up, when a woman appears naked. One man's mind is filled with lust, the second man condemns her for immodesty, while the third puts a blanket round her because he sees that she is sleepwalking. We see what we want to see, what we expect to see.

Each method produces facts in the sense of meanings to the individual. In everyday discourse our senses are assailed with weak and strong facts (Capaldo and Zollo 1994), and we seek to make sense of phenomena by integrating data from many sources. In the end it is a matter of individual choice whether you accept/believe/act on the numbers emanating from a statistical survey as opposed to the conclusions from a series of conversations with individuals in the survey.

## ANALYSING THE ENVIRONMENT AND OUR PLACE IN IT

'The fish', someone remarked, 'is the last person to feel the water.' History does not recount, however, how he knew. Nevertheless, it is true that it is all too easy to become so focused on our internal world that we become unaware of the changing world outside, and in particular how our approach is different from others and is not the only, or right way, of doing things.

An important step therefore in any business planning is to examine the environment in which we operate to identify the factors that we must take into account in our plans. A useful mnemonic is PESTEL.[5]

*P*olitical

*E*conomic

*S*ocial

*T*echnological

*E*nvironmental

*L*egal.

In looking at each of these factors and how they affect our plan, consideration should be given to both the internal and external environments. Below is a checklist of questions to ask.

# Political

## *External*

What are the priorities of the government of the day?

If there is an election looming will these priorities change?

What are the policies that affect us? Can lobbying mitigate them?

Do our plans coincide with government policy? If so, are there grants or other resources available that might support our plans? If they are not coincident, are our plans strong enough to withstand disapproval? For example, the plan might be to build an office in a national park.

## *Internal*

What are the priorities of senior management?

Who has the power to change things?

What are the philosophies and ideas that underpin current thinking on the organisation's strategy?

What ideas do we value most?

Which part of the organisation is particularly favoured? Where is investment being made, and in what areas are costs being squeezed to pay for that investment?

# Economic

## *External*

What are market conditions like for the organisation's goods or services? In particular, will the plan enhance the financial performance of the organisation in the light of these economic realities? Assumptions about growth in income, for example, always need to be made with reference to the external market. It is much harder to grow a business in a declining market than in a growing one.

What changes in economic policy or other market factors might affect the organisation? For example, Bank of England pronouncements on interest rates, whether to join the euro, and global conflicts can all affect currency fluctuations, interest rates and stock prices.

### Internal

What is the financial reality of the organisation? If investment is required to deliver this plan, with what other projects must it compete?

What is the rate of return hurdle[6] that new investment must overcome?

How significant is this project in the context of the financial performance of the organisation?

## Social

### External

Social trends can dictate fashion and lifestyle choices. What are we assuming in our plans about people's behaviour and preferences? For example, assumptions about moving staff to a different location these days are more affected by the reality of dual careers and concerns about children's schooling than they were a decade ago. As organisations encourage staff to take more personal ownership of their careers, so organisations have less influence on staff movements where they may not be in the staff member's interests. For busy managers, the travel industry reports a trend towards longer weekend breaks rather than long holidays. It has found that the fear of being away from work and the fear of returning to a mountain of e-mails are driving this trend.

Social trends on work–life balance may affect willingness to work unsocial hours; healthy eating may affect demand for canteen services. The box 'Lifestyle trends' highlights some of the lifestyle trends that result in a rather different pattern of market segments, compared with typical socio-economic groups.

---

### Lifestyle trends

- 'Downshifting' – dropping out.
- 'Cocooning' – the nester/couch potato.
- 'Down ageing' – live longer, act younger.
- 'Egonomics' – treat me as an individual.
- 'Fantasy island' – let's escape.
- '99 lives' – the jigsaw puzzle of life.
- 'SOS' – save our society.

---

- 'Treat myself – I deserve it.'

- 'Staying alive' – health has to be earned.

- 'Vigilantes' – don't fool with us.

Source: Kotler (1999).

## Internal

Where do people's loyalties lie and to what parts of the organisation? What is the culture like? Culture, often defined as 'the way we do things round here' can sometimes facilitate or hinder change.

Johnson and Scholes (2001) describe their cultural web (Figure 3.1) as a way of understanding culture, and identify symbols as one ingredient. In one example, a company established a cost-saving committee who did some good work in identifying waste and other opportunities for improvement. However, one day the conference room was full and so the committee moved next door to a restaurant. Unfortunately for their image, it was the best restaurant in town. In the future, their recommendations were met with cynicism.

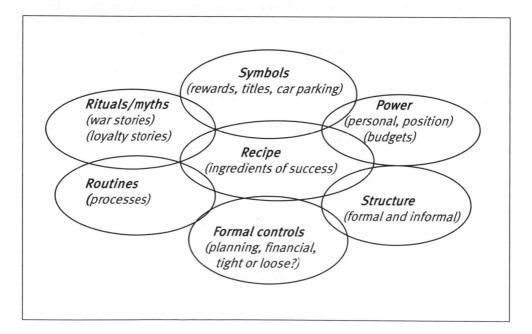

Figure 3.1 / **Cultural web**
  Source: Johnson and Scholes (2001).

## Technological

### External

The accelerating pace of technological change is a constant point for consideration. One consequence of the Internet is that it is lowering the barriers to entry in some businesses, such as music publishing, where anyone can now publish their work on the Internet and gain an audience. It is also changing some markets towards 'winner takes all', where there are few prizes for being second. Once you have got one online bookshop in your favourites list, how many more do you really need?

In developing any plan, consider the assumptions made about the technology used and how likely they are to hold in the future.

One group of businesses that is particularly subject to pressure from the Internet is intermediaries. Where customers can easily survey the market place electronically (and ever more sophisticated software makes the comparison easy for us), the role of a business charging the consumer for that service becomes harder to sustain.

### Internal

What technologies are available to us? Organisations make choices about technologies of all kinds. There may be competing options, the choice among which is affected by many factors (see Chapter 6). When a business case suggests a new technology to supersede an established base, the decisions will be harder to make than if we are using existing technologies, protocols, methodologies and vendors. (See the case studies in Chapter 7.) Indeed, it is a perennial problem of technological change: when do you make the switch? There is a natural reluctance to change from existing tried and tested technologies, especially when it is cheaper to make an addition. Yet the sunk costs of past technologies acts as an inhibitor of technological change, and if business performance suffers, they may result in decline such that the costs of changing become harder and harder to afford. A vicious circle is reached where performance suffers because outdated technologies are unable to deliver the cost-efficiencies required to generate funding for new investment. In addition, the competitive advantage of competitors that have adopted the latest technologies squeezes even further the ability of the business to invest – that is, if they are successful in earning the return that the potential competitive advantage should provide. A cartoon in a newspaper showed a new aeroplane, and admirers were saying that this is the future. 'I hope it will run on red ink' says the sceptic.

## Environmental

### External

Organisations that provide services – knowledge businesses – may think that they have no environmental concerns. Pressure groups, however, may have other ideas. Social responsibility and business ethics have become important issues. The WWF report *To whose profit* (Kemp 2001) points the way to arguing persuasively for sustainability. So the question that any plan must ask is: what impact does this have on the environment, and how well does this square with our social responsibility? Is this in line with an ethical stance?

### Internal

With increasing consciousness about environmental protection, employees may become vociferous if the basics are not addressed. How is waste disposed of? What commitment does the organisation make to fair trade? If it is a retailer, for example, has it adopted the code of the Ethical Trading Initiative?[7]

## Legal

### External

The rise of corporate fraud and the introduction of ever more stringent reporting requirements, such as those required by Sarbanes–Oxley,[8] point to demands for greater briefing and training along with surveillance and vigilance.

### Internal

The shift towards a more litigious culture means that people are less accepting of injustice and are more conscious of their rights. Do our policies and practices anticipate these pressures?

Now we have considered the environment in which the organisation currently operates and will operate in the future, let us turn to examining more closely customers and competitors.

## CUSTOMERS, COMPETITORS AND COMPETITIVE ADVANTAGE

Every time an enterprise moves from one person to several, it becomes an organisation. In its wake come the challenges and opportunities that organisations bring. At the heart of an organisation is the belief that additional people can add greater value – there is some synergistic benefit as a result of combining people. In some organisations one could be forgiven for thinking that the reverse is true.

In the commercial world, a business case rests on the assumption that some proposal is ultimately going to add greater value to the customer. A successful business plan shows how the investment of money and effort in making practical changes is rewarded by demonstrable added value, which is apparent to the stakeholders. An organisation presents to its customers a business proposition: here is a good or service, offered in return for some recompense. It is through the progressive adding of value to the business proposition that the organisation secures advantage in the market place. (See **Value chain analysis** in the Appendix.) While HR personnel may think of themselves as some way from the end customer, the actions and decisions taken about people – often the major cost of any business – will have a determining role in cost-efficiency and profitability, and so ultimately the organisation's ability to survive. In a competitive market where each and every other competitor is seeking to provide a better value proposition to customers and clients, every marginal improvement can be significant. Figure 3.2 challenges us to consider where our different staff categories might lie in the matrix. Competitive advantage does not necessarily rise with position in the hierarchy. Front-line staff, who can be quite junior in many businesses, can also hold the key to competitive advantage.

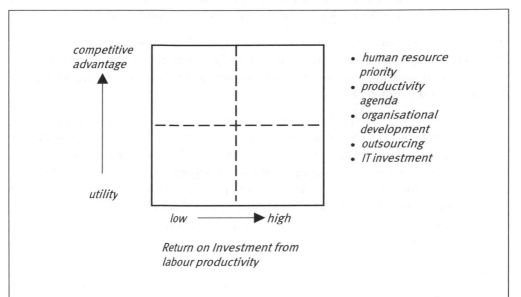

In this figure, we can map different categories of staff. Their position on these two axes will determine the type of activity listed on the right. For example, staff who are in the utility/low return box (such as canteen staff) might be candidates for outsourcing, whereas those in the competitive advantage/high return box (such as cabin crew in an airline) would probably be not. They are more likely to be a high HR priority worthy of investment in productivity and work climate.

*Figure 3.2 / **HR value to the business***

## Competition

A paradox of organisational life lies in the attitude to competitors. Markets encourage competition. Competition drives the search for competitive advantage, and ultimately customers benefit through new and better products and services at lower costs. Competitors are a vital driver of increased efficiency and ultimately wealth creation. Yet sometimes it does not sound like that if one listens to organisations. Competitors are ridiculed, for perhaps poor products, services or advertising. The psychology of motivating organisations to beat competitors encourages a view that you are superior and need not worry about competitors, or indeed the reverse, that the competitors are (unfairly) about to crush you.

Competition comes from several sources. Michael Porter at Harvard (1996) developed a five forces model to show how competition shapes markets. The first type of competition is amongst existing players in the market place. They are the easiest to research, maybe because some of your staff will have worked for them, and you may come across them in the market place each day, selling or bidding against you.

New entrants are harder to spot. They may start small, perhaps with a rather different proposition that can easily be ignored. They might even be ridiculed because of the differences, or seen as minor niche players. A high street bank once discounted Internet banking as 'only for techies'.

Substitute products are another form of competition. Our homes get ever fuller of gadgets that take the place of earlier approaches to enduring problems: the vacuum cleaner replaced the sweeper, which replaced the brush. There may also be substitutes in the supply chain: we might decide to do our shopping over the Internet, rather than go to a shop. Ultimately though we compete for a consumer's time and money, and there may be many alternatives for customers to spend both their time and money on. In a world where many consumers are very busy, we compete for time and attention with other distractions that have little or nothing to do with our service.

Suppliers have bargaining power, and in exercising it can influence the cost and specification of what they provide. This in turn affects an organisation's ability to compete. Staff shortages because of difficulty in attracting scarce and vital skills is a common example.

Finally, the bargaining power of buyers affects the transactions made. The power will flow back and forth between suppliers and customers depending on supply and demand. A challenge lies in understanding the segmentation of the market and finding a niche where a sustainable and defensible position can be secured, thus giving more power in any transaction. If you are the only trainer in a particular field, and it is a subject that everyone needs to know, then this is a more powerful position than a trainer who is one of many doing similar work.

Competitive advantage can be sustained by erecting barriers to entry. Securing patents or licences to unique technologies makes it more difficult for competitors to follow. Strong brands take time to emulate. Where an organisation has expended time and effort to create a facility, such as a shopping centre close to a motorway exit, it may be unattractive for a competitor to do the same, especially if it sees that the time taken is long and the final rewards are not substantial. The reverse can also occur, when competitors see potential customer flows, and can more accurately assess the return on their investment. A number of the risks of the unknown are removed when you can observe someone else having done it first. Competitive advantage, however gained, is rarely sustained for long. Cost advantages are eroded as competitors find ways of matching costs. Technological advantage is reduced as new technologies come along or patents expire. New technologies, particularly, have compressed the advantages of time and distance that used to be important before in some industries. Brand names can easily be tarnished and fashions change.

Jay Barney (1991) identified a number of sources of strategic assets that give a business competitive advantage. He described strategic assets as those that are simultaneously valuable, rare, inimitable and non-substitutable. Professor Cliff Bowman from Cranfield (2004) also suggested a list of potential candidates, given in the box 'Categories of strategic assets'.

---

## Categories of strategic assets

- Knowledge assets

  – Technical know-how, tacit routines, entrepreneurial insight, architectural knowledge.

- Relational assets

  – Trust, reputation, brand, contracts, switching costs, social capital.

- System assets

  – Operating, control, HR, information, co-ordination.

- Cultural assets

  – Creativity, co-operation, responsiveness, professionalism, learning.

- Tangible assets

  – Location, equipment, patents, information.

Source: Talk by Professor Bowman on 20 September 2004 at the Cabinet War Rooms.

---

Earlier, we identified from Becker *et al* (2001) (in the box on page 22) how HR can be built into a strategic asset.

## Customers

'Who are your customers?' is a familiar question to any marketer. The clearer you are about the characteristics of the customers you seek to serve, the more targeted you can be with your proposal, with corresponding benefits of less wasted time and effort.

When developing a business plan, there may be multiple customers. Let us suppose we are putting forward a proposal for buying an employee assistance programme.[9] Who are the customers? There are the customers of the service, potentially all staff, and to provide an appropriate service, a provider would need to know something about the types of staff, locations and possible problems. There are also customers for your plan, which may be your HR colleagues and the board. Finally, there are the end customers of your company, which may be impacted by the service. Hopefully happier staff might result in happier customers.

# AN OUTLINE STRUCTURE FOR GATHERING DATA

Once you have surveyed the external environment, the next stage is to gather specific data.

## What is data?

The dictionary defines a datum as an 'assumption or premise from which inference may be drawn', whereas information is defined as 'knowledge'. Our task therefore is to find data from which we can draw inference and so create knowledge.

The starting point for any data-gathering exercise is to identify answers to the following questions:

- What is the *purpose* of the data? What is the information gathered designed to show, and will it be of sufficient quality and rigour to pass scrutiny? For example, to prove a business case for more staff, data needs to be gathered on what they might do and how they might add more value. Showing merely the competences required is not sufficient to prove the case. If we are mindful of the future need of an OFR (operational and financial review) then we will need data on size and composition of the workforce, retention and motivation of employees, skills and competences required, remuneration and fair employment practices, leadership and succession planning.

- What is the *product* or desirable outcome of our data gathering? In carrying out an attitude survey, you might want to be able to determine what aspects of employment conditions staff find demotivating. But to determine a business case for putting it right, not only do you need to ascertain what staff might see as sufficient to improve motivation, and thus be able to calculate the costs, you must also be able to estimate in some way whether fixing these problems will have an impact on retention or absenteeism, grievances or productivity.

- What is the *process* of gathering data and is it valid? One famous study reported that a high proportion of the population were suffering from mental illness, much to the consternation of health officials. However, it was only later disclosed that the study sample consisted of people whom doctors had referred to psychiatrists. Ensuring representative samples is of course a difficult task — ask any market researcher or political pundit who tries to predict the outcome of an election.

## Where do we get data?

### *Primary sources*

*Internal data*

Whatever the method of recording, every organisation will record details of employees, if nothing else for the purpose of paying them. This data will come invariably from the individual concerned, and should therefore be valid. Of course, people lie about their ages and qualifications, and forget to tell you when they move or change partners.

Other data might need to be gathered as well, such as qualifications, training courses attended and sickness records. Whilst these might still come from the individual concerned, or the training instructor or manager recording sickness, they have less reliability. Where there is a diminishing consequence for getting it wrong, data invariably decreases in its accuracy.

Data might also be gathered from mechanical sources, such as time recording or security systems.

Whatever data is collected, the organisation of data can affect our ability to draw the right analysis. Data on competence, experience or knowledge can be difficult to capture in a way that allows for easy analysis. Finding out how many people speak Swahili may be within the compass of your database search software, but identifying those whose language proficiency is sufficient to translate on a trade mission could be more difficult without further testing. In designing new systems, it is always worth keeping a record for some time, prior to detailed design, of what you would have asked if the capability had been available. Such insights provide clues as to the depth of data required and the best mode of classification.

Surveys can be a way of capturing opinion, but consider the costs, time, and impact on those surveyed. Satisfaction surveys can arouse expectations and engender beliefs that conditions are about to improve. There is usually an expectation that there will be feedback, which in turn will change people's perceptions. Referring back to the philosophical issues at the beginning of this chapter, we can see that data in this instance is not neutral, and the relations between researcher and researched will affect the data.

## External data

Data on current and historical labour markets are available from sources such as the *Labour Force Survey*, the *Employment Gazette* and other government publications. The Office of National Statistics has data on, for example, the national census, available electronically. Market data can be found from market research reports and surveys by trade organisations, commercial sources, and through business and university libraries. Financial accounts for public companies are publicly available. Anecdotal material might be found from press cuttings, brochures and discussions with former employees. Much data is of course available on the Internet.

A company wanted to improve its competitor knowledge at minimal cost, and identified 10 major competitors that it wished to track. Ten staff members were asked whether, in addition to their normal duties, they would act as a point of collection for any information about these major competitors. The plan was to establish a physical and electronic filing cabinet for each competitor. Staffs were asked to feed anything they came across about these competitors to the named individuals. Any information about these 10 competitors, wherever it came from, was directed to these individuals, who filed it. Data came in the form of press cuttings, anecdotes, discussion with friends, and catalogues. When anyone wanted to examine a competitor, there was an immediate source of data to start from. Within a few months, there was sufficient data for most queries to be answered.

## Secondary sources

Data might be gathered from reports and summaries where others have gathered the prime data before, in which case we then have to rely on their accuracy. A story is told in the academic world of a paper that was published to popular acclaim in an academic journal. It had many erudite quotes and included many obscure references that sounded plausible. This hoaxer enjoyed seeing these made up quotes and references appear in many other papers subsequently, the later writers falling in to the trap of not checking sources, or going back to primary sources where possible.

Representatives such as trade union officials, or account managers for a supplier may have particular biases and points of view that they wish to pursue.

In all instances, we must recognise that records of all types will be affected by time and context. For example, it is clearly wrong to assume a current level of absence based on last year's records, or an exam result some years ago to be a valid measure of current knowledge. Surveys also are greatly subject to change over time and place, and great care needs to be taken in generalising from such findings.

Data that is not administratively convenient to gather is also more likely to be the subject of corner-cutting as, under time constraints, the researcher will make approximations and extrapolations. We will examine the presentation of data in more detail in Chapter 5.

## Who gathers data?

While I shall argue later that the writing of the plan should not be delegated —after all your professional career might be on the line as a result of this — there is a case for drawing in others. It shares the load of data capture, it builds a common understanding of the problems and possible answers, and it creates a sense of involvement at the heart of the business. When things go wrong, people are more likely to stay with it and battle through, whereas if they have not been involved they may turn on you. So establish a timetable and responsibilities.

## Establish a timetable for the process

- Launch meeting.
- Data capture.
- Data analysis.
- Strategy formulation.
- Data refinement.
- Development of the business case.
- Understanding and acceptance of the rationale.
- Development of the business plan.
- Launch.

## Establish responsibilities

Determine who is to provide:

- sales data, eg market research
- financial data, eg financial planning.
- employee numbers, eg payroll/HR records section.

## How do we ensure that data is valid?

There are several points to check with all data:

- How current is it? Do we know when the date was gathered and checked?

- Consistency. Is labour turnover, for example, measured in the same way across the business units we are going to compare? The statistics could include all leavers or just those who are full-time permanent. The ratio of leavers to numbers employed could be taken at a point in time or as an average over time. These subtle differences will affect the ability to compare trends.

- Accuracy. What is the error rate?

- Validity. Are qualifications, for example, what they say they are? Can we verify the source of our data?

- Completeness. Are there gaps?

When connections are made between data, caution should be exercised in jumping to conclusions. Anecdotes can be interpreted as universal fact. Statistical associations can be seen as enduring causal relationships. Before these connections can be accepted as hard evidence, there has to be logic for the change, and the independent variable – the driver of the effect – must precede in time the dependent variable. Many associations in organisational life are affected by a myriad of factors. If we want to be certain of the cause and effect we need to find a way of holding these other variables constant so the true effect of the causal variable can be tested. Only then can we truly determine whether the investment in the causal factor is worthwhile.

---

A study of supervisors who had undertaken a management course showed a strong correlation with reduced turnover, and this was claimed to be as a result of the tactics learnt on the course. Further analysis of the data showed that turnover had dropped before the course, and the benchmark group against which the supervisors were compared was in a particularly competitive labour market in a different town. The high correlation had occurred by chance.

---

## Types of data

Typically there are four types of data we collect when developing a business case in HR:

- what people *believe* via surveys of attitudes and opinions

- what people *do* via analysis of jobs

- the *result* of the activity via performance data

- the *cost* of people.

## 1. What people believe – surveys

In reading some business plans, one will only find hard numerical data. However, data is only a representation of the views and perceptions of people, whether it is staff views on areas for improvement, customer complaints or suppliers' problems with the organisation. Surveys have a key intrinsic problem: people do not necessarily respond accurately to a survey, telling what they really feel. They may be affected by fears of discovery, they may respond in an aspirational way (in the way they would like to be), or they may respond in the way that they think the researcher wants, or even say the exact opposite of what they mean out of some perverseness. Suffice to say that there are many ways to 'lie with statistics' (Huff 1991), and we need to be especially careful in ensuring that the process of eliciting responses is as free from bias as we can make it. One way is to compare the same sample over time – at least the biases may be consistent. In one study of the reasons for labour turnover (see Table 3.1), it was shown that leavers reported rather different reasons to an independent researcher some three months after they had left, than the answers they gave to an HR survey at the time of leaving.

Table 3.1 / **Exit interview – company case study**
*A survey of 177 people who left over a six-month period*

|  | Reason given at termination interview | Reason given 3 months later |
|---|---|---|
| Pregnancy | 4 | 4 |
| Marriage | 1 | 0 |
| More money | 17 | 12 |
| Better job | 23 | 28 |
| Promotion | 5 | 2 |
| Leaving the area | 7 | 7 |
| Change of career | 4 | 3 |
| Wanted a change | 8 | 18 |
| Did not get on with boss | 2 | 11 |
| Working conditions | 4 | 10 |
| Domestic reasons | 15 | 3 |
| Dissatisfied | 12 | 3 |
| Training | 8 | 5 |
| Other | 18 | 22 |
| Non voluntary reasons | 49 | 49 |
| **Total** | 177 | 177 |

Nevertheless, when measured on a like-for-like basis, the reasons over time were reasonably stable, and gave a benchmark against which to evaluate strategies to improve retention.

There will always tend to be question marks over the validity of data about people, especially when it is based on perception and individual assessment. If data is consistently gathered over time using the same definitions, it is more likely that at least trends can be spotted than if it is not collected so systematically. Where there are changes in these trends, a more targeted analysis can then be conducted to probe the causes more deeply.

The motivation of respondents will affect response rates. Typically, respondents to any survey are those who feel strongly about the issues being surveyed – positive or negative. Those who are indifferent tend to respond less, giving potentially an incomplete picture.

## *A checklist on questionnaire design for surveys*

- *When using a sample, look for matching characteristics between the sample and the population, and ensure that at least the important ones are matched.* Clearly the larger the sample, the greater the opportunity for overcoming skewed sample characteristics. The characteristics that are important will be determined by the questions asked and the likely interpretations of the data.

- *In determining the questions to be posed, consider what is cause and what is effect.* Is, for example, absence a result of low morale because people no longer have the commitment to come into work, or is it a cause of low morale because people are having to cover for others' work?

- *Consider whether the data you wish to gather is best in a descriptive form,* such as, 'Tell me about what you enjoy about your job?' which gives a richer understanding and makes no assumptions about what the categories might be, but proves more difficult to analyse and compare results, or *more analytic,* for example 'Rate your satisfaction with your job from 1 – low satisfaction to 5 – high satisfaction', where comparison and statistical analysis are easy but interpretation is more difficult.

- *How independent are the variables?* Is there an underlying factor to which they are related? Many processes change over time, making time an underlying factor.

- *In designing the process is it going to be more helpful to take a cross-section* of the organisation at a point in time or to compare the same group over time?

## *Points to consider in questionnaire design*

- Ensure that the wording is intelligible and matches the understanding of the audience, and that the questions are in a logical sequence.

- Avoid inappropriate assumptions about prior knowledge.

- Consider a respondent's attention span. It can affect the maximum number of questions you can ask.

- Consider how response rates will be affected by the perceived attractiveness of responding.

- There are many issues that surround the validity and reliability of rating scales:

    - How should they be anchored? By behavioural statements?
    - Is the distance between points on a scale equal?
    - What are the mental constructs conjured up in the mind of the respondent by the words?
    - How fine can respondents discriminate on the scale? Are five points too few or too many?
    - Should there be a mid point neutral category, or should we force people away from the middle?
    - Should the favourable end be on the right or left?
    - How far should we get respondents to give a considered response or their first impressions?

- Avoid leading questions, loaded words, prestige bias, and embarrassing questions, and consider the choice of open and closed ones.

- Reflect on the interviewer/researcher biases.

- Are we only seeing what we want to see in the results? Is this a case of the self-fulfilling prophecy?

- In encouraging high responses, anonymity is helpful. What is the level of anonymity that participants perceive and what is it in practice?

### Sources of bias and error

- Non-response is not a random process. It is the result of a complex set of circumstances affecting the respondent.

- In longitudinal studies, it is difficult to determine what is the cause of the change. Comparison with a control group can sometimes help to reduce the possible range of causes of variation.

- Bias comes from many sources: respondent ignorance, unreliability, motives, reticence, mental maps, taboos and more.

### Selection of statistics and presentation tools

In Chapter 5 we will explore more fully some of the issues surrounding presentation. Suffice to say at this stage, that when presenting data to argue and justify a case, we have a duty to present the facts as clearly and in as unbiased a way as possible. 'Lies, damn lies and statistics' sums up the way cynics may feel about surveys and statistics. Ensure that your integrity is not compromised by biased presentation of the facts. The facts should always be neutral; the debate should be about the interpretation and the consequences.

The box 'Process of survey design' shows a summary of the process to develop a survey.

---

## Process of survey design

1. Decide aims and hypotheses.

2. Look at examples, review literature, discuss with informants and relevant people.

3. Design the survey to test hypotheses.

4. Select/design research methods appropriate to sample and consider what questionnaire design is appropriate. Select items and wording for clarity, validity and ease of analysis.

5. Pilot, analyse and revise – what are these questions actually measuring? Consider turning free choice questions into multiple choices for ease of analysis.

6. Select sample.

7. Collect data and maximise response rates. Consider mail versus interviewer coding and processing.

8. Statistical analyses of results – test hypotheses.

9. Draw conclusions and present.

10. Gain feedback on actual interpretation of the results.

---

Survey data helps to find attitudes and perceptions. There are times when we need to find out what people do. In job analysis we use a range of tools to complement perceptions.

### 2. What people do – the techniques of job analysis

In determining what people do in their jobs, there is a range of techniques.

#### Observation

Observation of the jobholder doing his/her work is the simplest and most straightforward approach. Depending on how repetitive the work is, time taken will vary to encompass the whole range of activity. It may need supplementing by, for example, an interview and a time log of activities. It still requires the observer to deduce the accountabilities and competences required.

Whatever other methods are chosen, observation of the jobholder is a useful supplement.

Samples may be taken at different times for a specific job or for a range of jobs at a point in time, and the results used as input into a structured job description outline, to check against a predetermined list of competences, or written as some narrative.

Note that observation may well affect the behaviour and performance of the individual (the Hawthorne effect[10]) and that you may miss critical activities that are only done infrequently.

### Diary

This method relies on the jobholder keeping a log of his/her activities over a period of time. This may be completed over a period of say every hour or day, or when there is a change from a regular activity, such when a machine breaks down, or by identifying the specific activities undergone, for example typing.

A diary has the advantage from the analyst's viewpoint of efficiency in data collection, but it suffers from the possibly biased perceptions of the jobholder (especially if the use to which the resulting description is put may have an effect on terms and conditions), or he/she may forget to record events. This can occur especially when the jobholder is busy or concentrating on a difficult task – the very time you want a record. Recognise also that people who are highly competent may not recognise their competence, because they find work easy, and so will not record activities of significance to a less proficient worker. Some will find it an onerous task to complete.

The resulting data still has to be analysed and inferences drawn.

### Activity analysis or hierarchical task analysis

This approach is intended to define the activities in a job. An activity analysis is often laid out in groups of activities to form a hierarchy of tasks, and can be produced by diary, observation and interview methods. The method starts with a definition of the overall purpose of the job, then proceeds to break this purpose down progressively into the tasks that have to be done to accomplish this purpose.

To identify competences, for example, the focus is on behaviour analysis. The behaviour to be observed is that which is relevant to the outcome, capable of being observed reliably and consistently by different observers, and ideally differentiated between positive and negative effects on the outcome.

There are three components to be borne in mind when looking at an activity. What are the inputs (such as information on requirements for the task)? What is the process that is going on (such as using a computer to produce a report)? And what is the output (for example, what is the contribution of this activity to the overall purpose of the job)? Note that it is easy to confuse 'busyness' with productive activity.

## Criticai incident (see Appendix for more details)

This approach is a procedure for collecting observed incidents that have proved critical to performance. It is particularly relevant in jobs where success or failure in performance is defined by a few key events. For example, the pilot uses little of his/her skill most of the time. It is when there is a problem that subsequent behaviour defines the successful performer.

The jobholder is asked to describe events that have occurred and his/her response. Comparisons can be made between successful and unsuccessful outcomes, and insights can be gained into what might improve performance in the event of a future occurrence.

Critical incident technique can be used to evaluate the effectiveness of training, when someone is asked to describe a time when he/she used what was learnt on a training event.

---

A water company ran a series of courses in facilitation skills and wanted to evaluate the benefit. Critical incident techniques highlighted incidents where meetings were more productive and quicker, problems were solved with greater buy-in and conflicts resolved successfully. The auditors, who did the study, reckoned on a 6:1 ratio of benefit to cost.

---

## Behavioural event interviewing

This method was derived by McClelland and his associates (1987) for developing the required competences for a job, and involves five steps pursued by interview with jobholders:

1. Introduction and explanation – a review of their career to date.

2. Job responsibilities – the key tasks and accountabilities.

3. Behavioural events – the five or six most important situations they have experienced in the job – two or three high points or major successes and two or three low points or failures (this is similar to the critical incident technique).

4. Characteristics needed to do the job – what it takes to do the job effectively.

5. Summarising.

*Structured questionnaire*

This approach is based on developing a set of standard questions, which ideally are asked of a sample of jobholders. The resulting data can be more easily compared than unstructured data. It should be noted where there are a range of jobs, there may need to be different questions relating to different jobs. Care needs to be taken to avoid a too mechanical analysis, which may miss some subtleties of the job. The standard questions form a starting point but good probing questions thereafter are essential.

## 3. The result – performance data

Ultimately what people do is only a stepping-stone to what is achieved. So, to complete the picture, we need to find measures of performance. This may be direct and hard, in the form of direct output of work such as boxes packed or customers served; or slightly more remote, such as budget variance in areas of responsibility, or customer complaints in area managed. 'Softer' data may include changes in morale, negative attitudes or anecdotes about mistakes. Figure 3.3 shows the choices that we can make about where our focus is placed, what precise objectives might be set and how we go about measuring them.

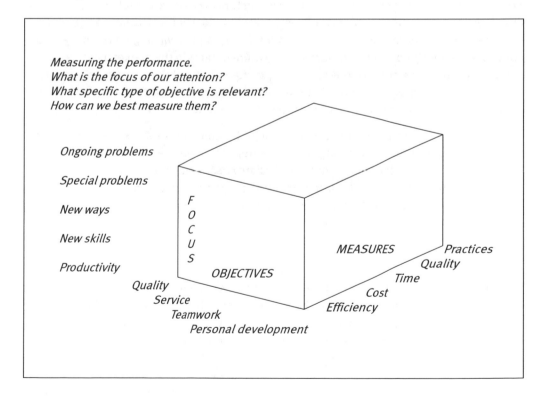

*Figure 3.3 / Measuring performance*

## 4. Costs

There are several ways we can evaluate costs:

### Current actual cost

If we want to explore the cost benefit of a new computer system we might compare the current salary costs of staff displaced with the cost of acquiring the new software.

### Historical cost

We might also want to take into account the lifetime costs of the project – all the costs associated with the project from start to finish. In which case, we would be gathering historical as well as current costs. If the computer system is to replace an existing one we might want to examine the historical costs – what it was before, in comparison with current costs. The evaluation of this cost of course will be affected by inflation over the intervening years and indeed the changing costs of technology.

### Replacement cost

So in comparing costs for a system today with historical costs we are reflecting the difference between replacement costs and costs that may exist in the accounts of a business. If we were to look at the lifetime costs of training, say, a pilot, we might take into account costs over several years. If there were already trained pilots in the market place, we might want to compare the costs of bringing in a qualified pilot and then retraining to our type of aircraft. So we are comparing lifetime costs built up of historical costs, with current costs of replacing the (in this case) person with a suitable alternative.

Where there is a shortage of a particular skill in the labour market, salaries tend to rise, shifting the bias towards training less experienced people as a more cost-effective option. See Appendix for more details on **lifetime cost analysis**. In Chapter 4 we will look at some accounting principles, in particular the need to avoid confusing readers with different bases of costing. If, therefore, you compare historical cost with replacement, make sure that each type of cost is clearly labelled.

### Opportunity cost

For our computer system, we might also consider what alternatives might exist for our time and money. The opportunity cost compares what we do with what we have foregone. Of course, you can change decisions and you can take actions in a sequence, but you can never get back the time spent. In a competitive market, where making the right decision today can make the difference between success and failure, you may not have the chance to reverse your decisions and survive. Change is always a choice, but survival is not a right and is never guaranteed. Once a competitor has gained some advantage, you have to work that much harder to win it back.

Even though it is sometimes difficult to measure, it is always a useful question to ask of any project. What is foregone by doing this project? What are the alternative uses of my time and money?

## SITUATION ANALYSIS

Let us try to summarise the previous sections into a checklist of headings. In carrying out a situation analysis the following areas need to be considered and answers to the following questions identified.

### 1. History

Starting a journey begins with knowing where you are, not where you would like to be. We are where we are, and the starting point to chart a route to the future is to understand clearly the current position. Travellers are only lost because they can no longer make a mental connection between their current position and where they have come from or are going to.

Analysis of the current situation starts with the history of where we have come from. Why are we here and what decisions brought us to this point? They may on hindsight have been good or bad. That is not the point. We cannot change history, only learn from it, and certainly as Santayana said, 'those who cannot remember the past are condemned to repeat it'. That history should include:

- Data on recent trends with a commentary. If labour turnover, for example, is a key issue, can we see any patterns over the recent past when it rises and falls?

- Theories as to why the situation has arisen. Note that there may be several theories and in our development of the business case for taking a particular action we will need to show how the plan deals with these theories. For example, if our theory about the rise in labour turnover is because of uncertainty amongst staff about the company's future, our business plan will need to show how, say, a new communications initiative will address the problem. In this example, we will also need to put in place measures to see whether the initiative is working. Recognise that there may be no right theory; indeed there may be several competing views. As Kurt Levin said, 'there is nothing so practical as a good theory'. The purpose of a theory is to explore the question why, and in so doing gain a deeper understanding of the subject at hand. The value of any particular theory can be judged by the use one can make of it to guide practical action.

- Identifying strengths, weaknesses, opportunities and threats (*SWOT*), as we have discussed in Chapter 2 and is more fully described in the Appendix, is a good way of summarising the analysis that has gone on.

Warning! In examining the past, history is on the side of the victor and it is all too easy merely to blame rather than explain failures on previous management. Even if the current problems are a product of incompetence, it is still necessary to show what the nature of this incompetence was and how current and future staff will avoid these problems.

## 2. Issues and challenges

- What are the issues we face right now?

- Why is this a concern at this time?

- Do we have a clear understanding of the *root causes*? For example, the issue might be that employment costs are too high, exacerbated by exchange rates in comparison to alternative suppliers.

In answering these questions we might use one or all of the following techniques:

- *SWOT* analysis (strengths, weaknesses, opportunities and threats)

- *CSF* (critical success factors – those things that we have to get right in order to be successful) including suppliers and key customers.

- *Core competences,* which give us competitive advantage.

## 3. Stakeholder analysis

- Who are the stakeholders and what do they want?

- Can we develop a strategy that meets expectations and reconciles possible conflicts?

- What power and influence do they each have? For example, some shareholders might want dividends, others might want capital growth, while staff might want pay and benefits that conflict with short-term profitability.

## 4. Market place and competition

- What is the structure of the market place? What is our market position and how do we compare against our competitors (market share)? (That is, are there few or many competitors and how do they compare in size? It is a very different market when there are one or two dominant players and the rest are minnows, than when there are many medium competitors.)

- What differentiates us in the market place?

- How does our marketing mix (product, price, promotion and method of distribution) compare with others?

- What is happening to the market? Is it growing or static? What is happening to market size and our share? If we are claiming market share growth in a declining market, we need to have a strong argument for our forecasts.

- How defensible is our position against new entrants in the market place or substitute products or services?

- What are our competitors doing about this issue?

- What do shareholders, analysts and suppliers say about us?

- What are the pressures we face and what are the emerging trends? For example, perhaps our competitors have outsourced all manufacturing to China, a growing trend among companies in our industry, and analysts are highlighting a profits warning for our organisation. The rights issue is under threat unless we get our costs in shape.

## 5. Customers

- Who are our customers and what do we provide to them?

- What are our customers saying to us right now?

- How prepared are our customers for changes in, for example, sourcing?

- Is price compared with service and quality an issue? For example, our customers are telling us that they want to support our desire to continue to manufacture in the UK, for the quality and flexibility it gives them.

## 6. Financials

- What are the current and historical trends in profitability, and in particular major cost areas?

- What are the latest forecasts?

- How much time do we have before our financial position becomes critical? For example, return on sales has declined from 15 per cent to 10 per cent and is forecast to decline to 7 per cent by the year-end. This ratio needs to be stabilised and improving within the next six months.

## 7. People and organisation

- What is the current organisation structure and headcount?

- What is the resource position and capacity for change (for example, money, staff, facilities, management quality, organisational capability and technology)?

- Do we have the management competence to carry through the plan?

- How do our employment costs compare with competitors?

- What flexibility do we have in changing the structure of our workforce? For example, from an analysis of our current structure and headcount, we estimate that our employment costs are 10 per cent higher per unit of sales than our most efficient competitor. Our contracts of employment are all full-time and we use few subcontractors or short-term staff.

## 8. Operations

- What are the measures of efficiency and effectiveness of our current mode of operation?

- What opportunities are there for improvement?

- How do we compare to the best in class? For example, we manufacture in product lines and we operate at 95 per cent utilisation. Measures of quality and waste indicate that we could improve our costs efficiency by 10 per cent. We are probably 20 per cent worse than the best in class.

## 9. Technology

- What generation of technology are we using?

- Where do we lie against competition – ahead or behind?

- How effective do we assess our use of technology? For example, we have installed the latest generation of assembly machine, though our oldest is 20 years old. Information technology is using the latest releases and we believe that we are comparable to the industry leaders in its use.

## PERSCO

At the away day in Persco, the team used several tools to explore their situation more carefully. They developed a *SWOT* analysis that showed:

*Strengths* – well regarded for their quality, effective teamworking sharing the expertise they individually had for the benefit of all.

*Weaknesses* – poor IT systems, too many managers reliant on them to do the HR component of their jobs.

*Opportunities* – two administrative staff were leaving, so there was a chance to avoid redundancy cost/recruitment costs.

*Threats* – the rate of change required would be too fast for them to develop systems and change attitudes and competence.

## SUMMARY OF THE KEY POINTS FROM THIS CHAPTER

Congratulations on reaching the end of this chapter! In this chapter we have explored several difficult areas, such as some of the philosophical questions surrounding information. The starting point for planning is to scan the environment, and an outline structure for gathering data was presented, including the use of PESTEL to provide a framework for our analysis.

This chapter has tackled the subject of data – its sources, validity and analysis. We have examined four types of data: what people believe, what people do, the result of their activity and the cost. We obtain data on these four areas from many sources, primary and secondary, and in many ways, including surveys and questionnaires. I have sought to show a number of techniques and principles to be adopted in designing the instruments for data capture.

These considerations about data finally led us to a situation analysis, where we sought to lay a foundation for considering future options.

So what should you do as a result of this chapter? Ensure that you have a thorough situation analysis and good quality data that will stand scrutiny.

# 4
# Getting to grips with the numbers

*A cynic is the person who knows the price of everything and the value of nothing.*

*Oscar Wilde*

## INTRODUCTION

The financial component of any plan will need to answer some specific questions about the amount of money needed and when it is required in order to plan cash flow. In some instances there will be questions concerning how the proposal is funded by, for example, raising money from elsewhere or diverting funds from other projects. It is at this stage that you need to relate to your finance function and be clear about who does what in preparing and presenting business cases.

This chapter sets out to describe the basic components of the financial plan.

## THE CONCEPT OF VALUE

When we purchase something it might be seen as expensive at £1 or cheap at £10,000. It all depends on the value we might place on the good or service in question. We place a value depending on a number of criteria:

*Need*. If it is a question of life and death, especially where we are emotionally involved, price becomes less relevant. So, for a pharmaceutical company, the consequences of not completing that trial on time or recruiting the right number of patients might result in delays in licensing and people dying.

*Alternatives*. Where the order of magnitude of the price of an article is broadly understood, for example, a car, we make comparisons between models and extras and features, rather than other goods or services. Often the context sets the price, which in other contexts might seem excessive, for example a car radio or a cup of tea in an exclusive hotel. We might also compare the cost against alternative ways of satisfying the need. Instead of driving to work we might take the train. In such an instance we might also consider the opportunity cost — what else we could do with the money saved, such as go on a holiday. Alternatives for a pharmaceutical company might be alternative suppliers, countries and protocols.

*The return*, financial or otherwise that we can make from the transaction. If by buying a better car that breaks down less often we are able to work more effectively, we might perceive a higher value in a more expensive car. In a drug trial, the quality of data might be considered versus the cost of obtaining it.

## ADDING VALUE IN EVERYTHING

In many time-management courses, a question is often suggested to participants that they should be asking throughout their day: 'What is the best use of my time right now?' In every job there is wasted time, but this is usually dwarfed by time that is spent on work that adds no value to the end product.

Organisations, as they grow, accumulate processes and rules that may have solved a problem at some stage but then become a hindrance to the future.

> When a visiting head of state visits the country, a ceremonial gun crew fires a 21-gun salute. One day, an onlooker asked why there were four people. 'One to load, one to fire, one to command and one to hold the horse in case it bolts.' 'But,' said the onlooker, 'there are no horses. You gave them up a century ago.' 'Ah,' said the commander, 'that's tradition.'

So it is with many of the processes in organisations. Subjecting each and every activity to the question 'Does this add value to the bottom line?' is the discipline behind every business case.

Any organisation is a chain of activities that culminate in a consumer gaining some good or service. 'If you are not serving a customer, you had better be serving someone who is' was an old maxim. In HR it is easy to become somewhat divorced from the end customer, as the value chain of HR work is sometimes quite tenuous in its connection with the end user. A good test of any business plan is, does it add value to the service the consumer gets?

In HR, the value chain is simple to understand but complex to measure. The net product of HR policies and processes should produce an organisation that scores higher on measure of productivity, morale, retention, discretionary effort, than without HR involvement.

Some ways in which HR can add value are:

- recruiting the right people for the job and thus enhancing the customer experience or avoiding the costs of dealing with poor performance

- delivering cost-effective training that significantly enhances skills and effectiveness in the workplace

- facilitating change to retain key staff and maintain morale and motivation

- providing timely and accurate advice such that line managers keep on the right side of the law.

Given that an organisation is a system of interconnected activities, anything that we do will have some consequences somewhere else within the organisation – both good and bad. Indeed one of the lessons from seeing an organisation as an interconnected system is to recognise that any action will have intended and unintended consequences. It is the latter that often nullify the intended benefits.

---

The purchasing department of an airline managed to negotiate a saving on plastic bags, which the airline used in large quantities, in return for using a thinner material. The bonus scheme for purchasing managers was based on their savings made against target. The sacks were used for rubbish collection on the aircraft and elsewhere.

However, the costs for cleaning the aircraft went up overall, exceeding the budget. The thinner sacks broke more often, spilling the contents and necessitating more cleaning. Cleaners then had to use double sacks, nullifying the cost advantage of thinner sacks.

Until the connection was made, purchasing staff were praised for their effectiveness while cabin service were criticised for exceeding their costs budget.

---

How do we know that we are adding sufficient value to keep us in the race? Measures of current profitability do not necessarily help understand what might occur in the future. The first technique is to **benchmark** our activities against others. Chris Nutt of the Manpower Society[11] says that the usual tendency is to benchmark current or last year's strategies and performance, that is, the end *result* of strategy making. By benchmarking performance *drivers* and *lead indicators* we are, in a sense, benchmarking for future performance.

The second technique is to develop a basket of measures, called a **balanced scorecard,** to identify some of the lead indicators that in time might have an effect on the bottom line. Invariably there is a lag between taking an action, especially in the HR arena, and the subsequent effect on the bottom line. See the Appendix for a description of these techniques. The concept that HR activities today will in due course have an effect on the bottom line tomorrow is now embodied in a new operational and financial review (OFR). The box shows an extract.

---

## Extracts from the OFR regulations

The OFR is intended to be a balanced and comprehensive analysis of the development and performance of the business, including the main trends and factors underlying the performance and financial position of the business during the year, and those which are likely to affect its performance in future years. The company's auditors will be required to carry out a review of the OFR.

The business environment is changing dramatically and at an accelerating pace. Companies are becoming increasingly complex and information needs are changing. Some of the forces reshaping the business environment include:

*Globalisation; Transparency and Accountability; Democratisation of Ownership;* [changes in] *Competition;*

*Changes in Business Assets* – increasingly intangible – some of the biggest contributors to business success are those that are the most difficult to quantify: people, customers, knowledge base, brand, and reputation;

*Stewardship* – business is being asked to contribute more to the well being of employees, customers, and communities.

Expected benefits include:

- lower average cost of capital

- 5–10 per cent performance improvement over five years

- better boardroom discussions and decisions

- improved ability to recruit and retain key personnel

- avoidance of reputation failure

- helps managers and investors identify and evaluate investment opportunities, reduce costs and ensure human and financial capital is directed towards investments with the highest returns.

Source: Nutt (2005).

---

## PLANNING TIME HORIZONS

*If you want to plan for a year, sow seeds, for ten, plant trees, and for a lifetime develop men.*

*Old Chinese saying*

Over what time periods should business plans be formulated? To answer the question, we need to resolve a dilemma. In a changing world any plan can easily be deflected by events, and so the longer the timeframe of the plan, the lower the probability that projections and assumptions will be valid. Yet, if we need to make decisions about longer-term change programmes (see Table 4.1), we must make some stab at the longer term. To reiterate an earlier point, the point of planning is not to believe that somehow we can make a better prediction of the future, but rather that by going through the process, the underlying assumptions and sensitivities will be more clearly understood, so when the plan does change it is much easier to recognise the consequences and update it accordingly.

The planning process is in the form of an iterative cycle (see box 'Planning cycle')

*Table 4.1 / **Human resourcing time frames***

|  | *Short term* | *Medium term* | *Long term* |
|---|---|---|---|
| *Needs* | *Budget forecast* | *Profit plan/ strategic plan* | *Strategic plans – market changes – product changes* |
| *Sources of supply* | *Existing resources and replacements* | *Current resources less wastage plus trainees* | *Predicted labour market – demographic – education/technical* |
| *Actions required* | *Overtime Temporary staff Recruitment Contractors* | *Flexible working Transfers Training Recruitment* | *Management development Organisational development Job restructuring Long-term training* |
|  | *0–12 months* | *1–3 years* | *5 years +* |

**Planning cycle**

| | |
|---|---|
| Agree | – where should we be? |
| Investigate | – where are we? |
| Identify | – the 'gap' |
| Plan | – the corrective action(s) |
| Implement | – the plan |
| Review | – and update plan |

## UNDERSTANDING THE FINANCIALS

This book is not designed to give you a course in accounting, but you should be aware of what kinds of information need to be presented for a proper financial appraisal:

- Investment required, both capital and revenue.

- The effect of the proposal on the income and expenditure statement of the business unit.

- In particular, if there are one-off costs upfront and benefits accruing later, a forecast over several years of the effect on the bottom line will be required. (See example in Figure 4.1.)

- A cash flow statement.

- Payback period.

Before we examine costs and benefits, it is important to view the financial case from the point of view of an investor. Whilst the origins of a business case may lie in investing in some new service or technology, the investor will be most interested in whether the market is there in sufficient volume and prepared to pay a price to achieve a profitable return. 'Investors want to put their money into market driven rather than technology driven or service driven companies' (Rich and Gumpert 1985). Even when focusing only internally, where customers might be staff, this is still a consideration when evaluating the benefit. While financial data is important, recognise that they are only the product of a set of assumptions about the future, and rest on the ability of people to deliver. Shrewd investors are more interested in the assumptions and the people.

Planning is different from budgeting. Business plans will look at different scenarios and will be open to change. Once agreed, there will no doubt be a budget struck, based on

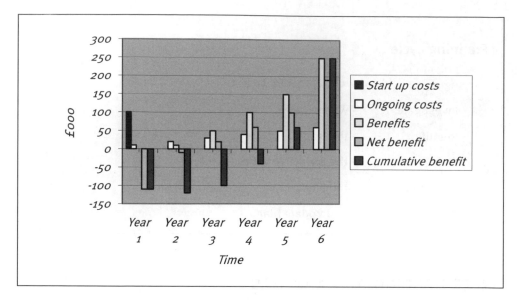

*Figure 4.1 / **Project costs and benefits over time***

the plan. Budgets tend to be for a year, focused on financial targets and for control purposes, whereas planning may look forward several years, over the life of a project.

In summary the process looks like this:

1. Establish a vision and a mission.

2. Determine a strategy to get there.

3. Build a business plan based on the strategy.

4. Identify individual goals and how these are to be achieved in line with the plan.

5. Establish a budget.

There are some accounting principles we should understand at the outset:

## Accounting principles

- *Matching.* When comparing costs against benefits, we should match those costs (and only those costs) incurred in generating that benefit.

- *Going concern.* The assumption is made that a business will continue and so the costs of closure are not usually factored into a plan, unless it has a specific fixed life. In risky projects, the costs of closure should always be calculated for reasons of prudence (see example below).

- *Consistency.* Costs should be treated in the same way throughout the plan. Mixing say historical costs with replacement costs confuses the reader.

- *Prudence*. We should take a cautious view of estimates of, for example, revenues or the value of assets.

- *Cost*. The cost of an asset should always be stated at cost or, if lower, the net realisable value.

## One-off costs and recurring expenditure

One-off costs, such as a training course to introduce staff to a new system, occur only once, as the name implies. But over a period of time a pattern may emerge, for example if training new staff in the system becomes a regular feature. An organisation might be prepared to consider a one-off cost for a less tangible gain, whereas recurring expenditure which will affect the ongoing profitability will need more financial justification. Recognising the difference between a one-off cost and recurring expenditure can help us identify the nature of the expenditure, and challenges us more specifically to identify what benefits arise.

Cost categories will depend on the specific project, but most will usually include:

- staff costs, including overheads such as pensions, national insurance and sick pay (see box 'Costs of human resources')

- property costs including utilities (heat, light, power)

- maintenance

- equipment and machinery

- IT (including depreciation on any investment)

- general overhead (eg management, finance)

- bought-in services (eg security, printing)

- materials.

Do not forget a contingency for unforeseen circumstances.

---

## Cost of human resources

- Remuneration

  - salary
  - bonus
  - fringes

- Recruitment

---

- Training
- Relocation
- Leaving
- Support services
  - social
  - canteen
  - medical
- Personnel administration

Source: Manpower Society Checklist.

Let us look at some of the start-up costs of a sample project.

## Example

This business was proposing to set up a new office.

### Set-up costs

Table 4.2 itemises the initial anticipated set-up costs.

Table 4.2 / **Initial anticipated set-up costs**

| Item | Cost (£) |
|---|---|
| Purchase of lease | 20,000 |
| Refurbishment | 25,000 |
| Furniture and office equipment | 25,000 |
| Professional fees for set-up | 10,000 |
| Relocation cost from old office | 5,000 |
| Recruitment cost of new staff | 5,000 |
| Cost of IT network and workstations | 5,000 |
| Telecommunication costs | 3,000 |
| Launch marketing and promotion | 5,000 |
| Total | 103,000 |

Of these expenses, some are clearly capital, including furniture and office equipment, as they have a life beyond the accounting period. Other costs are clearly revenue – professional fees – while there may be some debate about others such as telecommunication costs and refurbishment. While correct classification might not affect the decision to invest or not, it will affect how the expenses, once incurred, are shown in the company accounts, and so might affect the judgement of the wider world, such as financial analysts and journalists. Proper attention to accounting standards is necessary.

## Operational costs for new office

In evaluating the risk of the venture, the costs of closing the office at the end of year 2 were considered.

Table 4.3 / **Operational costs for new office**

| Item | Cost – year 1 (£) | Cost – year 2 (£) |
|------|------|------|
| Direct labour costs | 70,000 | 100,000 |
| Salary-related overheads | 17,500 | 25,000 |
| Office-related overheads | 30,000 | 60,000 |
| Total other overheads | 17,000 | 35,000 |
| **Total** | **134,500** | **220,000** |

## Exit costs

Table 4.4 / **Exit costs**

| Item | Cost (£) |
|------|------|
| Staff compensation | 13,500 |
| Legal fees | 5,000 |
| Termination of the office lease | 5,000 |
| Management time | ? |
| Fixed assets written off | 32,300 |
| Other fees | 500 |
| **Total** | **56,300** |

Of course, these forecasts might be pessimistic, as assets might be sold, staff transferred, leases assigned to someone else, all of which might mitigate the loss. Nevertheless, if the business case is viable on a pessimistic set of assumptions, then greater confidence will be experienced by the reader, which reinforces the case. It is also invariably true that additional costs emerge at time of closures that have not been forecast, particularly the time taken to achieve closure.

In Table 4.4 you will also notice 'management time'. You might value this in terms of the salary and overhead cost of an executive, but the opportunity cost is probably more important, as there might be more productive use for the individual's time.

If our payback period was, say, three years for any new project, we could estimate the revenue or benefit required.

Table 4.5 / *Cumulative revenue of the sample project*

|  | Year 1 (£) | Year 2 (£) | Year 3 (£) |
|---|---|---|---|
| Start up costs | 103,000 | | |
| Operational costs | 134,500 | 220,000 | 220,000 |
| Total | 237,500 | 220,000 | 220,000 |
| Cumulative cost | | 457,500 | 677,500 |
| Exit cost | | | 56,300 |
| Cumulative total | | | 733,800 |

On an ongoing basis, cumulative revenue would need to have reached £677,500 to achieve a three-year payback. If the project had a finite life and exit costs needed to be included, the figure rises to £733,800.

## Overheads

Beyond direct costs any organisation will have a myriad of more indirect costs that need to be borne. HR in many minds is an overhead, and the assaults on HR to reduce costs are in part a result of a failure to understand how the function adds value. How might overhead be apportioned? There are several options:

- Retained as functional costs, for example central management, and consolidated in the company accounts. On this basis the rate of return of any operational project has to be higher than might be expected in order to ensure these 'invisible' costs are covered. For example, a company required any business plan to produce a 30 per cent return on investment. Once the central costs had been excluded the real rate of return was closer to 20 per cent.

- The levy of a management charge on each function. This approach makes the costs more visible to each function, but inevitably raises issues about the way costs are allocated, and brings greater pressure on the spenders of these central costs to justify them.

## The effect of experience

When the organisation first sets out on a project, cost is incurred as a result of inexperience. There may be mistakes to be corrected, work to be redone or a longer time taken. Later, with more experience and a greater understanding, negotiation with suppliers can be tighter, utilisation of resources can be squeezed and equipment used more efficiently. In addition, with a greater volume of activity, overheads are spread over a greater number of transactions.

When estimating costs in a project, a common mistake is to underestimate the start-up costs, and the experience effect later.

## Non-financial investments

Apart from direct costs, other categories of investment might include far less tangible elements. For example, one manager might invest more time and show greater skill than another in completing appraisals in a way that leads to improved performance as opposed to hurt and disgruntled staff.

Investing in communications such that each and every member of staff understands the strategy of the organisation and how his or her role fits in can lead to more focused performance, increased motivation and morale. Measures of benefit might be the extent to which every staff member knows the strategy of the organisation, confirmed by survey or anecdote.

Long-term development of staff is sometimes seen as an act of faith, in that it is nigh impossible to accurately identify what the bottom-line effect is of coaching a manager in, say, developing a strategy. But measures of the gap between the ideal competency profile of the organisation and actuality give a measure of the investment required.

## Benefits

Merely identifying the costs of, say, an appraisal training programme, without identifying what that training programme is seeking to do, gives only part of the story.

In Chapter 1 we highlighted several categories of justification and benefit:

- within current policy and budget determined by the overall organisation strategy
- cost saved

- retention of staff

- better-quality work

- time saved and opportunity cost

- critical incidents reduced

- alternative choices for the same investment

- competitive advantage

- against best practice benchmarks.

In presenting a business case the costs are often easier to measure than the benefits. Indeed it is easy to confuse costs with value. An organisation in which there has been heavy investment in HR may still be valueless if the market changes and the firm collapses. So we are often concerned with prospective value, rather than retrospective value.

## Justifying the unquantifiable

Cost–benefit analysis on measurable costs alone is often flawed. An old story, often repeated, is of a drunk who comes out of a bar and drops his ring in a dark gutter. He walks to the nearest lamppost and starts looking for it. When asked why he was looking there rather than the dark gutter, he replies, 'It is lighter here.' It is all too easy to only focus on those items in the equation that can be measured. So before concluding our case based on the numbers alone, we need to consider the other 'softer' factors. There are principally four ways to evaluate them:

- By attempting some measurement of their value. For example, convenience of access to a service can be measured in terms of time and this in turn can be evaluated by the salary cost of someone's time.

- Having evaluated the measurable criteria first, the intangible factors can be assessed on the extent to which they tip the balance for or against the project. In some instances the crucial test might be whether it helps to deliver the overall strategy regardless of the cost or benefit of the particular proposal.

---

A company that had recently expanded to become a global firm believed that it needed to demonstrate to staff and customers the diversity of the workforce. In particular, it wanted to move staff between offices to ensure a consistency of approach and to show a truly global workforce. The costs of transfers were unable to be justified on tangible grounds, but the company was prepared to invest £50,000 to facilitate this process because it believed it was the 'right thing to do'.

---

- By weighting the different elements in the criteria. So for example, in a case of deciding whether to relocate staff to a new site, the measurable criteria might show savings, but a key factor might be the availability of new staff. This might be rated more highly than the cost benefit, and be seen as 'a show stopper'. A response might be to examine again the cost–benefit calculation and see whether reinvesting any of the savings might solve the recruitment problem.

---

A company that outsourced an IT function to India was frustrated by a series of problems that arose out of the cultural differences between the United Kingdom and India. The solution was to get some staff from India working for a time in the UK operation, and for there to be a UK presence in India. However, the costs of such an exercise had not been factored into the original cost–benefit calculation, and management were reluctant to invest some of the (tangible) savings to solve some of the (intangible) problems.

---

- By viewing what our competitors do. While there is a danger of lemming-type behaviour, it is invariably wise to at least check what your competitors do and make a deliberate decision to follow or not. Nathan (2005), drawing on the work of King, suggests this approach in justifying career counselling.

## More tangible measures

In working with people, measures of improvement in attitude and competence are difficult to measure, but there are measures that we can focus on.

### Labour turnover

'The chairman has retired, hire another office junior' was the opening line of one historical treatise on the subject (Cannon 1979). In the days of little turnover and promotional hierarchies that pattern may have happened. It is inconceivable today in many organisations around the world. Indeed the shift in emphasis towards encouraging people to manage their own careers and keep themselves employable encourages turnover.

*Mike was a computer engineer and decided out of loyalty to his company to stick at servicing a particular type of computer. When it was phased out, Mike was made redundant. 'I now know that the best strategy would have been to forget loyalty and keep moving to keep my skills up to date and to show flexibility and adaptability.'*

*Cannon 2004*

What is the process that underpins turnover choices? Figure 4.2 is drawn from several studies and highlights the many factors that affect the changing balance of personal needs required from work versus the contribution that is required.

*Other morale measures*

- Absenteeism is both a measure of individuals' health and commitment to the workplace, and a measure of organisational health when viewing the workforce as a whole.

- Accidents are both a measure of safe working practices and management control, as well as an indicator of individual attentiveness.

- Work satisfaction, derived from surveys as discussed earlier, can indicate several different dimensions of morale; the extent to which individuals are in the right job, the adequacy of their training, provision of appropriate equipment, working conditions and other support mechanisms, demands of the job, style of supervision, public perception of the organisation and the extent to which people are embarrassed or proud to be part of it.

A summary of how we can evaluate the costs and benefits of HR activities is shown in Table 4.6.

*Table 4.6 / **A framework for evaluating costs and benefits of human resource development***

| Resource investments | Resource condition | Resource performance | Return on investment |
|---|---|---|---|
| *Acquisition* | *Competence* | *Output* | *Impact on the bottom line* |
| Recruitment and selection | Attributes Knowledge Skills and fit with requirement | Productivity ratios Benchmark comparisons Efficiency Retention | Profitability Asset values |
| *Development* | *Climate* | *Quality* | *Customer loyalty* |
| Induction Relevant experience Training Organisation development | Attitudes Flexibilities Motivation Communications Creativity Synergy | Mistakes Fit for purpose Standards | Repeat business Cost of acquiring new customers |

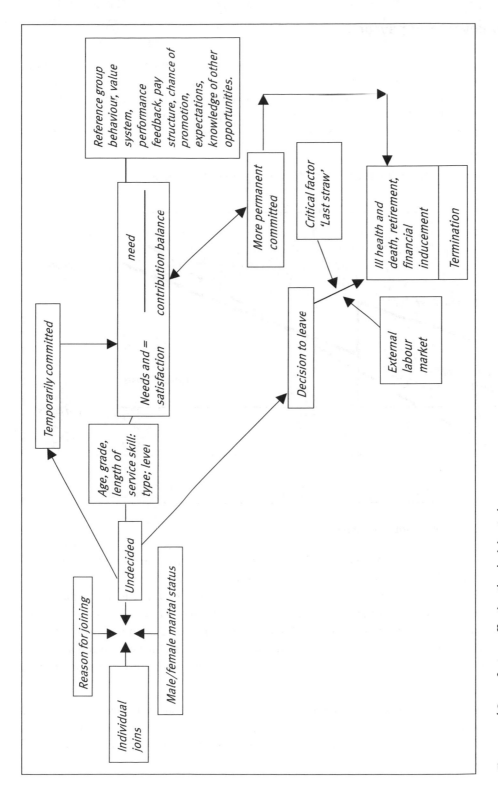

*Figure 4.2 / Some factors affecting the decision to leave*

## Breakeven and payback

When income equals costs we have a breakeven position. At the point in time when the accumulated revenue (or costs savings) equals the accumulated costs we have a payback period. In any business where there is an income stream from some activity, there is invariably the necessity of incurring expenditure before revenue arises. Some of that expenditure is of a fixed nature, and bears only a periodic relationship to the business being run.

Figure 4.3 shows a breakeven chart identifying the different types of cost.

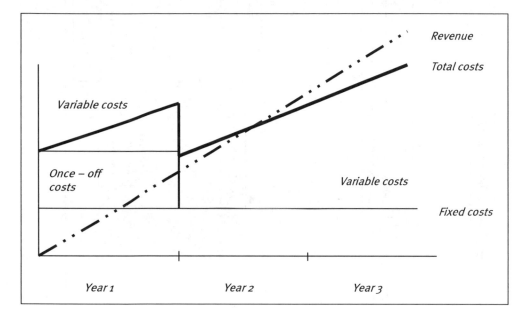

*Figure 4.3 / **Calculating the breakeven***

Once the business is started it is all too easy to forget the requirement for these periodic investments in facilities or equipment. Another problem, known as the creeping breakeven, arises when the breakeven only occurs when capacity is at its maximum. Just when the project becomes profitable, it becomes necessary to invest further, and the level at which breakeven is reached rises again. It points to the necessity of keeping costs under control and timing investment carefully. Make an investment too soon and the organisation will have underutilised assets; too late, and the business is constrained by a shortage of assets.

In developing a business plan any analyst will want to see breakeven as soon as possible after investment, and on conservative assumptions. In a changing world payback periods of more than one or two years are risky, because the assumptions can easily change.

## An example of a training centre

A company decided to set up a training centre and wanted to know at what volume of delegates and over what time period would the project break even. Table 4.8 shows the assumptions.

The following calculation was done:

**One-off costs**

*Fittings and furniture*              *£40,000*

*Launch costs*                       *£30,000*

These one-off costs are related to the maximum number expected, but bear no relation to the likely number of delegates that will arise. The following cost will also bear little relationship to numbers, but is of course recurring.

**Recurring cost**

*Lease on building*              *£10,000 per annum*

There are also some semi-variable costs. For example, utilities costs will increase with the number of delegates as they use more electricity and the like, but there are standing charges regardless of use, and indeed with no delegates there will still be some costs associated with staff employed there.

From Table 4.7 and Figure 4.4 we see that the project appears to break even in year 2, when total revenue begins to overtake total costs. However, if we look at the bank balance we see a different picture because of the one-off costs at the beginning of the project.

So in any project appraisal we need both an ongoing breakeven as well as a cash flow.

If we assumed that the variable costs vary directly with student numbers and we recompute Figure 4.4 (see Figure 4.5), a breakeven at about 250–300 students occurs. This assumption is not quite valid because costs are incurred (of a tutor for example) whether there are 5 or 15 students in the class.

Table 4.7 / **Profit and loss on training centre project (£000)**

| Number of students | 100 | 300 | 600 |
| --- | --- | --- | --- |
| Start up costs | 70 | – | – |
| Fixed costs | 55 | 75 | 95 |
| Variable costs | 20.5 | 55 | 112 |
| Total cost | 145.5 | 130 | 207 |
| Revenue | 60 | 180 | 360 |
| **Profit/loss** | **−85.5** | **50** | **153** |

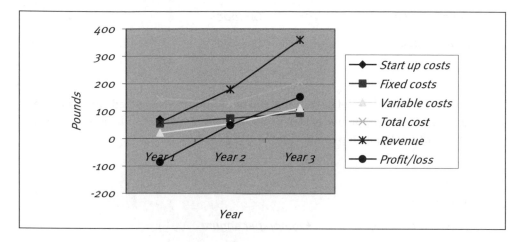

Figure 4.4 / **Profit and loss on training centre project**

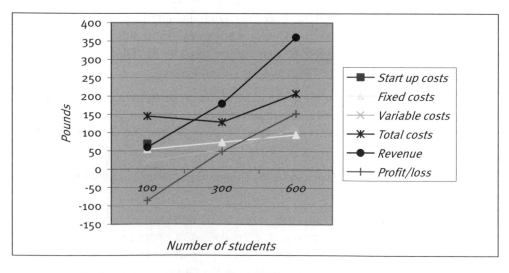

Figure 4.5 / **Profit and loss on training centre project**

Table 4.8 / **Business plan assumptions**

| Year 1 | Year 2 | Year 3 |
|---|---|---|
| 100 delegates | 300 delegates | 600 delegates |
| 9 courses on 3 subjects | 28 courses on 4 subjects | 60 courses on 6 subjects |
| 1 permanent administrator | 2 staff | 3 staff |
| 3 contract tutors, (only paid when a course runs) Paid at rate of £1,500 per course | 4 contract tutors | 6 contract tutors |
| Note: number of course tutors determined by type of courses run | | |
| Course fees £600 per 2-day course | | |

Table 4.9 / **Cash flow on training centre project**

| | Year 1 (£000) | Year 2 (£000) | Year 3 (£000) |
|---|---|---|---|
| Opening balance | 0 | -85.50 | -35.50 |
| **Costs** | | | |
| **Start-up costs** | | | |
| Fittings | 40 | | |
| Launch costs | 30 | | |
| **Fixed costs** | | | |
| Lease | 10 | 10 | 10 |
| Staff | 20 | 40 | 60 |
| Marketing | 25 | 25 | 25 |
| **Variable costs** | | | |
| Utilities | 5 | 7 | 10 |
| Course tutors | 13.5 | 42 | 90 |
| Materials | 2 | 6 | 12 |
| **Revenue** | | | |
| Course fees | 60 | 180 | 360 |
| **Closing balance** | **-85.50** | **-35.50** | **117.50** |

Table 4.10 / **Profit and loss on training centre project**

|  | Year 1 (£ooo) | Year 2 (£ooo) | Year 3 (£ooo) |
|---|---|---|---|
| Start-up costs | 70 | – | – |
| Fixed costs | 55 | 75 | 95 |
| Variable costs | 20.5 | 55 | 112 |
| Total cost | 145.5 | 130 | 207 |
| Revenue | 60 | 180 | 360 |
| **Profit/loss** | -85.5 | 50 | 153 |

You will see that the profit and loss and the cash flow are reconciled in the first year (Tables 4.9 and 4.10), but not in future years because of the loss brought forward. If this was a stand-alone business it would have its own balance sheet and we would see that loss being reflected there in a reduction in current assets. For the most part internal projects are consolidated, and only the overall figure is reflected in the balance sheet. There are other accounting technicalities such as depreciation, capital expenditure, changes in the net effect of creditors and debtors that affect the reconciliation of a cash flow with a profit and loss.[12]

## Capacity planning

To ensure maximum profitability, a business needs to ensure that it works at maximum utilisation of all its assets. Unfortunately assets rarely come in small incremental stages. Buildings require step changes in capacity, as do machines. People only come in a full-size unit (although of course you can buy temporary or part-time staff in incremental units). The problem for many operations is that in a business where the breakeven is close to full utilisation, profitability will never be robust.

Capacity planning seeks to find the optimum scale of the operation to achieve the objective with full utilisation of the assets deployed.

## Investment appraisal

Determining whether to spend money on an item or service is a choice most of us are making daily. However we sometimes regret our purchases because we did not consider all the alternatives; perhaps we found a better use for the money a little later. Once we had worked out the interest we paid on the loan, maybe it turned out not to be such a bargain. This in essence is investment appraisal.

All investment involves a sacrifice of present consumption in order to achieve a better return in the future. When the sums are small and interest rates are low, the cost of borrowing money might be small. In these instances we can think in terms of a crude payback period or rate of return.

> A group of staff was made redundant, incurring £280,000 of redundancy payments. The annual salary bill for this group was £140,000, so we can say that the redundancy process has a payback period of 24 months, or a 50 per cent rate of return.

However, this calculation does not take into account the timing of payments, a problem solved by the application of a technique known as discounted cash flow (DCF). 'DCF methods take account of the fact that earnings vary over the expected life of a project and that £100 due today is worth more than £100 due in a year's time' (*Investment appraisal* 1967).

To calculate a DCF, a cash flow statement is first produced. Then a discount factor is applied. In Table 4.11, it is assumed that the effective interest rate is 8 per cent per annum or 2 per cent per quarter.

Table 4.11 / **Discounted cash flow**

| Qtr | Redundancy | Salaries | Net cash flow | | Discount factor 2%/qtr | Discounted cash flow | |
| --- | --- | --- | --- | --- | --- | --- | --- |
| | | | monthly | cumulative | | monthly | cumulative |
| 1 | −280 | −35 | −315 | − | 1.00 | −315.00 | − |
| 2 | − | −35 | −35 | −350 | 0.98 | −34.31 | −349.31 |
| 3 | − | 35 | 35 | −315 | 0.96 | 33.64 | −315.67 |
| 4 | − | 35 | 35 | −280 | 0.94 | 32.98 | −282.69 |
| 5 | − | 35 | 35 | −245 | 0.92 | 32.33 | −250.36 |
| 6 | − | 35 | 35 | −210 | 0.91 | 31.70 | −218.66 |
| 7 | − | 35 | 35 | −175 | 0.89 | 31.08 | −187.58 |
| 8 | − | 35 | 35 | −140 | 0.87 | 30.47 | −157.11 |
| 9 | − | 35 | 35 | −105 | 0.85 | 29.87 | −127.24 |
| 10 | − | 35 | 35 | −70 | 0.84 | 29.29 | −97.95 |
| 11 | − | 35 | 35 | −35 | 0.82 | 28.71 | −69.24 |
| 12 | − | 35 | 35 | 0 | 0.80 | 28.15 | −41.09 |
| 13 | − | 35 | 35 | − | 0.79 | 27.60 | −13.49 |
| 14 | − | 35 | 35 | − | 0.77 | 27.06 | 13.57 |

As the table shows, a simple oversight of the current month's pay will lead to breakeven not occurring until the beginning of the twelfth quarter and if we apply a discount factor the breakeven occurs between the thirteenth and fourteenth quarters.

## Profit and loss

A profit and loss account will typically have several elements: see Table 4.12.

Table 4.12 / *Elements of a profit and loss account*

| | Example (£000) | Notes |
|---|---|---|
| Revenue or benefit | 1000 | – |
| (Costs of achieving the benefit) | (600) | Direct costs related to benefit |
| **Gross profit** | **400** | **40%** |
| (Salaries) | (200) | These indirect costs do not vary with the volume of revenue |
| (Utilities) | (50) | |
| (Promotion) | (50) | |
| (Administration) | (50) | Services, property costs |
| (Depreciation on equipment) | (10) | The cost of £30 invested in equipment, spread across its expected life of three years |
| **Operating profit** | **40** | **4%** |
| Interest charge | (5) | Cost of borrowing money |
| **Profit before tax** | **35** | **3.5%** |

For most projects, this is as far as we might go. To get to the figure for retained profit, a calculation on tax and for a public company, dividends, will be made.

### Analysing the example

If we had been presented with this income and expenditure statement as part of a business plan, would it represent a worthwhile project?

Gross profit margin (gross profit divided by sales) is 40 per cent. To determine whether this is good, several factors have to be taken into account:

> The level of start-up funding or existing assets that were used, but not accounted for. Businesses that have high start-up costs need higher margins to recover some of those costs, and to build up reserves for future investments.

The subsequent overhead that needs to be borne. Operating profit is only 4 per cent.

Alternative uses for investment moneys. Profit before taxes is 3.5 per cent, which is comparable to placing the money in the building society. This may not be an adequate revenue stream compared with safer options.

However, if the only investment is say £30 in equipment and because the indirect costs are already there and are fixed, we get a good return on the investment (ie $100 \times 35/30 = 116$ per cent).

## FUNDING REQUIREMENTS

In preparing a financial case, keep separate the income and surplus, or trading profit (that is, after all expenses except interest) from issues about funding. The latter is dependent on wider concerns about funding the business. If your project requires new computer equipment, the question of whether it is leased or bought relates to a myriad of factors surrounding the balance sheet and tax position.

In developing a business plan for internal purposes, it is easy to think that money is 'free' and available. Yet funds deployed on one project mean fewer funds for other projects. Cash flow has to be financed from existing resources or raised through overdraft, existing shareholders or the financial markets. Smoothing income and outgoings to achieve a cash-neutral position is a worthy aim.

## SENSITIVITY ANALYSIS

Once the ranges of options are identified and before a decision is finally confirmed, a sensitivity analysis is a worthwhile exercise.

In the business plan of a residential care charity which received money from public funds, it was stated that: 'If income per resident could be increased by 10 per cent then at the projected occupancy our surplus would double.' How can this be? In an operation which has a high fixed cost, but little variable cost (only food in this case), then once the fixed costs are covered, the additional income is mostly surplus. Such operations are highly vulnerable to any fall in occupancy, because it is very difficult to flex their costs to match variable income.

Sensitivity analysis, then, is a series of 'what if' calculations to see the impact of variations in income and costs on the bottom line. Plans which show that costs can be varied according to revenue (or savings) are likely to be more robust and less risky. If your plan is set up as a series of spreadsheets showing costs and benefits, then playing 'what if' is straightforward. Don't confuse the reader with endless permutations, though. Focus on the biggest risks and the most likely vulnerabilities.

## HUMAN CAPITAL

In 1845 Edwin Chadwick remarked that:

*In general, every adult trained labourer may be said to be, in this pecuniary point of view as valuable as two hunters or two race horses, or a pair of first rate carriage horses.*

A hundred and fifty years later, the Kingsmill Report (2003) set out to encourage reporting of human capital in annual accounts, and from 2005, the accounting standards will require companies to report by way of an operational and finance review (OFR). Human capital management (HCM) is 'an approach to people management that treats it as a high level strategic issue and seeks systematically to analyse, measure and evaluate how people policies create value'. This concept has been attempted before, with a joint IPM/ICMA report back in the 1970s on human resource accounting (Giles and Robinson 1972). Also at that time there was an American company, the Barry Corporation, which did include a calculation showing a balance sheet value for its human assets.

These earlier attempts were based on four competing methods:

1. *Tracking investment in human development.* This approach, used by the Barry Corporation and others, 'represents the investments made to acquire and train people to expected levels of effectiveness for their respective occupations, less the amortisation of this investment based upon expected tenure' (from the 1970 annual report of the RG Barry Corporation).

2. *Accounting for human assets.* In 1972 the then IPM and ICMA formed a joint working party and developed a scheme known as human asset accounting. This approach derived an asset value by adding up all the emoluments and adjusting them by a multiplier based on the price earnings ratio (Giles and Robinson 1972).

3. *Systems modelling.* In 1974 an accounting professor at Birmingham University demonstrated a tool to link social processes with accounting data and so measure the consequences of management actions relating to the effectiveness of the workforce (Gambling 1974). In some recent work on the **balanced scorecard** (Kaplan and Norton 1996) and the HR scorecard (Becker *et al* 2001) these earlier ideas have been revived.

4. *Competitive bidding.* Hekimian and Jones (1967) proposed that managers of investment or profit centres should bid for their staff like other assets, and the resulting bid price should be added to their capital base. The performance of these managers would be based on return on assets. The bid price would reflect the cost of alternatives, such as buying in a consultant, or the income/ increased value that they bring in to the team.

Apart from footballers, these ideas were not found to be practicable. These attempts foundered on several theoretical issues. Was a person truly an asset in the same ways as other assets when he/she had the freedom to leave with far shorter notice than the average depreciation period for most equipment? If human assets were supposed to enhance investment decisions, it is a curious effect when we see that reduction in numbers of people has a quicker effect on cash flow and profitability, resulting in an *enhanced* investment prospect. Several practical issues also emerged, such as how to establish the asset value: is it the accumulated lifetime costs of the current workforce? The replacement costs? The opportunity cost? How should experience be evaluated (Cannon 1979)?

In recent years the Saratoga Institute has produced a measure of value-adjusted profit per employee. Adjusted profit is revenue minus operating expenses for facilities, machinery, materials and supplies, and minus payroll and benefits costs. Human capital return in investment is derived from dividing adjusted profit by payroll and benefits.

The work of Becker *et al* (2001) has pointed to the very different nature of human assets. 'Human Capital is not owned by the organisation, but is secured through the employment relationship' (Scarbrough 2003). In particular, these intangible resources 'appreciate with purposeful use', have 'a short shelf life when not in use', 'cannot be bought or imitated' and are very different from the accounting view of an asset. The value of human capital in an organisation is continually changing, as it reflects the fit between the human potential and the market need for that combined capability.

The OFR is designed to identify drivers of performance, and submissions to the formulation of thinking in this area have pointed to items such as skill levels in the workforce, workforce development and experience and skills for the directors. Training costs should be reported.

Identifying which HR practices enhance the productive capacity of the workforce has been the subject of several recent studies. Guest (2000) identified that HR practices working in combination can impact employee behaviour, level of skills, attitude towards the organisation, and can enable staff to make fuller use of their abilities and so in turn affect performance. However, most studies are cross-sectional not longitudinal, and so causal links are difficult to make.

Finding measures that are robust enough to be included such that valid conclusions and comparison can be made is problematic.

The CIPD has recommended the following framework for human capital reporting:

- human capital strategy – the approach to acquisition, development, management and performance of human capital

- quantitative and qualitative data on the acquisition, development, management and retention of human capital

- performance of human capital (Scarbrough 2003).

It classifies indicators into primary and secondary. For a list see *Human capital: external reporting framework* (CIPD 2003).

It is too early to judge whether new thinking this time will develop new approaches, but it is an idea that will keep recurring. After all in most annual accounts, chairmen are fond of saying that 'people are our most valuable asset'.

## PERSCO – THE NEXT STAGE

The HR department was faced with a demand from the board to cut costs and improve service. At their away day, staff had decided to examine moving to a business partner model with a shared services centre and requiring investment in IT and training.

The MD had asked some key questions:

- Will your customers buy it?

- What is the evidence that this change has worked elsewhere?

- What will you need by way of investment?

The team then set about answering those questions. The first question required a dialogue with HR's customers. These included line managers as well as staff.

The director began a series of exercises to ascertain firstly what his customers wanted. He conducted a questionnaire (see example in the Appendix) and set about running a series of focus groups. In the focus groups customers were asked:

- What do you want from HR?

- If you had to pay for the service you currently get, what would you no longer buy?

- What is your ideal of a good service?

- Where do we currently not meet your expectations?

The staff then started a process of research to look at alternatives. They **benchmarked** themselves against others, they looked at literature and talked to academics, they studied their competitors and those they rated as successful in their field. The result of all this analysis was a strategy based on centralising administrative functions using better IT systems delivered over an intranet, along with some specialised advisors at the centre and more expert advisors in the field alongside managers. The business case would be based on lower costs through less staff, and more focused services on those aspects that customers valued, and monitored through a service level agreement. Key measures for the shared service facility would be costs per transaction and the speed of response. In addition some functions such as training delivery and recruitment would be outsourced.

Having ascertained the strategy, the nest step was to work up the business case. The information staff needed to gather for the case included:

- costs of the current operation

- data on alternative arrangements

- examples of how others have done it

- potential benefits.

The first exercise was to identify the costs of the total HR function together with an analysis of the activities undertaken. Some functions were partially handled by other departments, such as payroll, and some already outsourced, such as pension administration. Costs such as recruitment were also partially borne by some departments. So the first step was to get an accurate picture of the costs and activities of the HR function, and where those costs and activities were currently conducted. Figure 4.6 sets out the headings they used.

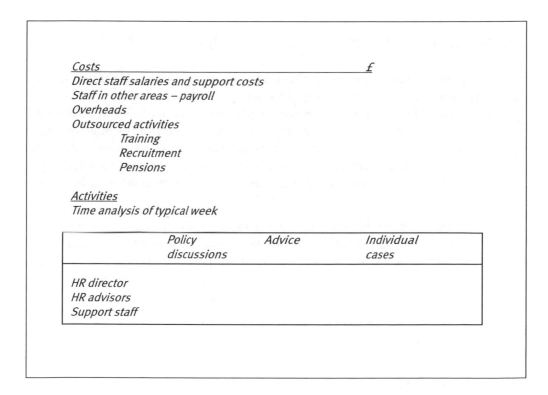

*Figure 4.6 / **A framework for evaluating costs and benefits of human resource development***

They then prepared a proposition and a business case that could be shown and discussed with line managers.

**Restructuring HR to provide cost reduction and services that will add value to the business.**

In line with the demands placed on every department, HR has been considering its strategy to achieve cost reduction and maintain essential HR services. We are proposing to save £50,000 in a full year by a reduction of two staff and by investing £50,000 in improved IT systems, training for HR staff, training for managers in basic HR activities and processes, and in particular how to improve the management of absence, recruitment and on the job training. The role of HR will become more advisory helping managers to manage HR issues for themselves. There will continue to be a service centre that will handle payroll administration, contracts of employment and staff records.

## SUMMARY OF THE KEY POINTS FROM THIS CHAPTER

In this chapter we have explored the financial elements in developing a business plan. We started with looking at the concept of adding value, and the variety of views about how value might be assessed. If a business plan does not deliver extra value to the organisation, however measured, then it is not worth the paper it is written on. When we examined the different approaches to measuring costs, we recognised that help might be needed from professional accountants, especially when we are looking at more complex financial arrangements that affect the balance sheet or tax position of the company.

Several examples of the financial schedules required are shown, including start-up costs, payback period, cash flow and impact on income and expenditure. Turning to the benefits arising from the investment, I highlighted both the tangible and intangible benefits, and pointed to the need to consider both. Just because something does not have a number attached, that does not mean it is not important.

Towards the end of the chapter I looked at human capital, an idea that keeps recurring. With the current interest in OFRs, it remains to be seen whether this idea will again come to the fore.

Finally we looked at the next stage in the Persco case.

So what now? If you are not confident about working with financial data or do not know your way round the company accounts, then this certainly is the time to seek the assistance of an accountant and submit your strategies and plans to a thorough financial appraisal.

# 5

# Turning a business case into a business plan – writing and presenting the plan

*Words are but leaves falling from the tree, actions are the fruit of our effort.*

*Anon.*

## INTRODUCTION

A common misconception is that the writing of a plan can be delegated to a junior manager, or worse to an external consultant. The writing might be more polished in such circumstances, but much of the value lies in the planning, as I said earlier, and this is lost when outsourced. In addition, a plan is only as good as the result it produces, and that often means tough decisions and hard work. If there is no real conviction borne out of personally grappling with the issues, then commitment is likely to fall away when there is resistance. Business leaders win through by clear goals, flexibility to adjust to changed circumstances, good leadership and the courage of their convictions.

## CULTURE OF THE ORGANISATION

Culture, sometimes defined as 'the way we do things together', is based on a shared set of beliefs about the right set of actions in any context. For those who have recently joined a new organisation, culture is all too apparent as the newcomer faces rules and processes that seem strange. Soon, the new starter becomes socialised and no longer questions the ways of the organisation. As we come to write a business plan, the acceptance of our ideas will be influenced by several dimensions of culture:

- Are we following the rules, processes and protocols laid down? If not, and we deliberately seek the role of maverick, our case must probably be stronger to overcome the 'noise' surrounding our approach.

- Are we conscious of the politics and who has power and precedence? If we flout hierarchies and the order in which people should be consulted to give their approval to plans, our chances of success are reduced.

- How do we interpret the biases of the organisation? Is there a greater focus on new ventures and entrepreneurism, or a more conservative attitude towards careful control of existing businesses? Where does the balance lie between concentrating on short-term day-to-day issues and the longer-term trends in the market?

- How hard-nosed is the organisation? Where does the balance lie between commercial pressures and social responsibility?

- Are we conscious of national differences? Fons Trompenaars (1999) highlighted in his international studies the problems caused by differences. For example, cultures differ in the value they place on being on time, or individual or collective rewards.

- Are we conscious of individual differences? A dimension of Myers-Briggs is concerned with sensing versus intuition. The high-sensing person will find it difficult to appreciate the big picture unless the detail is right. The high-intuition person, on the other hand, will find the reverse and be irked by diving into the detail before the big picture is clear.

## STYLE OF WRITING

There is a dilemma we must resolve, and it is one which most presenters of all kinds face: whether to 'slow reveal' or 'cut to the chase'. In the first approach, the case is built step by step with the conclusions right at the end. It has the advantage of showing the logic of the business case, and is especially useful when the conclusions seem at first sight to be counter-intuitive. It has the disadvantage that audiences may lose interest halfway through and may not give you the benefit of the doubt. The alternative is to present the conclusions and then work backwards showing the reasons for your conclusions. It has the advantage that your audience know where they stand immediately, but it has the disadvantage that people may make up their minds immediately and fail to read or listen to the supporting arguments.

Studies in the psychology of decision-making point to a universal human characteristic in our dislike of ambiguity. There is a tendency therefore to move towards quicker, and sometimes more extreme, reactions. Two reactions are either to insufficiently weigh all the evidence, or alternatively to procrastinate, with 'analysis paralysis'.

There is a further factor in our decision-making, known as 'hindsight distortion' (Fischoff 1975), where we seek to reinforce our decisions by filtering out any recollection of evidence that contradicts our belief that we were correct. In a typical ambiguous situation, our desire is to make the choice and so reduce the anxiety surrounding the ambiguity.[13] Once made, we filter out those observations and other data that would deflect us from our choice. If a presentation of a plan therefore poses more questions than it answers, it is likely to be greeted more negatively than if a plan is clear and unequivocal. Even if it is a finely balanced judgement, it can still be presented in a way that helps the reader make up his/her mind, by showing the logic of the case and the rationale of the argument.

A mathematician was explaining a complex theory to a colleague by the use of many symbols on a blackboard followed by an 'equals' sign to the answer. 'What happens here?' the colleague asked. 'A miracle,' said the mathematician. It is natural that your audience will be looking critically for the flaws, and will be less than impressed if there is a 'miracle' connection. If the argument is weak, say so, and show both why you have accepted the weak argument and what you have done to compensate.

## The use of active language

'I set out in the proposal the current situation and the results of the research my team conducted. I go on to show why the solution we suggest is best for the business and how we will implement it' has a better impact than: 'The current situation was researched and possible solutions formulated. Implementation of a preferred option is discussed.' The latter style is more favoured in academic work, but a business case is there to persuade an audience to a course of action rather than to just to present evidence.

## Provide evidence for your claims

The logic of the argument is the cornerstone of your presentation. Consider the following statement: 'We have a huge problem with leavers, because we don't pay the market rate.' It begs many questions in the mind of the reader. Instead the following has more credibility:

> *This year the number of people leaving us voluntarily increased by 20 per cent compared to last year. We now lose 19 per cent of our people every year.*
> *According to a survey of similar jobs in the region, the norm for organisations like ours is just 10 per cent. We looked at the reasons people give for leaving us, and money is the most frequently cited factor. This has been steadily increasing over the last two years, and this year one-third of all leavers cited low pay as their reason for leaving. We recently participated in a salary survey and found that our market position was lower quartile.*

Where there are differences between your proposal and others, internally or externally, explain the differences and why your proposal is better. It gives the reader much greater confidence in your proposal if he/she can see the comparisons. There is a view which says you should leave comparisons between options to the reader, but I would argue that the reader expects you to help guide him/her through the alternatives.

*This proposal to reorganise on the basis of customer segments differs from our current arrangement by.... It also differs from our competitors by .... Each of these organisation structures fails to address the needs of the newly emerging and growing sector, which our proposal does. We anticipate saving £x through a slimmer structure and through increasing penetration amongst these new customers by y per cent. These estimates are based on a pilot project in the North West.*

Consider another example:

*I propose we change this computer system to a newer version for an investment of £250,000 including implementation costs. The savings will involve two staff at a saving of £50,000 a year and a net saving of maintenance of £10,000 a year.*

On this basis it looks like this proposal has a payback over between four and five years (250,000/60,000 = 4.16 years), which is not very attractive. But then consider the opportunity cost.

*If we do not make this investment, we will not be able to capture the records on customer preferences which Sales estimate might be worth a further £50,000 a year of value. The current system is slow and is at capacity. Sales forecast for next year indicate that 5 per cent growth is expected in transactions and with the new product line, an increase of a further 5 per cent of transactions will be expected. To handle the extra load overtime or more staff will be required.*

*Staff are frustrated with the current arrangement and one resignation has been received, necessitating recruitment cost.*

A different picture has emerged, so ensure the whole case is included, some of which is difficult to measure fully, but nevertheless adds weight to the argument.

Consider another statement where more detailed statistical proof is required: 'Morale has suffered significantly since last year.' This begs the question as to how it is measured. Is it merely anecdotal? If so, it is likely to be open to much debate depending on individual perception. Morale might be measured by questions such as, 'How have your feelings about the company changed since last year? Rate your view on a 1 to 5 scale from better to worse.' 'Significantly' might be explained statistically. For example:

*The decrease in morale has been measured by an average decline of 2.4 points on a five-point scale for the five questions covered in the morale survey. This result could only occur 5 in 100 times by chance.*

'There is nothing so powerful as an idea whose time has come' highlights the role of timing in the launch of all new initiatives. Your proposal may be the same as everyone else's, but the time is now ripe. If this is the case, explain why. In an effort to show why this proposal is different to what has gone before, it is easy to focus on everything else other than timing.

## Other points to check

Check grammar, punctuation, spelling, formatting, page numbers. There is no excuse with modern technology. Of course, the closer we get to our work, the harder it is to spot the mistakes. Ask a colleague who is fresh to the subject to read it. They are bound to spot an error probably in text that you have read a dozen times.

Provide a structure – title, contents with page numbers, section headings, layered and maybe numbered.

Allow space in the document, so when bound, it can still be fully read. Space between sections is easier on the eye for the reader and for those who might read it on the move. Space also allows the opportunity for writing comments and questions on the document.

It may appear to be a trivial point, but always ensure that you maintain good document control, dating and numbering versions. Invariably, a business plan will go through many iterations and revisions, and it is all too easy to put in an earlier table with later revised text.

Reference sources of data, quotes and other documents, so the readers know your sources.

There are other subtleties that can cause doubt in the mind of the reader. A document poorly laid out, with typos and other mistakes, is unlikely to inspire confidence, especially when the plan calls for detailed and meticulous controls to achieve successful implementation.

Embedded in our culture and upbringing is the notion of the story. Yet the turgid nature of many business documents forgets this fact. There is likely to be a more ready understanding from a reader if the case is presented in a story, where the early sections tell the history and set the scene. It should draw readers in to the situation, and maybe excite them with possibilities of some business improvement. In the middle sections are the issues and the difficulties to be overcome, followed by the ways in which these can be overcome. The finale shows why the proposed solution is the best solution to the problem and establishes the expectation that, if it was achieved, 'all would be happy ever after'.

Finally, clarify in the document what you want – approval, money and/or support.

## Show why the plan will succeed

Venture capitalists are often faced with making judgements on business ventures based on market and financial data, when they really want to base their judgements on the person's track record. When it is a totally new venture in which the individual concerned has no direct experience, it becomes much more risky. In these instances, the proposer will often be advised to find ways of making further progress with the idea, before seeking funds.

While the detail may be in an appendix, always provide the opportunity for readers to get into the detail if they wish. 'The devil is in the detail', and many a plan has failed to be executed because of attention to detail.

Imagine your reaction to the following words in a business plan: 'We will train our customer service reps to sell more effectively.' We can be sure someone will ask about the nature of the training to yield higher sales and how the writer can be sure. The following paragraph shows in more detail how it is to be done, and gives more confidence to the reader that there is likely to be a positive gain from the investment in training.

> *The training, to be delivered by an experienced sales training consultancy, focuses on three areas of current weaknesses, identified from customer feedback surveys and mystery shopper experiments: product knowledge, especially where there are linked accessories and supplies (eg DVDs, plugs, cables, software with DVD players); customer rapport (eg knowing when to approach customers and how to do so effectively) and closing the sale.*

Where the decision-makers do not know the staff involved, you may wish to present the team, or at least to ensure that their relevant qualifications and experience are in the appendix. A track record in delivering similar types of project always gives greater confidence than if it is the first time (see the case studies at the end of Chapter 7). However, in a changing world this is a counsel of perfection, so always show experience that might be equivalent, or has relevant aspects.

Where there is a known weakness in the team, you might consider being open about it and how you will address it. It is much more convincing than if it is challenged in the presentation. Often a decision has to be made on the basis of trust. Do we trust the people involved to deliver, and if it is going wrong, to tell us in sufficient time to put it right?

If the plan entails launching a new venture, a number of skills might be necessary: marketing, finance, HR and operations. Do not assume that an audience will be impressed by a belief that those involved will pick these up if they have had no experience beforehand. A safer strategy is to assign, on a temporary basis at the launch maybe, more expertise than might be required in the longer term. Once competence in the new roles can be assessed, secondees can then be released back to their part of the business.

## TEMPLATE FOR A BUSINESS CASE

While the following sections can be used as a template, the author of a plan has to convince an audience, so do not be constrained by these headings if they do not tell a convincing story. Every plan needs to be relevant to the subject at hand. It rarely impresses a seasoned business audience if it appears to have been 'painted by numbers'. The Office of Government Commerce has published on its website a useful checklist for writing a business case.[14] It is focused on the public service, and some categories are unlikely to be relevant in anything other than major business planning exercises. Nevertheless, it sets out a comprehensive checklist. In summary, it suggests the following headings:

- Strategic fit

  - business need
  - organisational overview
  - contribution to key objectives
  - stakeholders' position
  - existing arrangements
  - scope of the project
  - constraints
  - dependencies
  - benefits
  - risks
  - critical success factors

- Options appraisal

  - bare minimum option and others
  - innovative possibilities
  - service delivery options
  - implementation options
  - detailed options analysis
  - risk quantification and sensitivity analysis
  - benefits
  - preferred option

- Commercial considerations

  - output required
  - sourcing options
  - payment mechanisms
  - risk allocation and transfer
  - contract length
  - TUPE[15] and other HR issues
  - implementation timescales

- Affordability
    - budget based on whole life costs
    - financials (income and expenditure, balance sheet and cash flow)
    - achievability
    - evidence of similar projects elsewhere
    - project roles
    - procurement strategy
    - project plan
    - contract management
    - risks
    - benefits
    - post-implementation reviews
    - contingency plan.

## TEMPLATE FOR A BUSINESS PLAN

### Front page

Title

Author(s)

Contact details (address, telephone number, e-mail)

Date and version number

Copy number or person to whom given (useful to control who has it especially if it is confidential, or subject to quick revision)

Confidentiality requirements (if applicable). This might include to whom the document can be shown and the uses for which the information in the document can be used.

Status (eg 'Subject to approval by board. To be submitted on 23 February').

### Second page

List of contents

Appendices – data to further support the argument.

### Third page – executive summary

Imagine you spent your life reading business plans – maybe as a bank manager or business advisor. You have a dozen in the post that day and have funds for only one.

You turn to the summary with expectation, and within a couple of minutes you need to decide whether to study the plan in more detail or move on to others.

Even if this is not the sort of situation you work in, it is a good frame of mind to be in when writing the summary. Every word must count, the case must be strong, the layout and presentation crisp and the language clear. 'Less is more' is a good maxim, because the less there is, the more likely it is to be read. More than a page or two and you have probably lost the readers. I saw one proposal written on scented notepaper. When I queried the choice of paper, the author said that he had written it at home on his wife's paper, as he had nothing else to hand. His dedication might have been praiseworthy, but his judgement about the impact he made was somewhat lacking.

Busy executives learn how to speed read and be selective in what they read. Invariably thick documents do not get read to the last page, hence the need for effective executive summaries. Some advocate writing a summary first, so that you are clear what you are trying to say, then writing the plan, and finally going back to the summary and amending it accordingly.

Business plans can easily seem like a collection of tables and charts. A business plan tells a story of a how a business case can be translated into practical action with data carefully presented to support the argument. So what should it include?

Whichever way you do it, the summary needs:

- *The current position* – the issues we face, particularly identifying the view from customers.

- *Proposed strategy* – what are we proposing to do and why? In some instances we need to show why this is different from others (competitors, or plans that have gone before).

- *Summary of the business case* (see checklist above):
    - *Strategic fit* – and for most commercial companies how this proposal benefits the customer.
    - *Options appraisal* – the choices to be made. You may also consider including how this was arrived at and with which stakeholders.
    - *Commercial considerations.*
    - *Affordability*, including the key financial assumptions.

- (*Key market and financial data*. In some instances the summary might include the vital figures on costs, benefits, returns and investment needed.)

- *Any risks*, and how they are to be minimised.

- Decisions required and action to be taken – by whom and by when.

Some prefer to write the document as a narrative, telling the story, while others prefer numbered or bullet paragraphs. Once it is written, show it (the summary or indeed the whole plan) to a friendly critic to challenge your assumptions, be sceptical of your enthusiasm that all will go well, and focus on the weak spots. A critic should look for:

- weaknesses in the argument
- missing or inconsistent facts
- typographical mistakes.

And check that you have got people's names and job titles right!

*Global has missed its trading plan over the last three quarters. Major causes have been significant vacancies in the sales force and a high level of complaints in customer service.*

*This plan proposes a restructuring of the sales force and a closer integration of customer service, supported by enhanced IT support and investment in training.*

*Creating linked customer service representatives to deal with sales and after-sales enquiries, with a territory salesperson, is a key strategic objective. This new structure will reduce communication errors, enhance the service given to customers because of a greater knowledge of customers in an area, and provide support to customers while recruitment is under way.*

*We have looked at the only real alternative option, which would be to recruit additional salespersons. This option would not produce the customer service benefits required and especially not in the short term.*

*The plan calls for an additional £30,000 in recruitment and restructuring costs and should be completed in four months. On an estimate of a return to forecasted sales, the payback is six months.*

*The major risk lies in our potential inability to recruit the right staff.*

*Authorisation is required to spend the additional moneys not in the budget.*

## The main body of the plan

### Introduction

Here you may wish to flesh out the current position, identifying the main features of the business, if it is not known or obvious to the reader, and signposting what the proposal is about and maybe its structure.

### Terms of reference

The reader needs to know what you will cover, so be specific. There is an ever-present danger that readers will make assumptions about the scope of what you are proposing which are at variance to what you are suggesting in practice. Better to disabuse them at this stage, rather than disappoint them later. Invariably people's area of concern is bigger than your area of influence (Figure 5.1). Inevitably, when we are at the stage of exploring possibilities and new visions, our reach will be longer than our grasp; but the business plan must be firmly within our grasp.

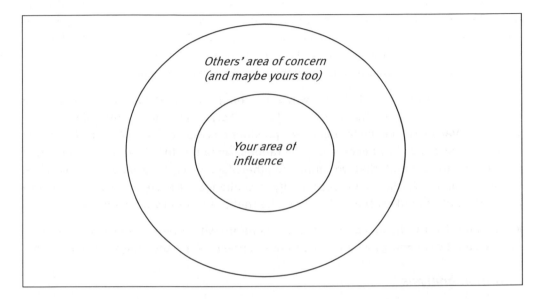

Figure 5.1 / *Influence and concern*

Consider, for example, the following terms of reference: 'To analyse the current position, including objectives, strengths and weaknesses and to develop appropriate strategies to meet current needs and future objectives.' It is not specific enough to give clear guidance about how far the remit goes. What is included in the current position? What are the current needs? What are the future objectives?

In cases where you have been given a specific brief, clarify this for the reader, especially pointing out things that are not covered or where this proposal links to earlier work.

## Vision and mission

In Chapter 1 we explored the notion of a vision statement, and clarified the nature of an organisation's mission. In essence, a vision statement is a summary of what you want to be in three to five years' time, whereas a mission statement sums up what your organisation does right now and the reason why it endures. Be warned, though: vision and mission statements can be controversial. Some will dismiss them as irrelevant while others will argue that they are the vital starting point. So know your audience. If your terms of reference have been considerably more restrictive than readers might have expected, clarifying the current mission and overall vision for the future is useful.

They set the business plan in the context of where you are and where you ultimately want to be, thus helping to allay fears that you have somehow missed the big picture.

## History

What is our history and how did we get to today? Every business and indeed every individual is today the sum of everything that has gone before. It leaves a legacy that can help and hinder our future and can sometimes explain why we do things in the way we do. Where there have been mistakes, be honest. After all we learn much from our mistakes. Then go on and explain how the mistake will not be made again.

History is sometimes used to justify why some things are impossible, 'because we have never done it that way'. Those arguments are likely to get short shrift from a critical audience. Václav Havel, the former Czech president, is reputed to have said: 'If we argue for our constraints they become our limitations.' meaning that if we seek to defend a position on the grounds that we cannot do otherwise, in time it becomes an impassable barrier. A business plan is the opportunity to challenge the sacred cows, but recognise and anticipate the likely scepticism from the traditionalists in your audience.

We summarise the historical perspective therefore with a view as to what we need to take account of in going forward – the things to preserve and the things to leave behind.

## Situation analysis

In Chapter 3 I identified a checklist of areas to consider and in the Appendix I outline a number of tools to help analyse the internal and external environments. We looked at *SWOT* and PESTEL and others all designed to identify more clearly what is happening to the organisation in the context of what its customers want and how it is responding in a changing and competitive world. In summary, the areas to be examined are:

- history – discussed above
- issues and challenges
- stakeholder analysis
- market place and competition
- customers
- financials
- people and organisation
- operations
- technology.

A question that is implicitly asked when any proposal for change is presented is: why?

There is a hidden bias towards the status quo (see Chapter 6), so our analysis needs to show why change is necessary. Key reasons that will be of interest to most readers are:

- Efficiency is improved leading to lower costs, higher margins and/or better value for money.

- Customers (internal or external) want us to offer a service/make a change, and are prepared to pay for it.

- Competitors are offering the product/service and we risk losing customers if we do not compete.

- Without a change, the trends indicate future financial disaster.

## Strategy formulation

From the vision, mission and analysis of the current situation will come the goals for the period of the plan. This section needs to answer two questions:

- What do we want to accomplish?

- What are the alternative options to get there (including doing nothing)?

In this part we might use a number of tools such as **scenario planning**, **decision tree** and **core competence** to explore options. We will want to explore for each scenario:

- the pros and cons of each

- risk analysis of each option

- resource implications of each (capital and staff requirements).

And if it has not been covered in the situation analysis, we may need to do a **stakeholder analysis** to anticipate what might be the reaction from different stakeholders.

## Proposed strategy

This section identifies the choice of route to achieve the goals.

- Explain what you are proposing to do in sufficient detail for the reader to get a clear idea of how it will be achieved. Background and supporting data can be put in appendices.

- Explain the logic of the strategy. Why is this the best route forward for the organisation? Have other options been considered, and why have they been rejected?

- Give the assumptions upon which the proposal is based, such as sales projections, price of commodities and inflation. Try to uncover and articulate the hidden assumptions. For example, a fashion retailer will have a different mix of stock and staff, depending upon the time of year, so one needs to identify the period of the plan. Where assumptions are weak, make sure you identify in the *risk analysis* the consequences of making the wrong assumptions. Quote external reference sources where they might be seen as authoritative. Always ensure that the assumptions are reasonable. They will be open to challenge by an intelligent reader, and if you are unable to justify them, the credibility of the whole plan suffers.

- A *sensitivity analysis* showing the impact on the outcomes of differing assumptions (particularly factors such as pricing, wage costs, time delays for hiring or moving to new premises).

- *Critical success factors* in delivering the strategy.

- Any legal issues (such as licences, planning permission and patents).

- Expected outcomes – what will success look like and why will the plan succeed?

## The business case

At a bare minimum, the costs and benefits of the proposal need to be included. In addition, an analysis of the reasons that this case is most suitable, including showing why the status quo is not acceptable and the expected rate of return from any investment, should be included. The checklist of possible headings in a business case, discussed earlier in this chapter, can be a guide for any further sections that might be helpful in explaining the case.

## Operational plans

This part of the plan sets out in detail how the strategy will be implemented. It will contain a resource plan (for example, money, facilities and equipment) and especially details of an organisation chart showing responsibilities and the structure of reporting relationships and general staffing.

This part of the plan may also indicate operational processes and specific procedures, especially where these are different from current practice. If procedures compromise ISO9000 or IIP certification,[16] ensure job descriptions and other procedural paperwork are revised in the correct format.

An HR operational plan might set out the training and recruitment needs arising from a gap analysis of supply and demand. In the Appendix there is a template for a *human resource plan*. Specific information that will usually be required includes:

- Details of any significant people and their experience and track record, especially if the plan relies upon these people to deliver it successfully.

- Any specific skill gaps that might be addressed through training or new recruitment. (Note: have these actions been factored into the costs?)

- Organisation chart. You might need to include details of interfaces with other parts of the organisation or external agencies. Invariably new initiatives place heavy burdens on a few key individuals. Anticipate the question of how they will cope.

The marketing plan might show the launch of different activities as in the example in Table 5.1.

*Table 5.1* / **Marketing and business development plan – an example**

*The timetable for the marketing activities would be:*

| Activity | Time |
| --- | --- |
| Develop potential customer database | Q2 |
| Segment potential customers by priority | Q2–Q3 |
| Identify key opinion formers in priority 1 targets | Q3 |
| Visit priority targets | Q3 |
| Mail shot 1 to all potential customers (office launch) | August |
| Opening event with priority 1 customers | September |
| Credentials presentations with Priority 1 & 2 targets | Q4 |
| Mail shot 2: invitation to launch event | September |
| Launch event | October |
| Mail shot 3 (services offered) | November |
| Mail shot 4 (Diary) | December |

The financial schedules, including cash flow, profit and loss effect, investment required and maybe balance sheet will need to be presented in sufficient detail to be able to modify (if necessary) existing budgets and forecasts if and when the plan is approved. Check to ensure that headcount shown ties up with amounts budgeted. Recognise the different audiences who read the plan might be looking for different things. Bankers will be concerned about the ability of the business to repay the loan and interest, and, if the worst happens, what assets there may be that can be sold to repay the debts. Those who have, or might provide, equity will be concerned about the long-term sustainability of the business and its ability to deliver dividends over the longer term, providing a return that is at least comparable with, if not better than, other places where they might invest their money. They will be concerned about how they exit with their money if necessary.

## Implementation plan

If the suggestions in Chapter 2 have been followed, there is likely to be a greater degree of acceptance than if the plan was written in secret and presented cold. This part of the plan, detailing implementation, will lay out the process for engaging staff in any change, anticipate any resistance and show how this will be overcome. Communicating the plan to employees in an effective way can contribute to retention and motivation by showing that the organisation, or this part of it, has a future. Demonstrating an awareness of the problems, how they are to be addressed, and showing a willingness to tackle them, places current day-to-day problems in a broader context, helping staff to understand some of the dilemmas senior managers face.

A timetable for action needs to be outlined, as well as operational details such as changes to systems and procedures and the impacts these might have on customers, suppliers and indeed the product or service. In the timetable there should be **milestones**, which are the critical points to take stock, assess progress and make any adjustments.

This section should include a section on the methods of evaluation of the outcomes to indicate how readers will know if and when they have achieved their goals.

## Risk analysis

This section will cover **sensitivity analysis** (if not already covered in the proposed strategy above), to different scenarios and possibilities. Some plans will also require an exit strategy, or at least what is required and what it would cost if it were necessary to close down the plan. See example in Chapter 4.

## Key decisions to be taken

Clarify what decision is being sought. Is it an outline authority to proceed perhaps to the next level of detail in planning, or in principle to start negotiating with a company, or maybe full authority to press ahead and commit resources?

## Appendices

Some examples of information that might best be set out in the appendix include:

- glossary of terms
- more detailed research, to prove key points in the proposal
- maybe cases of where others have successfully done what is proposed
- CVs of key people

- detailed financial reports

- technical specifications of equipment.

## CHECKING THE PLAN

The final step in writing a plan is to check it, or preferably have it checked by someone else. Successful plans have a number of characteristics. These include:

- A clear and exciting vision.

- Realistic financial projections. Be aware of the 'self-serving bias' that can occur when approval is earnestly desired.

- Sensitive and risky elements of the plan are highlighted and suggested action is shown to overcome the possible problems that might occur.

- Where funding is required, the source is clear. If internally, how this project justifies switching resources from elsewhere.

- Information in both text and appendices is sufficiently detailed to understand the proposal, the market and customer requirements and why this strategy is better than other alternatives.

- There is evidence that those responsible for implementation have sufficient experience and competence to achieve a success.

- The writing format is clear and unambiguous.

- It is of interest to the reader!

## PRESENTING THE CASE

> *I keep six honest serving men (they taught me all I know); their names are what and why and when and how and where and who.*
>
> *The elephant's child,* Just So Stories, *Rudyard Kipling*

### To whom are you presenting?

'In fourteen hundred and ninety two Columbus sailed the ocean blue', ran the rhyme to help children remember the date of his Atlantic crossing. As we recognised in Chapter 1, if you had observed that ship, the sailors would have been doing the same things as they had done before. The only difference was the mental map in the captain's head about the shape of the world and the assumptions he made that the world did not end at the horizon. When we think of presenting any case, our starting point has to be the mental maps of our listeners. Recognise that any deviation from the status quo is bound to be questioned (see Chapter 6). So how can we overcome this?

- Be clear what the purpose of the plan is.

- Understand vested interests.

- Recognise and work with people's fears.

- Show how risk is mitigated.

- Demonstrate real benefits – to the listeners.

- Ensure your assumptions are conservative and the maths is correct.

In presenting a business case there are many audiences – seen and unseen. The '6 Ws' is a checklist to help.

---

## The 6 Ws

- Who is the audience?

- Why are they here?

- What do they want from me?

- When and for how long?

- Where is it happening?

- With whom am I working?

---

As we identified in Chapter 2, there is the decision-maker, maybe your boss who needs to be convinced; there is the decision-taker, maybe your boss's boss who has the budget authority; and there are those who influence the decisions. There may be other managers who have a vested interest or are just respected, or just need to be convinced, such as the finance manager, bank manager or analyst.

HR managers may well be shielded from the need to confront shareholders and banks. Nevertheless it is a good discipline to imagine that you have to face them and argue your case.

The financial community will be interested in particular information. This includes:

- projected earnings and cash flow

- required borrowings

- security

- resilience of the plan to changed market conditions

And in addition, for investors:

- the structure of the proposed deal
- exit strategy
- management competence.

The story is told of a financial analyst who listened to an eminent hotelier explain that their business strategy was to move the chain of hotels more upmarket. It was explained with much jargon and sophisticated charts. At the end, the analyst was left wondering how this would be executed, and being near one of their hotels, went into the bar. He asked the barman what the strategy of the hotel was, expecting little comprehension. However, much to the analyst's surprise, the barman explained that the hotel wanted a clientele with more to spend, and his job was to add some exotic cocktails to his repertoire. Translating the strategy and business plan into action that is meaningful to employees at the customer interface is the key to success.

A good exercise is to jot down those who need to be convinced, choose the most sceptical, identify what you think they need to know to make a decision and see whether the business case passes their test. Recognise that gaining acceptance is not just a matter of logic. There may be an emotional component to the reaction that might hinder the case, however logical it is. Your audience might be jealous because you thought of the plan before they did. They may be irritated by you, your accent, your language or jargon. It may offend their values or beliefs and in their inability to articulate why the proposal is not to their liking, they may merely appear antagonistic regardless of what you do.

One good test is 'If it was your business, would you accept this case?' If you buy a business, advisors will often say 'Hasten slowly' and 'Investigate the track record.' Decisions often come down to whether one trusts the judgement of the proposer and his or her history in the past of delivering. Venture capitalists will just as much back the person or team as the idea.

What is in it for me (WIFM) is another good test. If the key opinion formers gain some advantage from this project then it is more likely to be accepted. (See *interest mapping* in the Appendix for a more specific tool to identify the consequences of differing interests.)

Looking more broadly, an OFR (operational and financial report) will provide shareholders with information about the company's objectives, strategy, past performance and future prospects, which will be of use to several groups:

- employees, customers and suppliers
- environmental groups because the report will discuss any impacts
- societal groups to assess other societal impacts.

So if the business case suggests that a proposed increase in training will improve the future prospects of staff, the proposal may well find itself read by a wider group than just the boss.

Every function develops its own jargon and TLAs (three-letter abbreviations). When used amongst peers they are convenient shorthand; when amongst others they can be interpreted as a put-down ('you must be ignorant if you don't understand this acronym') or a rather unnecessary irritation. Maybe with a mixed audience, a glossary at the back of the document can serve to remind people who are unfamiliar.

## What do they want to hear?

Typically, presentations seek either to educate, entertain and inform, or a combination of all. It is unlikely that an audience for a presentation on a business plan wants to be entertained, nor for that matter to be educated in the finer points of discounted cash flow. They do wish to be informed, but it is likely that each of your audience may be interested in different aspects. To retain maximum interest, it is better for the audience if you initially keep to the overall arguments without too much detail. Turn to the more detailed data in response to questions. You may have 50 PowerPoint slides, but it is likely that you will engage your audience if your presentation includes about 25, with 25 slides of back-up and explanatory material available to be turned to if specific questions are asked.

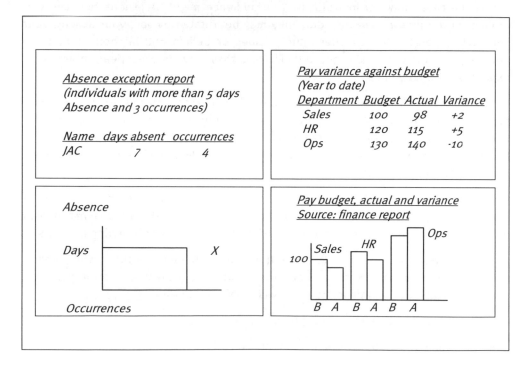

Figure 5.2 / *Reporting examples*

'A picture is worth a thousand words', so use diagrams and charts as well as numbers, as for example in Figure 5.2.

As we noted in Chapter 2, statistics can be misleading, and Figure 5.3 shows some of the ways figures can be poorly presented. These are obvious examples, but always remember that the presenter has a responsibility to present figures in a way that leads the audience to a fair interpretation.

## What are you going to tell them?

'Tell them what you are going to say, tell them, and then tell them what you have told them' is an old adage amongst presenters. In summary, the audience will need to understand:

- what you are proposing to do
- why it is a valid use of the organisation's time and resources
- how you will do it
- where and when will it happen
- the problems you anticipate and how you will overcome them
- what you are asking the audience for.

## So what do you really want?

If you start with the end in mind, you will have considered the response you want from each audience. It may be support from your team or other departments that are involved, in which case it may need to show the benefits for them. It may be a financial sign-off that you require, in which case the financials might be emphasised. Remember that it is your commitment to seeing the project through to a successful conclusion that is key to a successful argument of your case.

While the written document might be cautious, our enthusiasm (or desperation) to get approval when arguing our case can lead to a trap. It is easy to become a hostage to fortune and promise beyond what is reasonable. It may be in the form of underestimating the pitfalls, adjusting the numbers to make the case or over-optimistic assumptions. The estimate of a revenue stream can easily be talked up, whereas costs become much more tangible and less easy to adjust. 'We will deliver 20 per cent increase in productivity in a month because we will all work harder.' Such a statement smacks of wishful thinking rather than sober logic.

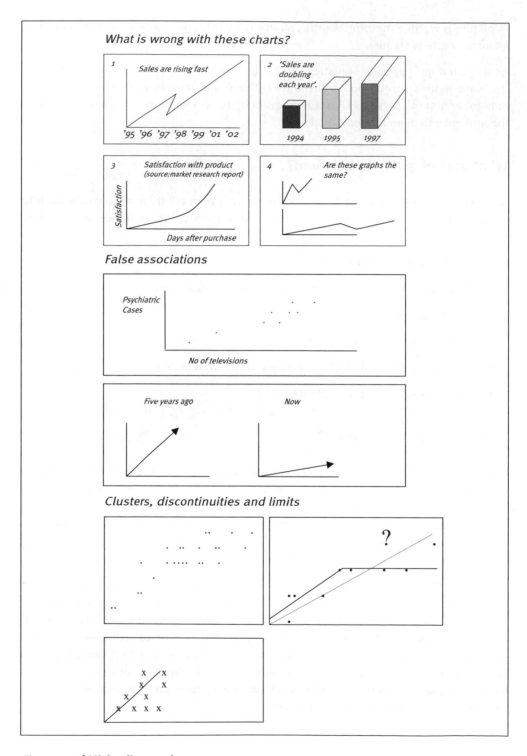

Figure 5.3 / **Misleading graphs**

## SOME PRESENTATION PRINCIPLES

### Dealing with difficult questions

There are likely to be several questions that any audience will ask of a business planning presentation and it is well to prepare for them:

- How well does this proposal fit with the stated goals and strategies of the organisation?

- What is required by way of investment (for example, people, money and facilities) and what impact will this have on the other projects the company might be interested in pursuing?

- How does this affect our relations with stakeholders – customers, suppliers, shareholders, staff?

- How practical and robust is it? Can it really be accomplished with the resources and experience available?

- If it is not pursued what will be the consequences, good and bad?

However well you prepare, there will always be those unanswerable questions. Beware, they are a trap and many a well-formed presentation is spoiled by waffling, avoiding the questions, lecturing or a 'put-down':

- In your preparation try to anticipate likely questions.

- Know your stuff.

- Ensure you have your back-up material or original research with you to refer to.

- If you cannot answer because of lack of information say so, and tell the inquirer that you will find it afterwards.

- Don't waffle.

- If you cannot answer because you feel it is not the right place, develop a form of words that you are comfortable with, such as, 'I would like to consider your question carefully and give it some thought. Can I come back to you?'

- If you are the wrong person to answer say so, for example, 'That is not a question I am qualified to answer. Perhaps we could ask Mr ... for his views?'

### Preparing a business plan presentation – some questions to ask yourself

1. Do you know exactly what you want to achieve – think of the 6 Ps, *purpose*, *people*, *proposition*, *PowerPoints*, *process*, and *payoff* – for the audience?

Sometimes, your purpose may be to get agreement that day, maybe to lay out the options to build towards a future decision, maybe to influence some of the audience both to you and to your proposition, maybe to impart some knowledge. So why are you there and what are the outcomes you want accomplished with the audience as they walk away at the end of the presentation?

2. Do you really believe in your case? If you do not, drop it at once, otherwise it will soon show, or get yourself to a position that you can believe in.

3. Have you got all the facts that support your case – and the ones to deal with the questions from the objectors? Have you checked the facts?

4. What are the strongest arguments for your case?

5. What are the benefits to your listeners? Note: the answers to 4 and 5 should be identical. No argument has more power than one where the audience benefit.

6. Why must the present position be changed (if that is the purpose of your presentation)? What is their problem – theirs rather than yours?

7. Who else is affected by any proposals. Have they been considered and any objections taken account of in your presentation?

8. Is there an alternative to your proposal? Can you give options? At least let inquirers see that you have looked at other options and the logic of why they are not suitable.

9. What are the arguments against your plan? Do not attempt to dodge this question. If you are not prepared to demonstrate that your proposal outweighs any others, then you are vulnerable. Get someone to give a critical view of your presentation before you give it, and in time for revisions if necessary.

10. What do you know about your audience, their preferences, peculiarities and concerns? Who are your allies and your opponents?

11. Is your case financially sound, with budget available, arithmetic checked, assumptions valid?

12. Have you got appropriate supporting material such as overheads, handouts, models and maps?

13. Is the timing right? It should be not long enough to be boring, nor too short to include sufficient detail.

14. How will you sum up? Practise this.

15. How will you end to achieve the desired effect? Plan and practise it.

16. Are you ready for questions, particularly the ones you dread?

17. Have you practised it before a friendly critic, or at least the mirror? As you travel to work, imagine giving the presentation in your mind.

## SUMMARY OF THE KEY POINTS FROM THIS CHAPTER

Despite the assertion in Chapter 2 that the process of engaging the organisation in a way that builds consensus lies at the heart of creating a plan that will gain acceptance and support, this chapter suggests that a well-prepared written document is essential too. In this chapter I have sought to identify the essential ingredients in a written document. Without a good written plan, it is doubtful whether any organisation would grant approval for substantial investment.

To help the task of writing I have included a checklist of factors to be included in a business case, based on that published by government, and a template for writing a business plan.

A counsel of perfection would hold that 'a good wine needs no bush' and a good plan needs no presentation. In the real world you will invariably have to stand and argue your case. I have laid out a number of tips and tactics to help make it a persuasive presentation, including a checklist of questions to ask yourself before going on stage.

So what now? Prepare a draft plan and find a friendly critic to look for holes in the argument and typos in the text. When you feel you are ready, prepare a presentation and rehearse.

# 6

# Reviewing the options and making the decision

*We must become the change we want to see.*

*Mahatma Gandhi*

## REVIEWING THE OPTIONS

Decision-making starts with the recognition of the need to make a decision. If there are no options, there are few if any decisions to be made. In Chapter 1 we described the concept of strategy as about articulating choices, some of which may be hidden. So at the outset of decision-making we may have to search for the alternatives, and ensure that we have exhausted our search for all possible plausible alternative courses of action.

If decision-making involves choices, what is involved in making a choice? Some choices are more important than others, and we have to weigh up the consequences of those choices, particularly thinking about the unintended consequences. Do we solve the problem or live with it? A woman MP recounted a story on the radio of how she faced the choice between a three line whip on a vote and attending her son's prize giving. A colleague asked her, 'Who was the home secretary 20 years ago?' 'I don't know,' she replied. 'Neither will anyone remember the vote in the house in 20 years time,' said her colleague, 'but your son will remember the time his mother was not present when he won a prize.' Choices often involve courage to face up to tough consequences, so review your choices if you are taking the easy option.

One way we avoid facing up to the difficult choices is to imagine we are in a different position. Margaret Silf (2004) describes an important part of making choices as getting to 'square one'. 'Square one', she says, does not mean: 'Where you wish you were, or where you think you ought to be, or where other people want you to be, or where you might have been if only ...'.

Some choices are not yours to make, so focus on those that are yours and redirect or leave alone the others.[17] Some decisions can only be solved partially, or at least for now.

Choices imply options, but it is difficult to sometimes know whether you have identified all of them. It is easy to dismiss options because they seem impracticable, yet innovations of all kinds often bear the mark of the inventor that defied the odds.

SIlf (2004) suggest that there are two sources of information to inform our decision-making: tuition and intuition. Our decision-making will rest on what we have learnt and what we sense. As we wrestle with a decision therefore consider what biases have entered our thinking as a result of what we have read, our prior experience and how we have been taught. In a world of lifetime learning we are urged to review every day what we have learnt. We rarely consider what we have chosen not to. The latter points to our biases and will be the source of our ignorance. Our intuitive choices point to our values. Indeed, we really only know our values by the choices we make.

Roger Niven[18] once suggested that every manager needs a clock and a compass on his or her desk. The clock is there to remind them of time and the need to prioritise in a busy life where it is impossible to do everything. Limited time forces us to continually focus only on the things that matter. The compass is to give a sense of direction in helping make those intuitive choices. In the Senate hearings associated with the collapse of Enron, a senator remarked[19] 'No regulation on earth will succeed if those in command have no moral compass.'

Everyday we make decisions in our lives, which are based on a mixture of information, intuition and feelings. Even the most rational decisions are subject to biases of all kinds. These biases come from some psychological processes, such as cognitive dissonance, discussed earlier, where to avoid living with ambiguity, we make a decision and filter out information that disagrees with our decision. Our personality can also influence the way we make decisions. One of the scales in the Myers-Briggs inventory[20] ranges from a style of decision-making based on logical thought, to one based on how we feel. Does our heart or our head rule? Which predominates in making our decisions? Some decisions might require more right-brain thinking – intuitive, non verbal, visual and creative, as opposed to left-brain thinking – logical, sequential, verbal and analytical. Some people will find it easier to switch modes whilst others will find it difficult.

## PROCESS OF DECISION-MAKING

Whilst it is a sad fact of life that persuasion is sometimes achieved by mere repetition, regardless of the truth of the case, business decisions require a more considered process. Decisions about choices require a basis for determination. What criteria and what logic will hold sway?

In the trial of Galileo, Francesco Sizi used the following argument:

> *There are seven windows in the head, two nostrils, two ears...so in the heavens there are two favourable stars, two unpropitious. From which and many other*

*similar phenomena of nature such as the seven metals, etc. which it were tedious to enumerate, we gather that the number of planets is necessarily seven.*

*Hempel 1966*

Clearly most audiences would not give much credence to this argument today.

But, as the trial of Galileo shows, it is the logic and values of your audience, those who have the power to decide which are important and it is your audience that you need to convince.

Choice can be clear between fixed alternatives: do we recruit this person or that. It can however be fuzzier. Do we, for example, feel comfortable making the decision today?

It is tempting to believe that no decision should be taken until all the analysis is done. It is however, more efficient of time and resource if analytical work can be carefully guided towards focusing on only the key questions upon which the decision rests, whilst taking care to avoid imposing bias or prejudgement. As the analysis progresses certain decisions may need to be taken to avoid unnecessary future work, as shown in Table 6.1.

*Table 6.1 / **Analysis and decision***

| Analysis | Decision |
|---|---|
| Assessment of the suitability of cost–benefit analysis. | Whether to invest the time required for analysis. |
| Enumeration of all costs and benefits. | Degree of detail required. |
| Estimate of probability of likelihood of benefits accruing and other outcomes. | Method of costing to be used |
| Calculation of net present value of investment streams. | Identification of significant benefits and how best to obtain them. |
| Presentation of results including: probabilities of outcomes, sensitivity analysis, pecuniary spillovers.[21] | Discount rate. |
| | Acceptance criteria. |

Any decision involves some risk, and a way of reducing it is to find some low-risk route of testing it in practice. If we are going to invest in an employee assistance programme, for example, can we offer it for a limited period to one division to test it out?

A professional firm wanted to introduce 360° feedback. The first year it offered a limited service and provided manual analysis. Once the system had been proved, the questions refined and the format of the report agreed and found useful, investment took place in developing a web-based system for capturing the data and automating the analysis, so that it could be rolled out more widely across the firm.

## CLARIFYING THE ASSUMPTIONS

Apart from the deaf, a skill that we all believe we possess is that of listening. Listening is like breathing for the majority of people. Yet studies of various kinds show that while we may hear the words, our interpretation is an individual phenomenon, and it is unlikely that any two people will interpret the same words in the same way. Our interpretation is affected by our prior knowledge and experience. When presenting a business case therefore, any uncertainty will be open to differing interpretations, especially where assumptions have been made that are not spelt out.

> *The proposed employee assistance programme will solve the possible growth in stress and so avoid tribunal cases.*

This proposal begs many questions:

- Why will it solve stress?

- Why will it avoid tribunal cases?

- What alternatives were considered and why is this the best?

In a proposal like this we need to both array the assumptions, the reason we are relying on that assumption and the logic of accepting it.

> *The proposed employee assistance programme has been modelled on a scheme run successfully in several companies (see appendix for research details). We are assuming that their experience will be similar to ours, and see no reason why ours should be different. In the three companies we studied, stress-related illness was reduced significantly by up to 20 per cent in one case and showed a continuing stable trend below the level operating prior to the scheme. In no instance had these companies had a tribunal case about stress, in contrast to our own experience.*

Organisation culture will also affect the assumptions people make. Some cultures will have a bias towards action, whilst others will take a more measured approach. A business plan in the former will be sharp and probably short, while in the latter it will probably be more detailed.

## CHALLENGING THE MENTAL MODELS

> Paper was invented by the Chinese some 2,500 years ago, the theory of flight was described by Leonardo da Vinci in the sixteenth century. So why did it take 2,000 years to put five folds in a piece of paper and make a paper dart?

Decision-making takes place in a context. For example, if I asked you to estimate the sales of a company you would probably give a different figure from the one you would estimate if I had asked you whether this company had sales of more or less than £100 million. How we anchor our decisions greatly affects our judgement. There are a range of hidden traps identified by Hammond *et al* (1998). The list is shown in the box.

---

### The hidden traps in decision-making

- Anchoring.

- Status quo.

- Sunk cost.

- Confirming evidence.

- Framing.

- Estimating and forecasting
    - Overconfidence.
    - Prudence.
    - Memory.

Source: Hammond, Keeney and Raiffa (1998).

---

So, what can we do to overcome the hidden traps?

## Anchoring

Where initial impressions, estimates, or data limit subsequent thoughts and judgements:

- View a problem from different perspectives.

- Think independently before discussing it.

- Be open-minded – value different opinions.

- Seek advisors with different views.

## Status quo

Where solutions that challenge the status quo or change radically existing arrangements are harder to choose:

- Stay focused on your vision of what you want to achieve.

- Always look for alternatives to any course of action.

- Be objective as you can be about the pros and cons of each option.

- The best option will change over time. Evaluate options both now and in the future.

## Sunk cost

Where greater weight is placed on justifying past decisions because of all the time effort and money put into them, rather than whether it is right now:

- Get those who were not involved in the original decision to assess the situation.

- Be honest with each other why abandoning a cherished project distresses you.

- Recognise the limitations of hindsight, don't blame actions in the past, cultivate a culture that is present and forward looking.

## Confirming evidence

Where information is selected that supports our existing point of view while avoiding information that contradicts it:

- Are you assessing all arguments with equal rigour?

- Find a 'devil's advocate' – the corporate jester?

- Be honest with yourself about your motives.

- Don't rely on advisors who tell you what you want to hear.

## Framing

Where questions or problems are defined in a way that biases the choices of possible outcomes:

- Do not automatically accept the frame of reference first posed – challenge the assumptions.

- Try to reframe where the losses and gains from each perspective are neutral.

- Test the solution against different frames of reference.

## Estimating

Where in the face of uncertainty, our minds struggle to calibrate the frame of reference for making accurate estimates. Our memory of past events guides us, so, for example, if we have a period of continued growth we become overconfident about the future and overestimate, and vice versa:

- Try to get feedback on your estimates and log them to see how robust a trend might be.

- Consider the extremes of your estimates.

- Build different scenarios, including worst and best cases. Avoid a linear view of the future.

- Get accurate data – don't rely on memory.

- Make all figures and assumptions behind them transparent for others to question.

## WAYS OF PERSONAL DECISION-MAKING

As we have observed, individual differences will affect how we make decisions. We should also remember that all decisions require some degree of courage and, once made, persistence to see them through to successful conclusion. To decide to step out into the unknown relies on judgement, which has an emotional component not to be ignored. Does a decision feel right as well as measure up to more objective criteria?

Some ways to make decisions:

1. *The balance sheet.* List the pros and cons. Keep the sheet in a prominent position for a few days and add to it as you think of things. Invite others who know you well to add to it. Don't forget to factor in the unintended consequences of your choice.

2. *Make the decision and sleep on it.* Then see how you feel about it in the morning. Try making the alternative decision and see if you sleep any easier.

3. *Argue your case.* Imagine you had to argue with someone who was sceptical. You may find that some options are easier to support.

4. *Balaam's ass.*[22] Try to argue against each option, highlighting all the unattractive features. Which option comes out most unscathed?

5. *Occam's razor.*[23] Choose the simpler of the options.

6. *Describe first the ideal solution* and then compare each option against it. Look at the solution which has the least gaps with the ideal.

7. *Imagine a typical working day in each option.* In your mind, walk through the day. What do you do? Who with? What do you see, touch and hear? Note your feelings as you go through this day in your mind. Do you feel more excited about some options than others?

8. *Flip a coin!*

In Table 6.2 is an example of using a matrix of factors against options for someone making a career choice. For each option, use words, ticks or crosses or a numerical weighting system to fill in the column. If you do not like the outcome, try to work out why; you may have discovered some deeper factor that is affecting your choice, which needs to be explored further.

Table 6.2 / **Deciding between competing career options**

| DECIDING FACTORS | | OPTIONS | | | | | |
|---|---|---|---|---|---|---|---|
| | Current job | Retrain | Downshift | New job A | New job B | etc. | |
| Salary | | | | | | | |
| Location | | | | | | | |
| Training | | | | | | | |
| Prospects | | | | | | | |
| Culture | | | | | | | |
| Language | | | | | | | |
| Enjoyment | | | | | | | |
| Values | | | | | | | |
| People | | | | | | | |
| Skills used | | | | | | | |
| Interest | | | | | | | |
| Development | | | | | | | |
| Family | | | | | | | |
| etc. | | | | | | | |

# GROUP DYNAMICS

Many business decisions will be taken in a group of some kind, whether it is a formal committee, or colleagues informally chatting. In a study of effective decision-makers (Eisenhardt 1999), certain features were apparent. The more successful teams created strategies for performance improvement by:

- Building a collective intuition amongst opinion formers that enhances the ability of the top management team to see threats and opportunities sooner and more accurately.

- Stimulating quick debate to improve the quality of strategic thinking without sacrificing significant time.

- Maintaining a disciplined pace that drives the decision process to a timely conclusion.

- Defusing political behaviour that creates unproductive conflict and wastes time.

Groups of people can also have an impact on the quality of decision-making, in contrast to individual decision-making. Several group features affect decision-making:

- In groups, people sometimes are so concerned about doing what they believe that everyone else wants, that they deny what each individually believe is right. In the end, the group concludes by doing those things that no one wants. This is sometimes called the Abilene paradox.[24]

- Groups shift their risk-taking behaviour, compared with individual positions. Groups can become more *risk-taking* as they feel the protection of the group and its invulnerability, believing that strength of the group is a defence against the possible downsides; or more *risk averse* as they act to protect the group against possible threat. Either way their judgement of risk can become distorted.

- Under the guise of democratic processes like voting, responsibility and accountability can become diminished. Group members can hide behind group decisions.

- In the desire for unanimity, those who disagree are shunned or pressurised by the group to conform to some group norm. This phenomenon can result in a loss of independent thought and objective analysis. In such circumstances people are persuaded that 'black is white' and a lack of reality takes over their discussions and decisions.

## WAYS OF GROUP DECISION-MAKING

Building on the work of Robbins (2003) several styles are suggested:

1. *Directive.* This style can be characterised as power-oriented, where there is little room for discussion and a low tolerance for subtle nuances. Often used where fast decisions are required.

2. *Analytical.* Here there is a concentration on data and looking at theories as to why things occur.

3. *Mathematical.* By taking the average of members' opinions, consensus is reached. For example, this approach might be used if you asked a group of HR managers what is the percentage wage increase that is likely in the future.

4. *'The classic chairman'.* Having heard all contributions the chair sums up and makes the decision.

5. *Democratic.* Voting can sometimes be a helpful way to make a decision especially where equality of all the parties is important. The result is invariably seen as fair, always provided that the process of voting is fair.

6. *Conceptual.* Creative solutions and lateral thinking are much in evidence in this style. Models and mental pictures are part of the conversation.

7. *Behavioural.* The focus here is on building consensus. The process of gaining commitment is as important as the substance of the decisions.

These different styles have their pros and cons.

## Advantages and disadvantages of decision-making methods

### 1. Directive – decision by authority without discussion

*Advantages*

Applies more to administrative needs; useful for simple, routine decisions; should be used when very little time is available to make the decision; and when the group members lack the skills and information to make the decision any other way.

*Disadvantages*

One person is not a good resource for every decision; advantages of group interaction are lost; no commitment to implementing the decision is developed among other group members; resentment and disagreement may result in sabotage and deterioration of group effectiveness; resources of other members are not used.

### 2. Analytical – decision based on analysis by expert member(s)

*Advantages*

Useful when the expertise of one person or a small group is so far superior to that of all the other group members that little is to be gained by discussion; should be used when the need for membership action in implementing the decision is slight.

*Disadvantages*

It is difficult to determine whom the expert is; the experts might have too blinkered a view and be less open to radical ideas; no commitment to implement the decision is built; advantages of group interaction are lost; resentment and disagreement may result in sabotage and deterioration of group effectiveness; resources of other members are not used.

### 3. Mathematical – decision based on the average of members' opinions

*Advantages*

Useful when it is difficult to get group members together to talk; when the decision is so urgent that there is no time for group discussion; when member commitment is not necessary for implementing the decision; when group members lack the skills and information to make the decision any other way; applicable to simple, routine decisions.

*Disadvantages*

There is not enough interaction among group members for them to gain from each other's resources and from the benefits of group discussion to be built; unresolved conflict and controversy may damage group effectiveness in the future.

## 4. 'The classic chairman' – decision by authority after discussion

*Advantages*

Uses the resources of the group members more than previous methods; gains some of the benefits of group discussion.

*Disadvantages*

Does not develop commitment to implement the decision; does not resolve the controversies and conflicts among group members; tends to create situations in which group members either compete to impress the designated leader or tell the leader what they think he or she wants to hear.

## 5a. Democratic – voting and the decision made by majority control

*Advantages*

Can be used when sufficient time is lacking for decision by consensus or when the decision is not so important that consensus needs to be used, and when complete member commitment is not necessary for implementing the decision; closes group discussion on issues that are not highly important for the group.

*Disadvantages*

Usually leaves an alienated minority, which damages future group effectiveness; relevant resources of many group members may be lost; full commitment to implement the decision is absent; full benefit of group interaction is not obtained.

## 5b. Democratic – voting and the decision made by minority control

*Advantages*

Can be used when everyone cannot meet to make a decision; when the group is under such time pressure that it must delegate responsibility to a committee; when only a few members have any relevant resources; when broad member commitment is not needed to implement the decision; useful for simple, routine decisions.

*Disadvantages*

Does not utilise the resources of many group members; does not establish widespread commitment to implement the decision; unresolved conflict and controversy may damage future group effectiveness; not much benefit from group interaction.

### 6. Conceptual – developing a theoretical rationale

*Advantages*

Develops a more robust basis for future debates; can generate innovative solutions and 'breaks the mould' of previous thinking.

*Disadvantages*

May be too theoretical; ways of making decisions may need to vary with new circumstances and so any perceived benefits may be illusory in practice. May swap one orthodoxy for another.

### 7. Behavioural – consensus

*Advantages*

Produces an innovative, creative and high-quality decision; elicits commitment by all members to implement the decision; uses the resources of all members; the future decision-making ability of the group is enhanced; useful in making serious, important and complex decisions to which all members are to be committed.

*Disadvantages*

Takes a great deal of time and psychological energy and a high level of member skill; time pressure must be minimal, and there must be no emergency in progress.

## Decision rules

David Oxtoby in a recent presentation (Oxtoby 2005) drew on the work of Vroom and Yetton (1973) to describe several decision rules to protect the quality and acceptability of a decision. He describes them under two headings as:

### Decision quality

- *Leader information rule.* Where the leader is short of information, a directive style is inappropriate. The use of the other styles is more likely to yield a better result.

- *Goal congruence rule.* Where participants in the process are striving for their own interests at the expense of the group interest, consensus is less likely. Voting approaches are more likely to gain acceptance.

- *Unstructured problem rule.* If the problem is complex and there is a need to harness the collective intelligence in the room, the democratic processes are less desirable in favour of the analytical and conceptual.

### Decision acceptability

- *The acceptance rule.* Where acceptance of the decision and commitment to carry it through is of paramount importance, consensus is most useful. A directive style is unlikely to succeed.

- *The conflict rule.* Where there is disagreement about how decisions are to be made, democratic methods are more likely to be acceptable. Conceptual approaches might be able to find an innovative solution.

- *The fairness rule.* If the outcome is less important than the way the decision is reached, then democratic and maybe consensus (if you have the time) methods are more acceptable.

- *The acceptance priority rule.* Where acceptance of both process and content is crucial and maximum commitment is required, then the pursuit of consensus is the ideal approach.

# PROCRASTINATION

'Procrastination' said Christian H. Godefroy, 'is one of the most widespread diseases known to man!' Procrastination is a tendency to avoid decisions and put things off until tomorrow. It reduces the time we have to do the things we need to do, we should do and we want to do. It is likely to leave us feeling pressurised, stressed, annoyed. We put off unpleasant tasks, particularly those involving people. We avoid making difficult telephone calls, avoid starting difficult projects, shy away from the unfamiliar and so on.

Procrastination can delay decisions. They may then be rushed or not completed to the best standard. However, not all procrastination is bad – it can be a creative way of delaying work to achieve a better outcome. This is normal. The symptoms of procrastination are many and varied! For example:

- daydreaming
- allowing interruptions
- doing low-priority activities
- taking long breaks
- constantly finding excuses
- insisting on delaying a job until all the documentation (information) is available

(remember the 80/20 rule – it is likely that only 20 per cent of the information will be necessary to get the job done!).

## Causes of procrastination

There are several causes of procrastination:

- *Doubt:* procrastination arises from a belief (often mistaken) that the decision requires greater wisdom or ability to make it than is currently possessed. Doubt might also exist about the ability to carry the decision through and do a good job. Therefore, the decision is avoided.

- *Perfectionism:* procrastination is a way to avoid failure. The perfectionist sets impossibly high standards and because he or she believes they are unattainable, avoids the decision all together. Maybe it is felt there is insufficient information required to complete a plan in the mistaken belief that nothing can be started until everything is in place.

- *Rebellion:* procrastination is a way to express defiance. By procrastinating you demonstrate your control of the situation. Constant crises and problems both of which are then solved, often at the last minute, show control over the events.

- *Socialising:* by getting involved in gossip, nonwork related conversations, distractions or trivial tasks the start or finish of a task is delayed.

- *Lack of commitment:* where there is doubt about the wisdom of the action required, procrastination prevents what is deemed unnecessary effort.

## Dealing with procrastination

There are some steps that can be taken to avoid or deal with procrastination:

- Accept that it is common! You are not unique. We procrastinate because we fear failure. Fearing failure is perfectly normal and generally there is no real foundation for this.

- Recognise that you only procrastinate in certain situations. It usually means the problem is smaller than you think.

- Discipline yourself – do little things in your area of procrastination. When you know where your weak areas are, then you need to concentrate on these. The *'do it now'* technique can be a very powerful one when you know where to focus your effort.

- Always be positive in the face of procrastination and reward yourself when you succeed and boost your morale when you need to do it.

- Adopt *'single-handling'* – each piece of paper should be handled only once!

## RISK ASSESSMENT AND CONTROL

Before deciding to press ahead with your business plan, carry out a *risk analysis* on each part of the project. Risk exists where there is prior experience to draw upon to determine the likely outcomes, whereas uncertainty occurs where there are novel situations with little or no history to guide us. To start a risk assessment, first identify each element of the plan and make an assessment of the likelihood and impact. A format is given in Figure 6.1.

| Project element | Risk | Evaluation | | | | | | Control measure |
|---|---|---|---|---|---|---|---|---|
| | | Likelihood | | | Impact | | | |
| | | H | M | L | H | M | L | |
| | | | | | | | | |

*Where the evaluation can be either high, medium or low of the event occurring and of its impact if it does.*

Figure 6.1 / **Risk assessment and control format**

Major sources of risk are those over which you have little or no control. Examples include:

- Sole suppliers where there is no quick or easy alternative.

- Unique materials – supply and price.

- Development lead times for a system, especially when it is bespoke.

- Government/legal regulations.

- Quality of key staff and management. Can they deliver?

- 'Events'.

Dealing with risk first requires judgement about the assessments. Are they material? If the likelihood is low and the impact low, do not put too much effort into guarding against it. At the other end of the spectrum – high likelihood, high impact – the business plan will need to address how to counter this. For example:

> *There is a high risk that we will not be able to find the technical and language skills required to bring the new facility in China on stream at the planned time. The impact of slippage would be to disrupt supply of the new product, which currently*

*cannot be made at any other facility. We have therefore increased the contingency fund in the plan to allow for bringing in contractors for a period from elsewhere to support the plan.*

## Finding low-risk routes to test the way forward

In assessing risk, there may be options to manage the risk. Computer systems can be provided with back-up. Staff can be trained to be multiskilled and so become flexible to respond to changed needs. Insurance can be taken out for possible disasters and contracts can be written to limit any damage.

The combination of many factors can soon become a complex 'tree' of probabilities. A **decision tree** can be a useful tool to use in these instances. To construct one requires thinking systematically of the full range of possible alternatives and events that can occur under the range of conditions expected. In essence, one is thinking forward into the future and trying to imagine all the possibilities.

It can be equally useful to look back for a time. What can be learnt from past failures and successes? How have others before you dealt with the unexpected? Hindsight allows one to construct theories about what has caused the events and the way people have responded. Gaining a deeper understanding of how our world works helps us to make more considered judgements about risks and rewards of any course of action.

The next stage in risk management is to increase readiness to respond if and when the risk becomes real. At its simplest, it involves building greater awareness. It may also entail budgeting for a contingency as above, or putting more effort into planning each detail. Training the people involved and finding low-risk ways of simulating what will occur helps to test the validity of an approach.

While there is a natural reluctance to consider that all will go wrong, working out a recovery plan helps to build confidence. Such a plan might include:

- early assessment of the impact of variations to the original plan

- rehearsal of options for recovery

- training in key skills

- arrangements with outside agencies to provide temporary support

- communications to key stakeholders.

## SUMMARY OF THE KEY POINTS FROM THIS CHAPTER

When a man renowned for his dithering and vacillation was asked whether he had difficulties making decisions, he replied, 'Well, yes, and no.' Ultimately a business plan presents a choice. Sometimes, the choice is a 'no brainer', but that is usually the exception. Business decisions invariably involve risk and as the litter of failed companies testifies, success is not guaranteed. In this chapter we have explored how to make decisions and some of the pitfalls involved. Nowhere in our human experience is there more potential for the battle between the head and the heart. 'The heart has its reasons, which reason knows not of,' said Pascal and anyone faced with the conflict between their logic and gut instinct will know what he meant – they are incompatible ways of decision-making. Myers-Briggs, discussed earlier, suggest that if we can find a way of integrating these two ways of seeing decisions we have a far more powerful tool.

Despite these difficulties, there are decision-making processes for both individuals and groups that help us in this task of integration. There is however no ideal formula, and I lay out the pros and cons of different approaches. Finally, no decision in business should be sealed without a risk analysis of the decision made.

So what now? Use the processes individually and collectively to determine your decision. Remember, whatever you decide, the sun will still rise tomorrow.

# 7

# Working the plan

*Vision without action is a dream*

*Action without vision soon fades*

*But vision with action can change the world.*

*Nelson Mandela*

## INTRODUCTION

In this final chapter we examine the ways in which we can ensure that a business plan is implemented successfully.

The Duke of Wellington was reputed to have asked for an assessment of his army before the battle of Waterloo. Reports came back that he had the best equipment and the most powerful guns, the finest army with the finest men. 'Yes,' said Wellington, 'but will they fight?'

The key issue to confront in any plan is whether it can be delivered successfully. Indeed, execution is as important if not more so than the strategy itself, as we discussed in Chapter 2 where we started with quoting an old song: "T'ain't what you do, it's the way that you do it'. Implementation of HR changes is critically dependent on the way of implementation, not the least because when we seek to implement change we invoke all the issues surrounding loss of old ways of doing things. Such loss takes people out of their comfort zone and into unknown situations where natural fears are revealed — fear of failure, of being exposed and looking foolish.

## TURNING THE PLAN INTO ACTION

The plan might well have been conceived as an integrated whole, which now needs to be broken down to its constituent parts such that tasks can be assigned in a form that allows clear accountability. The mark of a good plan is where it is communicated in such a way that each and every one affected understands what it means for their job. There are several steps in planning implementation:

- If the plan involves many people, break it down into manageable parts each of which has a defined outcome, and assign each part to someone with clear accountabilities.

- Identify critical activities, possibly using a critical path analysis to identify the points to really focus attention upon. A *Gantt chart* is a useful tool to lay out tasks, identifying the critical path and the linkages between elements in the plan.

- Where possible, measure performance against expected results and establish a way of reporting that is transparent and easily understood by all the stakeholders.

- Develop a style of managing that encourages problems to be surfaced early so that effort can be concentrated on the search for solutions, rather than the apportionment of blame.

# HOW TO CLARIFY ACCOUNTABILITIES AND SET OBJECTIVES

The purpose of setting objectives is to focus attention on the targets that need to be achieved in the shorter term, if an agreed strategy is to be met over the longer term.

Objectives are targets for the future, not day-to-day activities. They are milestones for managing change, not procedures for sustaining the status quo. They are designed to help individuals clarify priorities, understand their accountabilities, identify training and development needs around delivering business priorities, tease out overlaps or gaps in the organisation, and deal with competition for scarce resources.

Objective-setting serves no substantial purpose if there is no understood and valid overall strategy.

## The nature of objectives

Many people, particularly those who work in large organisations, spend a large proportion of their working lives enmeshed by habits. Their work becomes the systematic or routine application of old skills to old problems. The skills may be complex. The problems may be varied and difficult. Nonetheless, the emphasis can become centred on getting through the day, using the tried and tested, rather than on preparing for the future with the exciting, innovative or experimental.

The main purpose of objective-setting is to provide a co-ordinated, clear, and motivating set of targets for the future which are different, better, more challenging and more relevant to tomorrow's world. Objectives are motivating. This is because achieving an important goal is satisfying; so is the process of successfully negotiating a set of difficult objectives to reach an agreed group goal.

Most of us have objectives, even if they are fuzzy, opportunistic, minor, uncoordinated and personal. For objective setting to work effectively, it has to be demanding, relevant, important and create clarity.

The larger the organisation, the more this clarity has to become formalised. This means being explicit about assumptions, about the demands that the process will make and about the relevance to the organisation as a whole.

## A summary of objective-setting

It should:

- be observable, specific, job-related
- be focused on key results
- be quantified and/or verified
- answer questions about expectations
- be reviewed often
- have commitment gained through discussion.

## The six rules of objective-setting

### *Aims, output, standard, challenge, time span and review*

#### *1. Aim*
There has to be a general aim – connecting the associated objectives into the overall strategy.

#### *2. Output*
There has to be an output, a measurable and specific identifiable product or service, that someone somewhere wants, which adds value to what exists, and makes a genuine contribution to the overall aims.

#### *3. Standard*
There has to be a measure or a standard of performance. Typically these standards are about:

- *physical quantities*: such as products produced, or market share

- *money*: such as costs saved, or profit returned, or return on asset

- *time*

- *behaviour*: such as customer complaints, over-runs, or some other aspect of management effectiveness.

It is always best to have a standard that can be measured in a linear way, which is why people often search for numerical standards. However, using qualitative markers without being numeric, or even precise can also be used to assess levels of attainment.

## 4. Challenge

There has to be a challenge in the objectives set. If there is no stretch, then there will be no sense of attainment. There are two main ways of introducing challenge:

- *Targeting more than now*: for instance greater cost savings or greater market acceptance. Many organisations use the previous figures as a reference, but fail to recognise that such a strategy has a limited life. After two or three years of just adding more on more, people usually rebel.

- *Meeting new organisational needs*: a crisis of competitiveness, or of change in market conditions, can be translated into the new, more demanding needs on each individual. As these changed priorities and objectives cascade through the structure, they can provide highly motivating challenges.

Finding the right level of challenge for each individual is probably the most time-consuming part of the whole business. If it is too great, it will create despair and failure; if it is too small, it will serve no purpose. The most effective solution involves the active engagement of each individual at every stage of the process.

## 5. Time span

The time span has to be specified, as well as the other resources that are likely to be consumed, including the time of the manager setting the objectives. Conventionally, the time span is set as a calendar year, matching the company business plan for the organisation itself. However, it is probable that some of the objectives need to be achieved at specific earlier times. For more senior people, they are unlikely to be achieved until well beyond the period of review. The clear identification of the resources required has to be agreed and recorded as an essential part of the objective-setting contract.

SMART is a familiar mnemonic to remind us of the characteristics of good objectives.

- *S* – specific

- *M* – measurable

- *A* – agreed and achievable

- *R* – realistic, resourced and relevant

- *T* – timed.

And some commentators are adding:

- *E* – extending

- *R* – rewarding.

Some examples of SMARTER objectives:

- Improve productivity by x per cent by year-end.

- Streamline delivery procedures by reducing time taken by y per cent.

- Upgrade quality of new programmes to best industry benchmark.

- Gain industry-wide technical leadership, judged by independent panel.

- Improve employee relations by changing approach to staff problems, measured by change in 360-degree scores with a net result of reducing grievances by z per cent.

- Find and implement new ways of getting better interdepartmental communication, demonstrated by improved result from employee attitude survey.

- Increase cost-effectiveness through joint ventures, measured by reduced cost per case of b pounds.

- Strengthen co-operation between HQ and operation units, through establishing a weekly liaison meeting.

*Note*

An over-reliance on easily measurable, and especially financial, measures may cause blindness towards the important indicators. The balanced scorecard recognises the effect on these end financial measures of many other factors. Sustained performance comes from managing in a balanced way the basket of indicators, some measurable, some less so.

*6. Review*

Last, but by no means least, the objective-setting process has to include review procedures. These are needed for two reasons:

- There needs to be a formal provision for changed priorities and individual responsibilities. In this way flexibility is built in at the outset and nothing is cast in stone.

- Each party must have the opportunity to check progress, to assess whether circumstances have changed. For example, the resources agreed at the outset may no longer be sufficient. Or maybe there is a need to reassess the level of challenge that turned out not to be what was intended.

These reviews should be planned in advance thus increasing the likelihood that they will take place at regular and appropriate intervals. Done this way, updating and adjusting can be done with minimal difficulty.

### Summary

Objectives should be formulated in terms of what is to be accomplished. Furthermore, they are ideally:

- verifiable at all times

- tied closely to one specific responsible individual, but clearly linked to other organisational goals

- written as concise and crisp statements; details of the 'how' are the substance of action plans, which are not the same thing

- formulated so that they can be reviewed continuously, to determine what progress has been made

- written so as to give a clear indication of timescale, priority, and urgency to anyone directly involved

- introduced in such a way as to gain both understanding and commitment between all members of the management team, creating individual challenge, but at the same time enhancing a sense of overall team ownership.

## The objective-setting meeting

*In advance*:

Decide your aims in advance, *be clear about* what you hope to accomplish.

Establish how the meeting should be arranged, and assemble all relevant information and paperwork.

**During the meeting**

*Introduction:*

Establish a friendly, positive climate.

Arrange the physical environment so that it facilitates the discussion.

Avoid giving the impression that objective setting is an ordeal, a necessary evil or something to be concluded as soon as possible.

Indicate how you would like to conduct the meeting referring to both content and method.

Ask the other person if he/she has any views about how the meeting is to be conducted.

Agree both the method and the agenda of the meeting.

*Exchanging information:*

Start the discussion by seeking information.

Review the overall intent of the business plan and your area of responsibility.

Offer information confidently and unambiguously.

*Contracting:*

Agree the conclusions arising from the information exchanged.

Share your subjective judgements, conclusions, and feelings and determine if the other person agrees with them.

(If not, re-examine the information and assess its accuracy and explore jointly the value basis of your respective judgements.)

Review overall aims, standards of performance required, and the individual contributions being sought.

Agree priorities and formulate objectives.

Agree performance standards, resources, dates and responsibilities.

*Concluding the meeting:*

Assure your team member of your desire to help him/her succeed.

Confirm your availability if assistance is needed.

Set a follow-up date to review progress.

*Throughout:*

Use every opportunity to maintain and enhance the team member's self-esteem.

Figure 7.1 shows the continuing process.

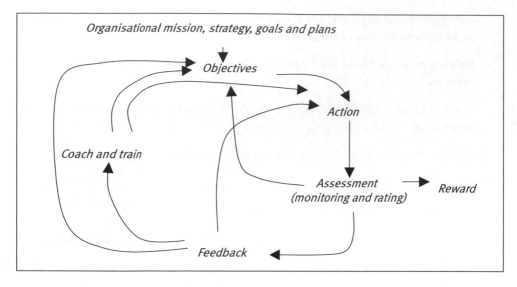

*Figure 7.1 / Objective setting and the appraisal process*

# SERVICE LEVEL AGREEMENTS IN HR

Another approach to ensuring that a plan is delivered is by the use of a service level agreement, whereby HR, for example, contracts to provide certain services for a defined level of resources. David Clutterbuck[25] has suggested a few points:

## What service level agreements do

1. Define expectations.

2. Create win–win situations.

3. Allow for continuous improvement.

4. Allow for joint problem-solving.

5. Build partnerships.

## What they should cover

1. Who does what:

    – the core services to cover basic needs, such as payroll and recruitment
    – support services such as communication, advice and guidance.

2. Roles of key personnel – on both sides.

3. How will the service provision be measured?

- deliverables
- intangibles – such as the attitude and style.

4. When and where service is to be delivered?

- response times
- how to change provision and with what notice
- period of agreement.

5. Problem resolution:

- consultation and review process when things go wrong.
- service guarantees?

## Making an internal service level agreement

### Step 1

Table 7.1 / **Making an internal service level agreement**

| Internal discussion | Customer consultation |
|---|---|
| What do we think the customer wants from us?<br>What help do they need to clarify their needs? | What does the internal customer say the needs are? |
| How do we think variation in our provision will affect the internal customer's performance? | What does the customer think? |
| What standards do we achieve now? | Does the customer have the same perception? |
| What standards could we achieve? | What standards would the customer ideally like? |
| What would it cost to raise our delivered standards closer to the customer's ideal? | What trade-offs/additional cost is the customer prepared to accept? |
| What measurements would tell us how well we are doing against the specification and standards? | What are the most useful and informative measures from the customers' viewpoint? |

*Step 2*

Negotiation between the parties is then conducted, leading to an agreement including clarification of milestones for implementation.

*Step 3*

Regular performance review and celebration of success with a periodic strategic review to address whether this agreement is improving the cost-effective provision of services.

## MONITORING PERFORMANCE OF THE PLAN

Two philosophies are apparent in the world of performance management. The first seeks to define gaps between where we are and where we want to be. The focus initially is on setting the standards and objectives. Recovery work is all about accurate assessment of current performance and closing the gap to the ideal.

The other philosophy sees a world of infinite possibilities and performance as a journey of continuous improvement. A supporter greeted Yehudi Menuhin, aged 6, when he came off the stage after a rapturous reception to a solo performance, with the words 'You are a star, that was perfect.' 'But,' Menuhin replied, 'I can do better.' He embraced the idea of continuous improvement, however good he was, and continued throughout his life to develop. 'Show me a craftsman,' said the old Japanese woodcarver – a national living treasure, 'and I will show you someone who is permanently dissatisfied.' It is this quality of constructive criticism of everything that is done that drives the true craftsman in whatever walk of life.

We see the same differences of philosophy in the way in which organisations are managed and developed. On the one hand there is gap analysis where the focus is on identifying the difference between where we are and some ideal standard, and on the other, the philosophy of appreciative enquiry.[26] The latter approach seeks to build on what is good and done well, so as to encourage further improvement.

For our purposes both philosophies have value in our quest for implementing effective business plans.

### Control

One of the enduring tensions of organisational life is that between freedom and control. Give people freedom and room to move and it encourages initiative, responsibility and fosters the continuing search for better ways of working. Yet, it also encourages individuality and variability and so results in a lack of consistency in performance. Conformity and consistency have however the unintended consequence of inappropriate actions when people are faced with a changing and unpredictable world. Following the rules, regardless of how inappropriate they may be in the circumstances, and an unwillingness to look creatively at their work or to take ownership, results in compromised safety, waste and frustrated customers.

A feature of successful businesses therefore is their ability to manage this tension. They do this by several critical processes:

- Clarity for everyone about what are the non-negotiable rules – and these are kept to a minimum.

- Encouragement to people to think for themselves, through an empowering style of management. Where mistakes occur, these are used as learning opportunities rather than reasons for apportioning blame.

- An understanding of what the ideal outcomes are in any situation and a focus by management on communicating clearly goals and expectations.

- Common values that are consistently applied. Where there are contentions between them, there is an understanding about what takes precedence.

- Balance between single-minded resolution to deliver despite the obstacles, with an openness to change if the circumstances change. The story is told of two people hacking their way through the jungle. After a while, one of them who had been focusing solely on cutting a path declared that they had covered 10 miles. The other climbed a tree to look round. 'Wrong direction in the wrong jungle,' he shouted.

Peter Drucker, one of the top management thinkers for decades, is reputed to have said: 'If you can't measure it, you can't manage it.' Control, wherever possible, needs to rest on accepted metrics. In addition, these metrics should be so embedded that they focus on the key levers of the business and show the impact on performance as the plan unfolds. Invariably there is a lag between the event, gathering data about it, reviewing it, taking action and that action taking effect. A recognition of possible time lags encourages us to identify wherever possible lead indicators and to keep the loop as fast as possible. Controlling an enterprise by using merely historical data is akin to driving a car by only using the rear-view mirror.

So there are several key financial indicators we should watch, identified below. Imagine if it were your business you would probably make sure at least that you monitor current and prospective cash flow and the factors that impact on it.

## Financial ratios

Financial ratios are often used as indicators of the financial health of a business. Examples include:

| For managing cash | Debtors in days |
|---|---|
| | Inventory in days of sales |
| | Acid test ratio or liquidity ratio = total current assets less inventory / total current liabilities |
| For a factory | Utilisation = number of hours used / total number of hours available or paid for |
| Productivity | Output per person |
| | Value added per pound of employment cost |
| For evaluating an investment | Return on capital employed (ROCE) = Profit before interest and tax / capital employed |
| Contribution | The sales less costs of a division/employee/product or customer |
| Overheads | Support or indirect costs/profit |
| | Indirect/direct employees (or costs) |
| Investors | Earnings per share |
| | Price earnings = market price of a share/earnings per share. |

## Keeping the plan on track

In keeping a plan on track it is important to keep in mind what successful implementation looks like. In one case a plan to deliver a new wage structure was implemented on time and according to plan, but with such animosity that no motivational advantage was gained. 'The operation was successful but the patient died.'

Try to identify therefore, the critical points in a project and identify what you would expect to see then.

---

In a company that launched a new 360-degree feedback system, attention was paid to the first participants. Early acceptance by some key opinion formers ensured a favourable response when it was more widely launched. If that had not occurred the project would probably have died.

---

Focus on the essentials. These are likely to be:

- Activities that are on the critical path for completion.

- Large expense items such as hire of a conference centre, or lower-value items where there are many of them, for example training consumables.

- Examine progress in detail at the predetermined milestones. Do not just accept that because things appear to be going according to plan, there are no lurking problems. Problems have a habit of only emerging at the end of a project when there is no money or time to recover the situation.

- Look at the early results in terms of quality and quantity.

- Gather a sense of, and from, those involved. Are they enthusiastic? Will they push on when the going gets tough?

- What is happening in the wider world of your organisation and the outside? Are there events that might derail progress?

## IF THINGS GO WRONG – GETTING A PROJECT BACK ON TRACK

Why do projects fail? The box shows a number of reasons.

---

### Survey of 120 organisations: major causes of runaway projects

- 51 per cent project objectives not fully specified.

- 49 per cent bad planning.

- 42 per cent inadequate project management methodology.

- 42 per cent wrong team members.

Source: *Project Manager Today*, March 2000.

---

No one likes making mistakes; it strikes at the heart of our self-esteem, our notions of our competence. Our culture is full of clichés designed to counter this problem. 'To err is human,' 'We learn more from our mistakes than from our triumphs,' 'If at first you don't succeed, try, try again,' and so on. Organisations espouse 'no blame cultures' yet continue to fire (or at least roast) the messengers of bad news.

---

One day an employee of a large company made a terrible mistake. It cost the company £50,000. Knowing something of the hire and fire reputation of the company and mindful of his career prospects if he was dismissed, the hapless employee presented his resignation to his boss, with a plea that he let him go with a reasonable reference. The boss tore up the resignation with the words, 'I have just invested £50,000 in your training. I am not about to lose you now.'

---

Apart from mistakes, projects of all kinds tend to get derailed because they run out of time. When faced with a project that is late, first consider the causes:

- Try to find out why it has slipped in terms of time and/or budget. Use *root cause analysis* and *fishbone diagrams* to investigate. Use *bottlenecking* to find those 'pinch points'. Then see if resources could be rebalanced to put more support at the bottleneck.

- Consider how corporate politics might have had an impact, particularly where professional rivalries occur (see *interest mapping*). There comes a time in all change programmes where a line has to be drawn.

A famous OD consultant once told a client, 'We either change the team, or we change the team.' In that organisation, the chief executive laboured for two years to break down silos and get people working together. One day he stood up at a meeting of all managers and said that it was here he was drawing a line in the sand: 'You are with me or you are not.' The following day many executives were asked to leave the organisation.

So in summary, what can we do to recover the situation?

- *Recover lost time during later steps*: If, in the early stages of a project, a step takes longer than planned, re-examine time allocations for the remaining steps. Use a *Gantt chart* to see where time might be found. Perhaps other time can be saved so that overall time on the project will not increase.

- *Renegotiate*: The simplest action when you need to redo some work or cannot make a deadline is to renegotiate the due date. Perhaps there is enough flexibility that a day or two longer will not really matter. Organisations often use deadlines that are wholly artificial in that nothing specifically hangs on them. They are useful to encourage a sense of urgency, but they may cause participants to cut corners, take risks or reduce the amount delivered. Consider whether an extension of time might aid the delivery of the project to the standard required. And finally, what revisions if any do you now need to make to the plan? If you have identified any changes to the plan you may well need to recontract with those involved (from our *stakeholder analysis*) their objectives and time lines.

- *Narrow the scope of the project*: Once it is underway you may find it will take longer to accomplish everything you planned. When time is critical, you may have to eliminate some non-essential things to meet the deadline. Can any part of the project be streamlined or simplified to bring it back on track? Maybe you can separate the 'nice to haves' from the 'essentials' and move the former to a later phase.

- *Deploy more resources*: Try to do more activities in parallel rather than in sequence. It allows additional resource to be brought in on parallel work, with a positive affect on the critical path. This option clearly increases the cost, so it represents a decision choice of weighing the cost against the importance of the deadline.

- *Accept substitutions*: When a needed item is not available, you may be able to substitute a comparable item to meet your deadline.

- *Seek alternative sources*: When a supplier you are depending upon cannot deliver within your timeframe, look for other suppliers who can. (You may choose to pursue other sources before accepting substitutions.)

- *Accept partial delivery*: Sometimes a supplier cannot deliver an entire order but can deliver the amount you need to get you past a critical point. After that, the remainder of the order can be delivered to everyone's satisfaction.

- *Offer incentives*: This option calls for going beyond the terms of an agreement to get someone you are dependent upon to put forth extra effort. It might be a bonus clause in a contract for on-time delivery, or a penalty clause for late delivery, or simply buying someone lunch to encourage extra effort.

- *Demand compliance*: Sometimes it is necessary to stand up for your rights and demand performance according to the agreement. Occasionally, an appeal to higher authority will produce the desired results.

- *Persistence pays off*: Today, in the garden of Thomas Edison's house in Florida grows Chinese bamboo, one of the materials he tried but subsequently discarded in favour of sewing thread from which he fashioned the carbonised filament for the world's first light bulb. He had evaluated hundreds of materials until he found the right one. What would have happened to the world if he had not persisted? The process of invention is described as '5 per cent inspiration, 95 per cent perspiration'.

## EVALUATING OUTCOMES

Financial outcomes will be monitored in many organisations by variances to plan, or if they have been set into a budget, against budget. It is the other elements of a plan that are more difficult.

If there has been a service level agreement then there may be other indicators to look for. A rerun of a **customer–supplier questionnaire** may also indicate changes in service level and customer perception.

In addition to formal measures, a review meeting might help to examine the process.

## Project review

The purpose is to:

- determine to what degree the project accomplished its desired outcomes

- achieve closure on a stage of the project

- be explicit about how the group is working together so members can make ongoing improvements for the future

- acknowledge what contributed to the project's success

- provide an opportunity for direct feedback to leader, members, facilitator and recorder.

What it consists of:

- Listings of what worked and improvements for future projects.

- Can be done a variety of ways, with greater or lesser detail.

- Variations from a light review (a few short comments at the end of a meeting) to a medium review (list of pluses and minuses), to an in-depth evaluation (follow-up interviews).

Principles for a project review:

- Ongoing project reviews are the foundation for groups taking responsibility to improve the quality of their activities.

- Use them as information to make choices about what to keep doing and what to change.

- Meeting reviews that are only done as a formality produce superficial information (for example, we liked the doughnuts; no coffee).

Capture the points in the format of Figure 7.2.

| *What worked* | *Needs improvement/do different next time* |
|---------------|--------------------------------------------|
|               |                                            |

Figure 7.2 / **Meeting review chart**

# WHY DOES INDIVIDUAL POOR PERFORMANCE OCCUR?

It is a reasonable assumption that the vast majority of people in organisations are trying to do a reasonable job. Yet good performance is by no means assured. Some of the reasons that plans are not brought through to fruition are a lack of commitment at the outset or maybe a confused presentation of information which left people bewildered and misunderstood. Time might have been too limited, the task just too difficult, or there could have been a reluctance to step into the unknown.

However, poor performance does arise and needs to be addressed. It is always a sensitive area, and particularly difficult if you do not have direct authority. Use the checklist below to help you determine the possible causes, which in turn can help in suggesting a course of action to improve the situation.

## Checklist of factors affecting behaviour/performance

*Competence*

> lack of training

> over-promoted

> wrong job

*Organisation*

> confusing structure

> inter-group conflict

> poor communications between geographically separate groups

> strategy not linked to structure

*HR practices*

> inappropriate reward package

> unfair/inadequate placement and promotion policies

> insufficient attention to maintaining morale

*Job design*

> span of control too large/narrow

> impossible workload

> unclear role/authority

> too specialised/generalised

*Supervision*

> demotivating style
>
> not clarifying expectations/standards
>
> poor work allocation – peaks and troughs
>
> lack of communication

*Environment*

> inadequate technology
>
> temperature, noise, light
>
> office layout
>
> furniture ergonomics

*Information*

> too much/too little/wrong sort
>
> too late
>
> one-way

*Non-work*

> personal relationships
>
> other demands on time such as moving house.

## BRINGING ABOUT CHANGE

It was Machiavelli (2005 edition) in his famous treatise on statecraft who remarked that there was nothing more difficult to bring about than change. It made enemies, he asserted, of those who had a vested interest in the current situation and only lukewarm support was forthcoming from those who might gain from the new. In this section I want to explore why change is so difficult and what we can do, both personally and when responsible for others, to bring about lasting change.

The first issue we must confront is who or what is to change. Organisations are bad at tolerating mavericks, yet a cursory glance at the history of inventors and innovators shows all too clearly that it may be the organisation that should change rather the individual. Organisations rely on people building collaborative relationships, yet for many there always seem to be some with whom there is a difficulty. Does the difficulty lie in them or the other, or maybe in the relationship and the way it has developed? We must be wary of assuming that it is always the other person who must change. Of course, change is always a choice, but survival is not guaranteed.

> *I feel so angry, frustrated and resentful – at myself mostly. We changed lots of things to become more efficient, but in the end it was too little, too late. We changed at a pace that was comfortable to us. We talked about 'planned and controlled evolution'. The market and our competitors changed faster, and now we are history.*
>
> **Executive talking about the closure of his company**

## Personal change

Charles Darwin, following his famous voyage, concluded that it is not the strongest or most intelligent species that survive, rather it is the most adaptive to change. To bring about adaptation to change requires six aspects to be aligned with the desired direction. These are self-awareness, competence, willpower, congruence with our values, positive and negative incentives, and a vision of the future.

### Self-awareness

It is a common human trait to see ourselves as different from the way that others see us. Indeed some might suggest that our lives are one long journey of getting to know ourselves. The differences in perception might be about appearance or intelligence, accomplishment or belief, attitude or behaviour. Change requires a minimum of self-awareness that our position is in some way different from what is appropriate or required in the situation. Too often we live in a protective bubble, denying the reality of the need for change. 'When ignorance is bliss 'tis folly to be wise' runs the old saying. When the environment around us in no way challenges our beliefs, there is little awareness of the need for change. Often it is only when we step out of our environment and habitual ways of acting that we become aware of differences. So the first step in the route to change is through feedback – maybe formally through appraisal and 360-degree feedback as increasingly practised in organisations, or more informally through experiential learning. Large organisations that have been successful in the past are often very successful in denying the reality of the present, and so continually need the challenge of external benchmarks. But self-awareness is not sufficient.

### Competence

In recent decades, organisations have sought to improve their customer relations through a bewildering array of strategies. From ever more convoluted ways of answering the telephone to empowering front-line staff to take more and more complex decisions, these changes have resulted in mixed effects. Telephones are encumbered with jingles and staff have become increasingly stressed. Building competence to change requires several components. First, there is the knowledge and skill required to do the new job, and second, the confidence needed to apply these skills in a sensible way beyond what the manual says. Yet we see in many bored employees the signs that they are just going through the motions, and if we are on the receiving end of the service in question, we easily see through it. True change only occurs when there is congruence with our beliefs – when there is a recognition that this change is for the better and one that we believe in. 'As is our confidence so is our competence,' said William Hazlitt, the eighteenth-century philosopher. This provides a clue that training in new skills requires more than the development of competence. It requires a transformation of our beliefs with an improved will to act.

It also requires a skilful handling of mistakes by managers. Learning is a risky business, and by the time middle age comes, we carry in our heads a catalogue of things we have no intention of trying because we tried them once and failed. Mistakes of course can be catastrophic for organisations, but they are the most powerful source of learning. If after a mistake, we can leave a learner with not only an understanding of what went wrong and how to avoid it in the future, but also a willingness to keep on risking failure in learning new things, then a foundation for lifetime learning and thereby continual change is laid.

The fear of ridicule, of fallen pride and loss of self-esteem provide strong incentives to avoid any challenge. Yet when we collude with our fears rather than confront them, it makes it harder next time. The boss who says that your words are 'not the answer I want to hear' presents a choice; do you have the courage of your convictions or do you back down for fear of losing your job? If you back down, where does that leave your fear or your conviction?

While the concept of lifetime learning is largely accepted as essential for survival in this fast-changing world, its practice is at best patchy. Ask busy executives how many books they read a year and any publisher will tell you it is a far from encouraging picture. In addition, learning involves choices and an opportunity cost, in that there are always alternatives for our time and attention. It is a powerful question to ask of anyone: 'What have you learnt today and what in your learning are you avoiding?'

## Willpower

There is considerable willpower required to change, as we all know only too well not long after those New Year resolutions. Some have suggested that in order to change a behavioural habit one must carry out the new behaviour over 30 times before there is any hope of it sticking. That needs willpower and support to bring about sustained practice. Willpower rarely comes from external exhortation alone, though it can be enhanced. It is more a function of our inner beliefs that this change is worthy of our effort (and maybe pain).

Willpower alone might produce motivation but it requires other ingredients. One way of looking at our lives is like a stream running down hill. It takes the easiest course, flowing round rocks and down gullies. So in our lives it is sometimes easiest to go round problems rather than confront them. Few people make a deliberate choice between good and evil: the choice is between what we want to do and what we ought to do. So building willpower rests on building our beliefs — both in the change to be accomplished and in our own capacity to accomplish it. Removing as many of the rocks in the way can help this, so that the stream has an uninterrupted flow. We should not however ignore the powerful positive effect that adversity has on willpower, but that usually only occurs when the rightness of the cause is well assured, otherwise rapid discouragement ensues.

## Congruence with our values

At the beginning of this book I mentioned Jean-Paul Sartre, the French philosopher, who remarked that we see our values in action by the choices we make. Our values about honesty and integrity are increasingly tested in business today, and it often takes courage to stand up for what is 'right'. So when change is urged upon us that conflicts with our values we become uncomfortable and find ways of making it more acceptable. These sometimes involve 'semantic gymnastics' or being 'economical with the truth', as some would call it. In other ways we see employees subvert systems and processes where they do not conform to their values. Recently I came across a canteen assistant who gave everyone good helpings because she thought portion control was not right, and a car hire assistant who ignored the customer survey questions she was supposed to ask me because she wanted to help me get away quickly. Her choice about customer service was right for me, but probably did not get much support from the market research department.

So the fourth strategy for change is to identify the values behind the change and how these will conflict with those of the people on the ground implementing new systems and procedures.

## Positive and negative incentives

Incentives are powerful levers of change. Incentives to gain something (the carrot) and/or to avoid some undesirable consequence (the stick) are a common feature of organisational life. We are used to incentive schemes designed to boost performance of individuals and teams, but success in business comes from many ingredients all working together successfully. So the problem with such incentive schemes is that they have to strike a balance between conflicting goals. On the one hand they must be simple to ensure that the rules are well understood and that participants know exactly what they have to do to win the award, but that runs the risk of focusing on a limited behaviour at the expense of others. The stories of sales personnel who ignore the more subtle aspects of customer relations in their bid to earn more money are legion. On the other hand, schemes must be sufficiently comprehensive to reflect the total range of behaviours required, such as helping colleagues or developing longer-term strategies beyond the bonus period. These schemes, however, run the risk of being so complex that no one can determine what they have to do differently, and so they lose any impact.

Perhaps the most powerful examples of the stick have been where job loss threatens and survival depends on sacrificing sacred cows. Creating a climate of crisis – 'the barbarians are at the gate' – has been used since time immemorial to galvanise people into actions that they otherwise would not have taken.

### Vision of my future

In Chapter 1, we discussed the importance of vision and referred to that most famous of vision statements: 'I have a dream …'. They are still some of the most evocative words ever spoken of a man's vision of the future. Martin Luther King touched a nerve of a nation and gave those in the civil rights movement in the United States a vision of what they could become. This gives us the final clue in a successful change strategy. If we can create a picture of what the change will accomplish in each person's life, such that each will say to him or herself, 'Yes, I can see myself doing that and it's what I want for myself,' then we will have created a condition that will sustain people through the pain and heartache of personal change.

Let us turn to some of the tactics for working with change.

## Practical steps to work with change

People can be energised and enthused by change. However when change is so great or uncertain that it threatens people's security, self-esteem and ingrained habits, then reactions can be shock, anger and resentment. Individuals and organisations often go through predictable stages in responding to major change. The 'loss curve' as it is sometimes called (Figure 7.3) comes from the work of Kubler-Ross (1969) on bereavement.

The reactions to change go through a number of phases, as follows.

### Surprise, shock and anger

When any major change is announced, there is an initial feeling of shock, which may last for a few moments or few weeks. It is partially a physiological reaction while the body comes to terms with what has been said and comes to conclusions. Is it good or bad news? Do I fight it or flee from it? Who are my friends and foes? During the time of surprise, sometimes experienced as 'freezing', rational debate is rarely possible and much of what is said or written is not understood. These reactions are a result of the limbic system in the brain becoming active and masking the neocortex or rational parts.

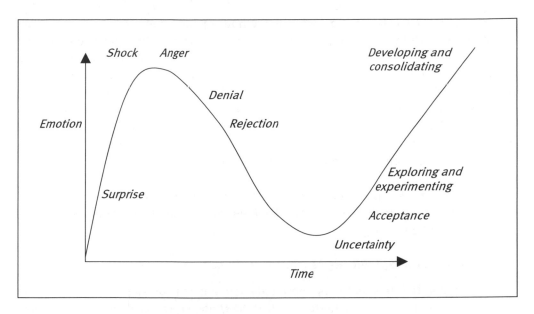

*Figure 7.3 / **SARA – shock, anger, rejection, acceptance***

Recognise therefore that the first step in managing change is to accept the need for careful, continuous and repetitious communication. So often, managers who have been planning some change for some time will be so conversant with what they are planning to do, that they overlook the time spent in turning the problem over in the mind and coming to grips with it. During the phase of announcing changes:

- Give time and opportunity for people to talk about what is proposed.

- Answer points of clarification.

- Encourage staff to come up with useful suggestions.

The problem for many is that having planned the change before announcing it, there is a high degree of emotional commitment to it. It is not easy in the tense moment of briefing everyone, to admit that there may be a better way.

Keeping people informed on a regular basis of what is happening builds people's confidence that you know what you are doing. If you are uncertain, use your colleagues and manager to build a sense of unity and purpose across the organisation.

### Denial or rejection

The next stage is denial. This can happen in groups as well as individually. It stems from the belief that by denying the change, or not hearing it correctly, that in some way the change will be made to go away. 'Perhaps it is all a dream and on waking, life will be the same as before'. For people who are dismissed because of their inability to cope with new changes such as technology, working methods or pace, denial can be a very strong reaction; after all they feel they are fighting for their life or at least livelihood. Expect there to be arguments for the status quo and detailed accounts of why they perceive all is well. Individuals may point to examples of exemplary performance that only recently were recognised – so why change? One of the tensions that always confound conversations about individual performance is a history of appraisals and rewards that seem to indicate no problem. Yet as we know the issue many organisations are facing is one of changed roles that demand more in the future than has been asked in the past. This may lead to even more strident arguments about unfairness:

> *I was hired to do x which I have done faithfully and now you are changing the rules. You can't do that. It's not fair, besides who will do all the important things that I have been doing?*

So what can be done? There are essentially three tactics:

- Engage in the debate. Spend more time listening than talking – 'If you wish to be understood, seek first to understand.' If the changes proposed are logical and well thought-out, in time you will manage to get the logic across. People may not like it, but they can in due course be brought to understand it and thereby give (albeit grudgingly) their acceptance.

- Focus on the key opinion formers before change is announced to ensure that the ground is laid and that there is a growing recognition amongst the most influential of those affected, of the need for change and the likely impacts. Shock and denial will then be minimised.

- Ignore it. Presenting a fait accompli sometimes can continue a momentum already started. It avoids protracted time before implementation and may ensure that the waverers or at least those not actively resisting the changes have no time to gather opposition. Its success as a tactic is based on the assumption that some changes are better once experienced, rather than when talking about them. The tactic runs the risk of generating considerable resistance, not the least because of ignoring genuine concerns however petty they may be.

Above all seek to behave consistently and in a way which encourages people to trust you. Keep to your word and if you have made a mistake that is obvious, don't deny it. Try to behave with integrity and calmness. This is a time when people can lose their heads and say things that may be regretted later. Seek to calm these situations.

## Uncertainty

Faced with uncertainty or new things where old patterns of behaviour may now no longer be appropriate, individuals can react with irrational behaviour. Knee-jerk reactions, lack of wisdom in judgements and actions, as well as slowness in carrying out new tasks are all characteristics. When learning about new technology, often the simplest misunderstandings can become major bottlenecks, only to be looked back upon in subsequent months with amusement that such trivial matters assumed such significance at the time. For example, instructions on how to log on to a computer may seem insignificant to some, yet the first time you did it, it probably seemed a great mystery.

Deal with this phase with care. How one reacts will determine attitudes and willingness to learn new things. Ensure that where new skills are to be learnt a programme of training is instituted. It is imperative that positive attitudes are engendered right from the outset. Do not shirk the responsibility of talking about the standards of competence expected, but signal clearly your understanding that it will take time and practice to attain these high standards. Exhibit by your behaviour those high standards you are seeking. For example, it is hypocritical to talk about customer service standards of say, answering the telephone after two rings, if the manager or his/her secretary never answers in this time. Look for examples of behaviour and attitudes that meet your standards and recognise them publicly, so that others can gain some insight into what you expect. Where confusion and ignorance continue, make sure that adequate information, sources of reference and help are available.

At this time clear leadership is vital, demonstrating clarity of vision of where the organisation is heading.

## Acceptance or letting go

The next phase is where acceptance of the changes begins. The danger at this stage is one of apathy and indifference. From now on greater energy is needed by the leadership towards accomplishing the changes rather than on justifying the decisions of why the change was necessary. In essence, at this stage, reality is beginning to seep in and there is a growing ability to see the world as it really is as opposed to how we would like it to be.

This is the time to capitalise on the reduction in emotional content and generate more focused energy, by getting behind those who will be affected and setting in train positive action. It may be the time to establish a teambuilding session with new colleagues, book-training courses, or to commit to installing new equipment, or for the person who is leaving to talk about the outplacement programme and what to do in the future. Let your energy, enthusiasm and certainty for the future come through. In the film *Gladiator*, the hero in his speech to his troops before the battle says, 'In three weeks time I will harvest my crops.' He does not say 'I hope to be …', or 'Perhaps if we are lucky.'

Work at giving new meaning to the new work. Help people rationalise and make sense of what they now have to do. There is an old story of a traveller who comes across three men breaking stones. 'What are you doing?' says the traveller. 'Breaking stones' was the reply from one. He asked another the same question and received the reply: 'Earning my living.' From a third came a different reply: 'I am building a cathedral.' We see our work through many lenses, and if we can be helped to find some meaning that lifts the tasks beyond the commonplace, we have the chance of sustaining the work at a higher degree of commitment.

## Exploring and experimenting

However well planned, there will always be the need for fine-tuning as changes become implemented. The essence of good change management is the ability to respond positively to new ideas and to experiments, taking the benefits, but not getting overly side-tracked which might cause time and budget overruns. Any process of innovation has to be a balance between getting practical benefits now, and waiting a little longer for further improvements to come through. Experimentation is also important for learning about the practical problems in a way that planning at the outset can never totally accomplish.

'If at first you don't succeed, try, try again.' Persistence and searching for ways to overcome problems needs to be the hallmark of any change manager. Folklore abounds in inspirational stories from Robert Bruce's spider to Thomas Edison's light filament. Demonstrate that the goal is non-negotiable. It is the means of getting to the place where creative ideas can be explored. By releasing people into a more experimental way of working, it can be a way of gaining people's involvement and thus commitment. During this phase, leaders need to be close to their staff, gaining insight first-hand into the problems, listening carefully to objections and those who may be wavering. Seek to energise by showing practically the way forward if they are stuck, bring people together in temporary teams to solve problems and encourage those who may be less committed. Don't be afraid to talk about problems openly, encouraging team members to do the same – don't 'shoot the messenger' – but make sure there is no doubt in your resolve to overcome them. Encourage a sense of ownership and responsibility within the context of teamwork. 'If we don't hang together we will certainly hang separately,' said Benjamin Franklin at the time of the American declaration of independence.

## Developing and consolidating

This phase is about establishing new patterns of working and building on them to achieve sustained superior performance.

Build on the sense of achievement and team spirit that can arise from going through a period of change. Make sure there is clarity of what is now expected, and encourage dialogue about the goals now being set. Be clear about new roles and responsibilities, and especially the relationships you may have with different departments. Try to install some basis of measurement so that all can see how much progress has been made.

## TWO TYPICAL CASES

In this last section of the book, we examine two cases of introducing new systems. Business plans invariably end with the introduction of change of some kind. New systems development is an area that seems particularly susceptible to problems caused rarely by technology, mostly by the human factors.

### Introduction

Despite the enormous resources devoted to the implementation of ever more sophisticated applications of information technology, there continues to be a wealth of case studies of failure. As expectations continue to rise about the benefits of IT so the disasters appear even greater when these benefits are not achieved. Failure can be defined in a number of ways, but commonly is found in an inability to fully realise the expected benefits or gain the acceptance and enthusiastic support of users and management.

### Case one

A retailer decided to upgrade its systems and embarked upon an ambitious plan to redesign its distribution and stock management systems. It employed consultants, established an experienced project team, had a clear user-defined system design and utilised project management techniques to control the redesign. In the end the first phase of the system was abandoned after almost 50 per cent more time than planned had been taken and response times were still unacceptable. What had gone wrong?

Three things emerged in the autopsy that were critical to the project's failure:

1. The size of the project was far greater than anyone had completed before, and estimates of the time taken to analyse various activities and come to sensible system solutions were hopelessly inaccurate. The size of the project also placed a strain on the management skills of the project leader, whose staff had tripled. He was not used to welding such a team together into an efficient unit. This took time during which the team lacked tight cohesion. Size meant also that new disciplines were required to keep hundreds of programmes and subroutines in properly controlled libraries, maintain change control disciplines, and manage a test regime that was logical and allowed a number of parallel test routines to carry on simultaneously.

2. There was little real experience of a system of this type. It was also to be implemented on a new database with a new language. This newness and

complexity meant that there was a long learning curve for both technical staff and users.

3. The end result was thought to be well defined, but it became clear that the detail was only hazily understood as the project progressed. It was to some extent a 'voyage of discovery', which required more time to fully understand all the likely conditions that had to be satisfied. In the end, time estimates were incorrect.

With hindsight, many of the problems could easily have been solved, but there is a natural tendency, with hindsight, to forget the effort that was expended for only seemingly modest gains. However, hindsight is easy and it is characteristic of system failure that there is enormous learning that goes on which might benefit future projects but at the expense of the failed system.

## Case two

An airline that was changing its accounting systems set about creating a user-driven project team utilising sophisticated technology. The project lasted some two years and by the end it was running over time and budget. The factors that again emerged were the three cited above of size, technical innovation and specificity of the end result. In this case the combination of a long complex project with new technologies which required substantial retraining meant that tracking the project was difficult. Estimating the time required to achieve certain milestones was highly variable.

A further factor emerged in this case, in that the strong user direction of the project blurred the edges between legitimate technical concerns and practical solutions. The user management had established a new vision for the system outputs, which bore little correlation to existing outputs. The resulting effort required to educate users into a new way of thinking and overcome the resistance to change detracted from the focus on getting workable software in on time that met the needs of today as much as the needs of the future. Users could not see the value of new more flexible reporting systems unless they could see what replaced the printout from which they extracted a vital piece of information.

## An analysis of the factors

Why do these factors have an impact on project success?

### Size of the project

1. Size increases the management task of co-ordinating more people and activities with more complex interactions involving potentially different locations, ways of working, functions and layers of management.

2. Size increases the chances that project management may not have experienced anything similar before. As a result it becomes a process of experiential learning with a reduced perception of the likely critical 'show stopping' stages that lie ahead.

3. Size means that any requirement for additional resource may be substantial in terms of money if real impact is to be made on project timescales. Hence there is a greater likelihood of the project being stopped or reduced in scope.

4. Size in terms of the number of programmes increases the testing task more than linearly because of the need to test a growing range of the interactions between different subroutines. This in turn can add complexity in understanding the potential outcomes from any given set of conditions and even more so when hypothesising about what might happen.

5. Finally size often means that the consequence of failure is greater and there is therefore greater attention to it within the organisation.

### Experience of the technology

Application of the technology to the particular project has a number of aspects:

1. New technology inevitably requires mastery to be properly utilised to the full. The learning rate at which this is assimilated will be different for individuals, and the degree of understanding and application will be different. In a world of jargon and heavy marketing, it is difficult to properly assess the true level of competence and the skill with which this new-found knowledge will be applied.

2. The combination of new technologies can pose problems that specialist technicians of each are unable to assess. The interaction of technologies can pose large matrices of possible outcomes and may cause particular issues about performance. All too often project teams have a high concentration on functionality at the expense of performance, especially where there is insufficient technical expertise. In a recent example an organisation in the public sector implemented a personnel system. Each element of the mix was state-of-the-art but as there was little experience of combining this particular recipe, bottlenecks occurred which were not understood and performance suffered.

3. Lack of experience of the technology and its application can lead to assumptions about its capability that may not be apparent. Systems like scanning technologies

and character recognition may not have the accuracy in practice that is assumed or even claimed.

4. Systems behave in different ways with different volumes, and those who have not experienced it before may poorly understand these phenomena.

## Degree of specificity of the end result

1. For many system developments, the process of analysis and design exposes inconsistencies and ambiguities that may have lain hidden in organisations, handled silently before by personnel using their judgement.

2. Project management by both users and IT staff may be at the level of senior managers who in reality do not fully understand all the logical alternatives that might arise. More junior staff have a more detailed knowledge, though they may not fully appreciate the bigger picture. Figure 7.4 shows the curve of influence, where the greatest influence can be exerted by middle managers – both in facilitating change and in blocking it.

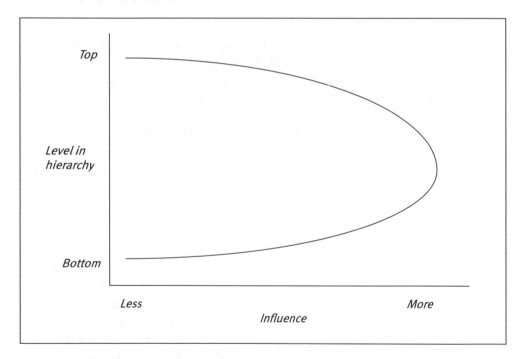

Figure 7.4 / *Where does influence for change lie?*

3. The precise specification may depend upon many other factors such as organisation, location, market structure or business priority, which may only be hazily known and may change during the life of the project.

## Risk assessment

Each of these factors is an element in the assessment of risk, shown in Figure 7.5.

The likelihood of failure increases as size increases, specificity decreases and experience of the technology is low. These factors can be further amplified by looking at other sub-factors that affect success. Some of these sub-factors can be similarly expressed in terms of increasing and decreasing likelihood of risk as shown in Figure 7.6.

| Task definition | Technical experience | |
|---|---|---|
| **High** | **High** | **Low** |
| large project | low | high |
| small project | very low | medium |
| **Low** | | |
| large project | low | very high |
| small project | very low | high |

*Figure 7.5 / **Risk assessment***

# Success factors

In considering why projects fail it is useful to turn to those projects that succeed and understand what factors have contributed to their success. There are four major factors that are apparent.

## *Successful projects have good project leaders*

Project leaders tend to be more successful when they combine high user acceptance, often being responsible for a major activity that uses the system once complete, together with an understanding of the technology and what is involved in making it

| LOW RISK | HIGH RISK |
|---|---|
| **TECHNOLOGY FACTORS** | |
| Used before | New |
| Single supplier | Multiple suppliers |
| Single technology | Multiple technologies |
| Replaces existing | New, additional functionality |
| Simulation of new system possible before going live | Not possible |
| High cost benefit | Marginal cost benefit |
| High clarity of solution | Unclear solution |
| 'Trailing edge' | 'Leading edge' |
| Adequate capacity/funding | Tight budget |
| **PEOPLE FACTORS** | |
| High IT literacy | Low IT literacy |
| Clear project authority | Incongruent authority for project size |
| Win–win outcomes | Greater number of losers than winners from project |
| Clear organisation | Low clarity of organisation objectives/processes |
| High commitment from top | Low commitment from top |
| High sense of ownership of system by users | Low ownership of system |
| Stable organisation and environment | High rate of environmental/organisational change |
| Technical competence | Low competence |
| Future working patterns clear | Low visibility of ways of working with new system |
| Little impact on organisation/power structure | High impact on structure |
| Sound and appropriate management | Poor project control |

*Figure 7.6 / **High and low risk factors***

happen. Project leaders have to be able to move across organisational boundaries and hierarchies, inspiring confidence and commanding support and action when required. They are doers, rather than thinkers, and they have a high belief in the vision of what it is they are trying to achieve.

## Successful projects go through several stages

A basic requirement for success is that the stages of project management are well understood by those involved:

- *Brainstorming*. The accent at the beginning is on being freethinking and seeking out a range of solutions.

- *Project start*. Resources are assigned for the first stage and top management signal that they are totally committed to the project.

- *Diagnosis*. Specific research is now carried out to identify the business processes that are to be computerised and how these are to change. This might involve a number of techniques such as data modelling.

- *Planning*. The route to implementing the ideal solution is a detailed activity which results in a carefully crafted implementation plan with costs of the project identified.

- *Formal start*. It is at this stage that managing with project control techniques becomes useful.

At several defined stages through the process there are quality control milestones with great emphasis placed on avoiding surprises at the final testing stage:

- *Implementation,* seen as an exercise that is as much about introducing organisational changes as about launching a new computer system. It involves understanding the impact on the socio-technical system. This involves identifying beforehand who wins and loses out from the system in terms of power, job interest and freedom to act.

A system once implemented is taken as the start of a continuing process of improving working methods thus gaining benefit. As organisational needs change, so continuing essential activities are maintaining the system in line with those needs as well as ensuring its operation is utilised to maximum advantage by the training of operatives.

The key test of any system is whether it survives beyond the life in the organisation of the original project team members.

## Successful projects are in control of the technology

Control of the technology is a key factor. Here, project teams understand the technical performance of the hardware and software and data on how it might perform in a new context is available.

## Successful projects are oriented to organisational processes that are well understood

The rules and procedures, especially in relation to exceptions and rare events are recognised and able to be incorporated.

From this analysis of failed and successful projects comes a series of general principles that, if implemented, are more likely to lead to successful systems implementation.

## *Some general principles for project success*

1. Keep projects small and of short duration before implementation. This ensures that the organisational complexity is reduced and the opportunities for slippage are small. Of course it is important that small projects are within the context of a strategic plan that is clear in its direction, relevance and benefit. However keeping each subsystem small encourages focus on those parts that have most relevance and are of benefit today.

2. Change sequentially. Where systems change is part of a wider process of change, seek to change parts in discrete phases. Try to avoid changing systems, people, facilities and work methods all at the same time.

3. Where systems are complex and users are unclear of the precise specification of their needs, prototype and run pilot schemes before main systems are developed. Build into timescales the opportunity for changing specifications in the light of user experience (Figure 7.7). It is a feature of the interactive and iterative nature of people and systems that a system will stimulate further demands for new development.

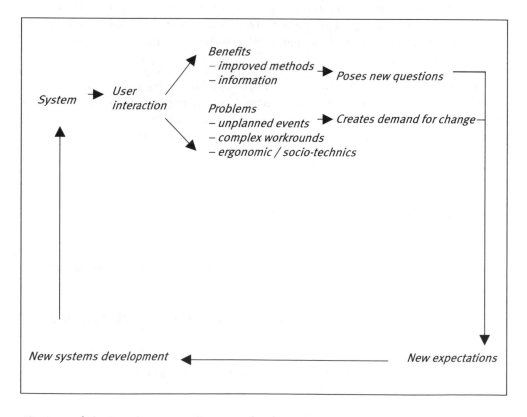

*Figure 7.7 / **The iterative nature of systems development***

4. Look for the 80/20 rule of 80 per cent benefit with 20 per cent effort. However recognise that many projects require core foundation building blocks with little perceived benefit other than providing a secure basis for future development.

5. Ensure top management commitment for the project, for funding and for managing the inevitable changes that will arise in organisation, job profiles and skills required.

6. Be wary of 'leading edge' technologies unless you are prepared for unpredictable timescales and funding requirements.

7. All projects require enthusiastic champions who are able to inspire those affected with a vision of the future. They need to possess sound persuasive skills and the necessary authority to command resources, overcome resistance to change and make the necessary decisions about project management. Sufficient technical literacy is also required.

A critical factor that emerges as intervening between people and technology is the approach and style of project management.

## Styles of project management

From the cases studied, there appear to be several models that are adopted:

### The traditional or formal approach

Here emphasis is placed on a clear specification at the outset of what is required, with milestones of achievement along the way which are monitored using a variety of numerical and graphical techniques. Stress is placed on achieving time deadlines, sometimes at the expense of system refinements. Techniques of critical path analysis are often employed, and the qualities of strong leadership are required in the head of the project. Invariably if the project slips, the response is either to allocate more resource or transfer functions into a later phase. This methodology is well suited to systems that are well known, have been done before, and where user needs and business processes are clearly defined.

Its weakness lies in the assumption that the time required defining all the parts of the system could be accurately estimated. Where there are new functions and where participants have not done it before, then such estimates are likely to be inaccurate.

In an attempt to improve the control of projects and to integrate the total process of design, programming, documentation and project control, emphasis has recently been placed on the development of sophisticated tools. These require considerable discipline and are based on the assumption that it is the lack of disciplined control that is at the root of many poor pieces of software. Clearly software development tools are at their best in well-disciplined environments with clearly defined projects. Where projects are less well defined and a more heuristic approach is required, the emphasis needs to be placed on higher degrees of flexibility and involvement to facilitate problem-solving.

### Natural work teams

These are based on a grouping of those who are directly impacted by an organisational process and who seek improvement. The emphasis is on improving work methods, of which a computer system may be but one part. Their focus is on problem-solving through building strong personal relationships across organisational boundaries. They may graft in technical skills and deploy project control methodologies, but time is not crucial as they seek continuous improvement rather than defined bursts of project activity. This approach has high benefits in terms of personal commitment to continuous improvement, but may suffer from a tendency to only select activities that are relatively easy to achieve and timescales can drift.

### Hybrid approach

A third approach is a hybrid, where against a background of natural work improvement activities, defined groups are detailed to achieve specific project goals.

## Conclusions

In conclusion, the research shows that there is a range of human and technical factors that interplay together to form a greater or less likelihood of project failure. Three factors stand out: size of the project, technical competence and experience of those implementing the system, and degree of specificity of the requirements within the organisational context in which it will reside.

## SUMMARY OF THE KEY POINTS FROM THIS LAST CHAPTER

In this last chapter we have explored ways to bring plans to fruition, by clear objectives and effective change management. I have shown the characteristics of good objectives, and a process to establish them and keep plans on track. When things go wrong, there are tactics to deploy to bring the plan back on track. Recognise that our focus is not about apportioning blame, but rather finding solutions for the future. That way, you are more likely to keep people engaged rather than demotivated and protective.

Change is always difficult, and many a good plan has failed because it failed to take people with the instigator. In this chapter I have identified several considerations that maximise the chances of success in the management of change.

Finally, I concluded with two case studies on implementing technological projects. They act as a both a warning as to what can go wrong as well as some encouragement that with careful planning and some insight into human frailties, successful business plans that involve radical change can be brought about.

So what now? The plan is formed, written and agreed. Now comes the tricky part: bringing about change. From this chapter, you will find many tips for bringing it about successfully, which are all concerned with dealing with human emotions. In our desire for rationality in this unpredictable world, it is easy to forget.

## FINAL THOUGHTS

Remember John Lennon's famous dictum – 'Life is what happens while we are busy making other plans' – so we must ensure that we are not so absorbed in our plans that we fail to live in the real world. Sir Edmund Hillary is reputed to have shook his fist at a mountain after an unsuccessful attempt on the summit, saying, 'You are as high as you will ever be, but I am still growing.'

The capacity of human beings to continue to grow and develop new skills and competences gives us confidence that, if managed in the right way, we can get extraordinary performance out of ordinary people. The key to success of any business plan is in releasing that extraordinary and discretionary effort. We are today the product of everything that has gone before, the choices we have made and the ones we have foregone. I hope that by the end of this book, you might in some way see your world differently.

# Appendix
# Tools and techniques of business planning

## INTRODUCTION

Archimedes, in explaining the concept of the lever, is alleged to have remarked, 'Give me a firm place to stand and I will move the earth'. In this Appendix, we examine a number of levers that help us to develop more informative business analyses and thus better plans. The following sections explain a number of tools, in alphabetical order, that can be of benefit when developing a business plan. As I explained in Chapter 3, business planning relies on identifying and gathering suitable information to make a case for change and to show how it can be accomplished. The tools listed in Table A1 are designed to help that process, though not every tool will be needed in every situation.

*Table A1 / **Tools for business analysis***

| Tool | Page no | Page no in the text where cited |
|---|---|---|
| Balanced scorecard | 196 | 88, 110 |
| Benchmarking | 196 | 5, 38 |
| Bottlenecking | 203 | 170 |
| Contingency diagram | 203 | 26 |
| Core competences | 204 | 82 |
| Cost analysis tools | 208 | – |
| Cost–benefit analysis | 210 | 244 |
| Critical incident | 212 | 5, 78 |
| Critical path analysis | 213 | – |

Table A1 / **Tools for business analysis** – **continued**

| Tool | Page no | Page no in the text where cited |
|---|---|---|
| Critical success factors | 214 | 21, 36, 128 |
| Customer–supplier relationships | 214 | 171 |
| Decision tree | 217 | 155, 240 |
| Fishbone analysis | 218 | 170, 242 |
| Gantt/milestone chart | 219 | 130, 158, 170, 251 |
| Human resource planning template | 221 | 128 |
| Interest mapping | 225 | 25, 30, 36, 133, 170, 246 |
| Lifetime cost analysis | 225 | 80 |
| Methods of forecasting | 229 | 244 |
|   Correlation and regression | 229 | – |
|   Time series and trends analysis | 231 | – |
|   Scenario planning and forecasting tools | 232 | 245 |
|   Validity and reliability of forecasts and estimates | 233 | – |
|   Dealing with uncertainty | 235 | 244 |
| Measuring change | 237 | – |
| Modelling | 239 | – |
| 'Niciling' | 241 | 52 |
| Problem-solving process | 242 | 202, 245 |
| Risk analysis | 244 | 130 |
| Root cause analysis | 245 | 170, 242 |
| Sensitivity analysis | 246 | 130 |
| Stakeholder analysis | 246 | 36, 82, 127, 170 |
|   Force field analysis | 247 | – |
| SWOT analysis | 248 | 7, 26, 34, 36, 37, 81, 82, 84, 126, 244 |
| Timelines | 251 | – |
| Value chain analysis | 251 | 37, 65, 208 |

## BALANCED SCORECARD

### What is it?

The balanced scorecard is more than just a technique; it is a philosophical shift towards recognising that financial results are only the product of a chain – a value chain of activities that eventually have financial consequences attached to them. In the same way that no driver drives by solely looking through the rear-view mirror, no organisation can move forward by only looking at historical data. If we can therefore measure the ingredients in the value chain, identify the connections and consequences, we are more likely to be able to influence the outcome before it becomes a problem.

### How does it work?

Kaplan and Norton (1996) argued that organisations have to satisfy multiple stake-holders if they are going to endure. In particular, organisations have to satisfy in a balanced way customers, shareholders, employees, suppliers, distributors and the community at large with its myriad of sectional interests. They set out a framework which identified financial, customer, internal, and learning and growth as the major components. The latter category has become increasingly linked with the measure-ment of human performance, and the linking of changes in the condition with an estimation of the impact on the bottom line in the future. Indeed some scorecards talk about the 'future view'. Figure A1 shows an example of how one business inter-preted the concept. Some of the key areas it seeks to measure are highlighted in each of the boxes.

A distinction can be made between those organisations that are gathering data on performance in all the boxes and use the scorecard as a convenient way of presenting it (some call it a performance 'dashboard' and apply red/amber/green distinctions to the data to signal where attention should be focused), and a few organisations that are moving to the next step, which is identifying the causal chains that affect each indicator. This next step differentiates those who really use the scorecard to identify the lead indicators and so manage more proactively. A danger that some have experienced is the desire to measure everything, leaving managers swamped by data and spending time on gathering data rather than managing better.

## BENCHMARKING

### What is it?

Among the many drivers of change for an organisation is the knowledge that there may be a better way of doing things, especially if it comes from a competitor. In these cases

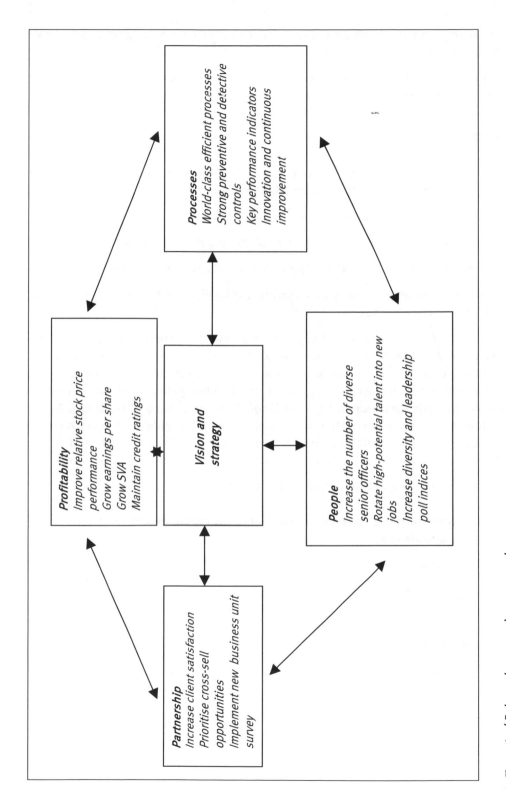

*Figure A1 / Balanced scorecard – an example*

there is an imperative to learn the lessons and to ensure that the competitive advantage of others is not gained for too long.

Benchmarking, an early proponent of which was Xerox Corporation, is a process for comparing processes and practices between organisations.

## How does it work?

There are benchmarking clubs to which some belong, such as Saratoga,[27] but the majority of benchmarking is done informally or bilaterally.

Benchmarking has a number of advantages:

- It challenges the conventional wisdom of the way things are done.

- It helps to separate out what *is* from what *should be* and what *could be*.

- It helps to establish a clear gap analysis between where the organisation is and where the best in class are.

Understanding any situation will always be subject to the interpretation of the viewer. As was highlighted in Chapter 3, we see what we want to see. Our background will highlight aspects that are more significant to us and not to others. Our frame of reference will determine our perception. A philosopher giving a talk once asked a woman to join him, whereupon he kissed her. 'What is going on?' he asked. To the psychologist, the kiss indicated a relationship, to the anthropologist it indicated rituals and customs, to the physicist it indicated the meeting of two bodies, and to the biochemist, the transference of microorganisms!

Benchmarking has been defined (Spendolini 1992) as

> *a continuous, ongoing, long-term, systematic, structured, formal, analytical, organised process for:*
>
> - *evaluating*
>
> - *understanding*
>
> - *assessing*
>
> - *measuring*
>
> - *comparing*
>
> *the:*
>
> - *business practices*
>
> - *products*

- *services*

- *work processes*

- *operations*

- *functions*

*of organisations, companies, institutions that are recognised and acknowledged as:*

- *world class*

- *best in class*

- *representing best practice*

*for the purpose of:*

- *organisational comparison and improvement*

- *meeting/surpassing industry best practice*

- *developing and driving product and process change*

- *establishing priorities, targets and goals.*

The process for benchmarking typically involves several steps.

## Determining what to benchmark

This may appear obvious, but the issue to determine is at what level to pitch the investigation and what precise aspects are to be covered. If you benchmark, say, the HR department with another organisation, there may be many differences in areas for which you are responsible, reflecting the unique features of your business. It may be difficult therefore to get a sufficiently useful comparison. If on the other hand, you benchmark the car parking system, you are less likely to discover anything that will significantly impact your operation.

A typical area in HR might be the recruitment process. When looking at quality, be mindful that it is often the subtle differences that you are looking for. Two car companies once agreed to share information, as one company's quality was better than the other. In comparing the assembly lines of each an observer initially saw no difference: same organisation, same work roles, and same speed of assembly line. But when he looked closer, he saw that in one company, after a worker had put his component on the car he had just enough time to stand back and pull on his cigarette before the next car came. On the other line, the worker in a similar role stood back but then checked and adjusted the component to see if it fitted properly before the next car came.

## Form a team if necessary

Members of such a team might share the load of data collection, perhaps look at different benchmarks and provide a source of challenge to each other to ensure standards of data accuracy and consistency. Make sure that in the team there is a balance of expertise and experience about the area as well as those with open minds.

## Identify benchmark partners

The search needs to be focused on finding those whose practices are better than yours. While the ideal is to find the world-class standard or at least best in your industry, in practice it is more difficult to do. Competitors are unlikely to share data, unless through some club. Indeed it can be difficult to decide who is better than you on the specific process you are interested in.

Sceptics say that benchmarking is impossible with your competitors, but it begs the question who are your competitors. One airline wanted to benchmark its reservation operation, where employees took telephone reservations using a computerised reservation system. Of course, other airlines might be reluctant to share details of their organisation, productivity measures or processes. The airline also wanted to progress from best industry practice to world-class processes. So it looked at many organisations that had similar processes. Eventually it found that the box office of a large stadium was a useful benchmark as it did exactly similar work. The only difference was that reservations were being made for a rock concert or football match, rather than for an aircraft seat. Through the comparison with a non-competing business, the airline learnt about more flexible staffing models and predictive algorithms to determine the likely booking patterns of various events.[28]

Competitors can be seen as a widening circle of differing types. In Figure A2, an example of a television station, the first thought of management was to see their competitors as other domestic television stations. However, television competes for our time and attention, not just with other programmes but also with all the other activities that might take our attention. The figure shows widening circles of competition.

## Collect and analyse benchmarking information

When starting a benchmarking study, there is a natural desire to get out there and look at other companies, but it is wise to study your own practice first. Without a clear understanding of what you do, why you do it and in the way that you do, there is a danger that you might not focus on the differences with others, and especially those that show some potential benefit to you. One company set up a benchmarking team

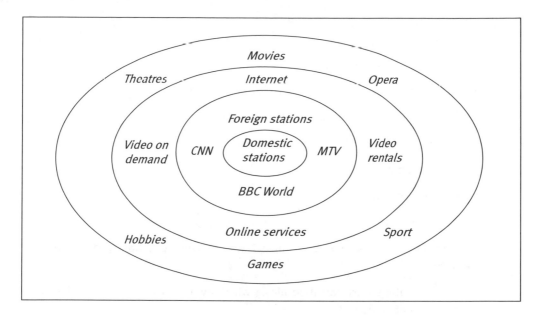

*Figure A2 / Understanding competition – an example of a television station*

who set about this exercise, only to find many opportunities for improvement before they had even gone out of the gate! Much of the value of benchmarking comes from turning a critical eye upon yourself, informed by a comparison of your own and others' practice.

There is an assumption that data can only be collected on site, but do not ignore the cheap and quick routes of telephone calls, publications and the media. Staff may have worked for competitors or in businesses, such as advertising agencies, that know your competitors. Care must be taken not to infringe confidentiality clauses or restraints that employees might be under, but much is in the public domain that goes untapped.

## Turn the data into action

The list in the box identifies the contents of a typical benchmark report. Writers including Spendolini identify this following structure.

### Typical benchmark report structure

Title

Executive summary

Statement of need/purpose

Project customers – who the report was for

Customer requirements – what did they want from the project

Project team members – and reasons for being there

Team process (see problem-solving process on p242 as an example)

Project timetable

Subjects benchmarked

Information sources

Methodology (such as surveys, interviews, observation, library data, desk research)

Results – numbers and narrative along with any assumptions made, missing data or suspect areas

Commentary on the overall picture presented

Analysis of the comparison with yourself

Conclusions

Next steps

For further information on benchmarking, see Phelps (2002) and the Manpower Society *HR Benchmarking Manual*.

## What to benchmark: Xerox's 10 questions

- What is the most critical factor to my function's/organisation's success (eg customer satisfaction, expense to revenue ratio, and return on asset performance)?

- What factors are causing the most trouble (eg not performing to expectations)?

- What products or services are provided to customers?

- What factors account for customer satisfaction?

- What operational problems have been identified in the organisation?

- Where are the competitive pressures being felt in the organisation?

- What are the major costs (or cost 'drivers') in the organisation?

- Which functions represent the highest percentage of cost?

- Which functions have the greatest room for improvement?

- Which functions have the greatest effect (or potential) for differentiating the organisation from competitors in the marketplace?

# BOTTLENECKING

## What is it?

The strength of a chain is defined by the strength of the weakest link. So it is with an organisation, which is a system of interconnected processes. Bottlenecking focuses on the end-to-end processes and seeks to identify where is the weakest point.

## How does it work?

Ways of bottlenecking include:

- Physically following, say, an invoice through the whole organisation and identifying what happens to it: where does it go, where does it get held up, what difficulties do people have as they handle it? On the way, people are asked for their ideas and suggestions of how the process could be improved.

- Process mapping, using paper or computer charting.

- Measuring the time each step takes and comparing it with the time of the total event. An activity might take only a few minutes to complete, but stay in that section for a week, because of a backlog or dependency on another process. The imbalance in resources or the structure of the system causes the bottleneck. The principles of *just in time* seek to balance all the processes to ensure minimum waiting time.

# CONTINGENCY DIAGRAM

## What is it?

A contingency diagram is a problem-solving tool that first defines what is critical to success and then uses the brainstorming technique to generate obstacles to success, followed by a prevention list to ensure the obstacles don't happen.

## How does it work?

The facilitator first identifies what is critical to success and then draws out all the obstacles, before developing a list of prevention activities. (See Figure A3.) The end result should be a checklist containing a thorough list of all that needs to be accomplished to avoid the obstacles. It often includes items such as:

- communication to key managers who need to 'buy-in' early

- identifying 'Plan B'

- implementation activities such as workshops and other events.

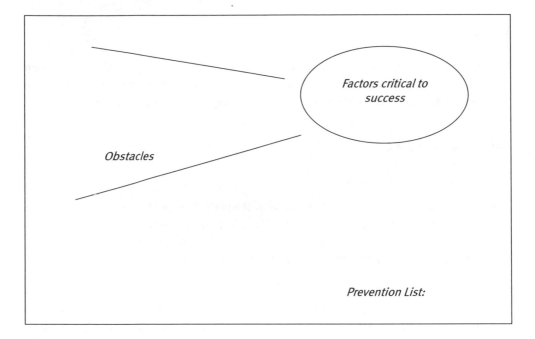

*Figure A3 / **Contingency diagram***

# CORE COMPETENCES

## What is it?

A core competency determines what an organisation does well.

## How does it work?

To identify what it might be, and indeed what it needs to be for the organisation to prosper in the future, a core competency should:

- provide significant value to customers and make a major contribution to the perceived customer benefits of the end product

- be difficult for competitors to imitate or procure in the market and thus create competitive barriers to entry

- enable a company to access a wide variety of seemingly unrelated markets by combining skills and technologies across traditional business units.

These are sometimes expressed as the 'driving forces' of the organisation, and typically there are nine classifications as follows.

## 1. Products offered

Where the organisation has unique or highly regarded products, and ones that are difficult to copy by competitors, its future strategy will be focused on line extensions and other product derivatives. It might also use geographic expansion of existing products as a means of growth.

Organisation capabilities will be constructed around product development, promotion and distribution. This is usually short-lived. An example is the Palm pilot.

## 2. Market needs

The organisation is driven by the needs of a particular market. Its expertise lies in understanding that market segment, anticipating changes and reacting swiftly with products and services that fulfil those needs.

Organisation capabilities will be organised around market research and highly flexible sourcing/resourcing to meet new needs as they arise. An example is the Virgin Group.

## 3. Technology

With access to and experience of a particular technology, these organisations look for applications of the technology in new ways as the core of their strategy. They may also license it to others to leverage its intellectual property quickly. Organisation capabilities will be focused on R&D. A current example is Intel, a historical example Sinclair.

## 4. Production capability

These organisations, though often not well known in the high street, use their skills of organisation and process control, together with assets of people and equipment, to produce a highly cost-competitive service. Examples are BT call centres and many factories in the Far East.

### 5. Method of sale or 'channel strategy'

These organisations attain distinctiveness in the market place by the way they distribute their products. These are usually more cost-effective than other methods. Future strategy focuses on how other products and services can be sold through the same distribution channel. The rise of the Internet has created considerable dislocation in traditional distribution channels as new options arise. Examples are amazon.com, Dell, and W H Smith book clubs.

### 6. Method of distribution

To be distinguished from the method of sale as a driving force, organisations that are driven by the method of physical distribution establish a service of getting products to end customers that is quicker, more convenient or cheaper than other methods.

Organisations that are driven by this have to be nimble as the economies are constantly changing between the use of wholesalers and distributors versus direct to retailers versus direct to customers. An example is Tesco Home Shopping.

### 7. Natural resources

These organisations are usually found in mineral extraction industries. Some would argue that developing countries see their cheap educated labour as a natural resource, and one that is the driving force for their quest for products and markets where that gives them advantage. An example is De Beers, Singapore.

### 8. Size and growth

It is argued that one consequence of globalisation is that one or two major players dominate more and more markets. The conclusion to be drawn is that the overriding strategy must be to achieve market dominance through size, achieved by rapid growth.

These organisations develop a competence in the aggressive acquisition of markets and customers. Such a driver is only for a period and can be inherently unstable because it is often based on highly geared funding and is susceptible to changes in market conditions. Examples are Vodafone, and historically, Lucent.

### 9. Rate of return

These organisations have no allegiance to any product, process or market. Their competence lies in deal making and spotting opportunities for releasing hidden potential. Examples are fund managers, and a historical example is Hanson.

Richard Stuteley (2002) summarises these drivers in 14 areas where you might find competences in the organisation:

- R & D

- product development

- management of supplies and suppliers

- production

- capacity management

- inventory control

- branding

- management of channels to market

- market research

- account management

- information management

- negotiating

- acquisitions

- international operations.

And for companies that outsource many operations, project management has become a necessary core competence.

In reviewing these nine competences and 14 areas, there are several questions to consider:

- What is your organisation's core competence? If an activity is not built around your core competence and it is not critical to your success, is it a candidate for outsourcing?

- Does your business plan nurture and enhance it? Leonard-Barton (1992) suggests that there are four approaches to improvement, by developing qualifications, norms and values, organisational competence and managerial competence. Each of these might require development in your plan.

- If your plan is about developing new competences, what gives you the confidence that you can do it sufficiently well to gain significant advantage over competitors who might already possess this competence?

# COST ANALYSIS TOOLS

## What are they?

There are several tools to analyse costs in more detail:

### Value chain analysis

This is a systematic examination of all the activities in an enterprise and how each impacts on the others to add value. Such an analysis can help in cutting out activities that might have been done for historical reasons, but no longer add value.

### Relative cost position

The process involves identifying the costs of each function relative to major competitors.

### Activity-based costing

The cost of each activity is identified across the organisation (as opposed to within a department or function) in order to determine the total cost. This analysis is useful for items such as training, travel and stationery where small amounts are found in many cost centres but when aggregated, can add up to substantial amounts. If the costs are apportioned in some way, it can enable a more accurate 'true' cost of products and customers to be found.

### Cost behaviour analysis

Modelling different elements allows determination of how functional costs behave in response to management policies. This is an important input into the evaluation of cost-effectiveness of a change in strategy.

### Activity value analysis

This analysis seeks to isolate costs of activities that contribute to customer value and those that do not.

## How does it work?

Selecting the last tool above, the process for doing the calculation is as follows:

- List the main activities of the area in question and identify the cost of each. A simple way to calculate costs is to identify the time spent on each activity and apportion total cost accordingly.

- Identify the customers, both internal and external for each activity.

- Rate each activity for value *from the perspective of the customer.*

- Use Figure A4 and the checklist in the box to determine action.

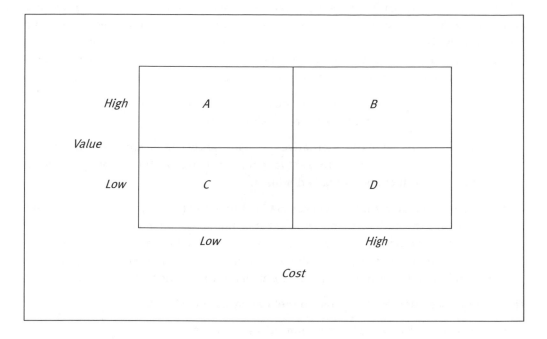

Figure A4 / **Value cost analysis**

## Value cost analysis

- A – Reinforce (this is your competitive advantage)

- B – OK (but vulnerable to lower cost alternatives)

- C – Examine – are they necessary (maybe contribute to higher value work)?

- D – Eliminate (reallocate resources?)

# COST–BENEFIT ANALYSIS

## What is it?

When we wish to evaluate the benefits of a course of action, we try to weigh up the pros and cons. So too with a business case, and if we are to win the argument we need to array as much hard evidence as we can. Cost–benefit analysis differs from conventional financial appraisal in that the former attempts to include social costs and benefits that are normally excluded from conventional investment appraisal. Cost–benefit analysis identifies:

- The problem to be addressed and the possible alternative options to close the gap between the current reality and the desired position.

- The characteristics of the alternatives – their costs of implementation, one-off and ongoing, and the impact these are going to make on the problem, such as improved productivity and raised morale.

- Units of measurement to allow comparison between the two, ideally currency, but not always the case with intangibles. For example two alternative training courses might be compared; one is £100 more than the other for the same syllabus. However one venue requires a longer journey and so the cost–benefit might be couched as: 'Is one hour of my time travelling worth £100?'

The benefits we might see in a cost–benefit analysis could be:

- Lower costs (for example, staff numbers are reduced).

- Higher output (for example, increased productivity).

- Change in behaviour, which has both quantifiable and non-quantifiable elements. For example, Nathan (2005) quotes a study where over a period of two years, participants in a career development workshop were half as likely to leave the organisation as those who did not participate. The change in the rate of turnover can be measured and evaluated in financial terms, but the underlying reason for this change might be the greater commitment of people to the organisation as a result of this workshop, which might have benefits in terms of discretionary effort and willingness to support the organisation through change. Nathan (2005) quotes the Audit Commission, which justified training a pool of line managers in career counselling techniques by reference to savings in outplacement fees as well as reinforcing a cultural shift towards staff development.

## How does it work?

Cost–benefit analysis starts from identifying all the costs of a particular course of action. See the box for a checklist of costs of people (first suggested by the Manpower Society) and comparison with the benefits.

## Costs of human resources

- Remuneration
  - salary
  - bonus
  - fringes
- recruitment
- training
- relocation
- leaving
- support services
  - social
  - canteen
  - medical
- personnel administration

Source: Manpower Society.

In Figure A5, we see that there are four types of information that should be considered, shown in the boxes. In addition to the advantages, the negative consequences to offset benefits and subsidies to offset costs should be included.

|  | INPUTS to the project | OUTPUTS from the project |
|---|---|---|
| ADVANTAGES (benefits) | Subsidies to project | Useful outputs |
| DISADVANTAGES (costs) | Cost of project | Bad consequences |
| TOTALS | Net inputs (ie sum of costs less subsidies) | Net outcomes (ie positive benefits less negative benefits) |

*Figure A5 / **Cost–benefit analysis***
Source: CIPD course on Human Resource Planning. Chart prepared by Ron Howard.

# CRITICAL INCIDENT

## What is it?

The analogy is sometimes made, maybe a little unkindly, between an airline pilot and a train driver. The similarities are obvious, and it can lead to the conclusion that they should be paid the same. The differences lie not in what both do for the majority of the time, but rather what they do when novel situations occur or things go wrong. Critical incident is designed to try to uncover those situations.

## How does it work?

As a technique it is often used in job analysis (see Chapter 3) and has its origins in the US Aviation psychology programme in the Second World War (Pearn and Kandola 1993). The process is as follows:

- The jobholder and others who know the job well are interviewed about specific incidents when things go wrong or right – in the past or hypothetically in the future.

- They may be observed or asked to keep a log or diary over the period of time to provide further information and examples of specific behaviours.

- Records are examined to look at historical incidents. For example, records of aircraft near misses might be analysed to identify the critical success factors in the performance of pilots and air traffic controllers.

The aim is to understand what the jobholder did that made his/her response effective or ineffective. Incidents might be analysed to find broad themes such as 'faulty diagnosis of a situation', or 'distractions', or 'anticipation of events'. These in turn might require further analysis and diagnosis to identify appropriate action to be taken to ensure the issue is no longer relevant. Typically, actions might include changes to the methods of selection or training, but they might also include changes to working methods, management style and other cultural determinants.

The conclusions of the exercise need to identify the action required, including time, cost and ease of implementation to ensure good outcomes are maximised and bad ones minimised until the risks are acceptable.

# CRITICAL PATH ANALYSIS

## What is it?

It is a technique for identifying the shortest time to achieve a project with multiple activities.

## How does it work?

To start with, all the activities in a project plan need to be identified and a decision made whether they operate in sequence or can be done in parallel.

Draw a network diagram as in Figure A6.

Then determine whether the plan is to be worked from today going forward to identify how long it will take, or whether you start from an end point and work back to identify where time and activities have to be squeezed to fit the time available.

To find the critical path, add the total elapsed time for each of the parallel paths

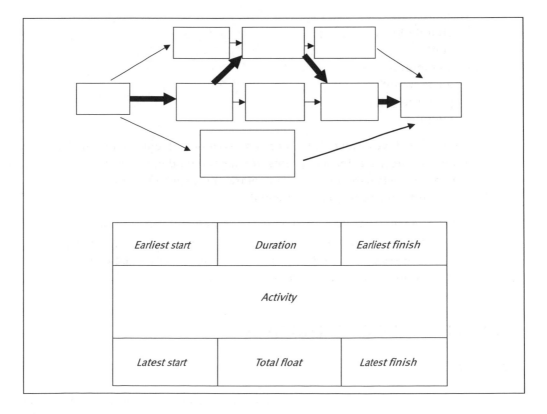

| Earliest start | Duration | Earliest finish |
| --- | --- | --- |
| | Activity | |
| Latest start | Total float | Latest finish |

*Figure A6 / **Critical path analysis network diagram and explanation of an individual node***

through the network and identify the longest. This is the shortest time for completion. There are a number of software packages on the market that automate these calculations.

# CRITICAL SUCCESS FACTORS

## What are they?

Critical success factors, as the words imply, indicate those few major things that an organisation has got to get right to ensure success.

## How does it work?

The process to establish the critical success factors is typically as follows:

- Identify the outcomes by which you will be judged by your different stakeholders, who might include:

    - customers
    - shareholders
    - staff
    - community
    - government
    - pressure groups
    - suppliers.

- Identify what drives those outcomes. For example, accuracy and timeliness for customer service, maximised profits for higher dividends, good work climate including extrinsic benefits (such as salary and benefits) and intrinsic rewards (fairness and opportunity) for staff morale.

- Establish measures for these factors that are sufficient. For example, in a market place with four major competitors, a rating on customer service by an independent agency that ranks you in the top two might be the minimum required in order to be taken seriously as a new entrant to the market.

# CUSTOMER–SUPPLIER RELATIONSHIPS

## What is it?

Tables A2 to A5 are designed to be used as a tool to stimulate discussion between supplier of a service and the customer. These might be internal or external to the organisation.

Table A2 / *Thinking about the general relationship between the supplier and customer*

| As the 'customer' | Strongly agree | Strongly disagree | As the 'supplier' |
|---|---|---|---|
| 1.1 We are well aware of what services are available. | 1 2 3 4 <br> Comments: | 5 6 7 8 | We keep our customers well informed of the services we offer. |
| 1.2 We know who to contact for the services we use. | 1 2 3 4 <br> Comments: | 5 6 7 8 | We ensure that the customers' staff know who to talk to about their problems and service needs. |
| 1.3 We feel they work hard to share with us what they learn with other customers. | 1 2 3 4 <br> Comments: | 5 6 7 8 | We work hard to share what we learn between customers. |
| 1.4 We feel that they only offer services they can deliver. | 1 2 3 4 <br> Comments: | 5 6 7 8 | We only offer services we can deliver. |

Table A3 / *Thinking about the choice of supplier and how we define and specify tasks*

| As the 'customer' | Strongly agree | Strongly disagree | As the 'supplier' |
|---|---|---|---|
| 2.1 We prefer to use the supplier department rather than give out work to outside suppliers. | 1 2 3 4 <br> Comments: | 5 6 7 8 | We think the customer prefers to use us rather than give out work to outside suppliers |
| 2.2 We feel it is cost-effective to use. | 1 2 3 4 <br> Comments: | 5 6 7 8 | We feel we are cost-effective to use. |
| 2.3 We put enough time and effort into defining our needs. | 1 2 3 4 <br> Comments: | 5 6 7 8 | We feel that the customer puts enough effort into defining its real needs. |
| 2.4 We involve the supplier enough in the specification phase. | 1 2 3 4 <br> Comments: | 5 6 7 8 | We are involved enough in specifying work to be done. |
| 2.5 We are confident the supplier will meet the agreed deadlines. | 1 2 3 4 <br> Comments: | 5 6 7 8 | We achieve agreed deadlines. |
| 2.6 We are confident the supplier will meet the agreed budget. | 1 2 3 4 <br> Comments: | 5 6 7 8 | We achieve agreed budgets. |

Table A4 / *Thinking about projects or tasks while they are running*

| As the 'customer' | Strongly agree | Strongly disagree | As the 'supplier' |
|---|---|---|---|
| 3.1 We have effective systems for monitoring progress. | 1 2 3 4 | 5 6 7 8 | We have effective systems for monitoring progress. |
| | Comments: | | |
| 3.2 We are kept clearly informed of the work's progress. | 1 2 3 4 | 5 6 7 8 | We keep the customer clearly informed of the work's progress. |
| | Comments: | | |
| 3.3 The supplier provides a clear point of contact for us to talk to if needed. | 1 2 3 4 | 5 6 7 8 | We provide a clear point of contact for the customer to talk to if needed. |
| | Comments: | | |
| 3.4 We provide a clear point of contact for the supplier to talk to if needed. | 1 2 3 4 | 5 6 7 8 | The customer provides a clear point of contact for us to talk to if needed. |
| | Comments: | | |
| 3.5 We raise problems quickly with the supplier when they occur. | 1 2 3 4 | 5 6 7 8 | The customer tells us about problems quickly when they occur. |
| | Comments: | | |
| 3.6 The supplier tells us about problems quickly when they occur | 1 2 3 4 | 5 6 7 8 | We raise problems quickly with the customer when they occur. |
| | Comments: | | |

Table A5 / *Thinking about what happens at the end of a task or project*

| As the 'customer' | Strongly agree | Strongly disagree | As the 'supplier' |
|---|---|---|---|
| 4.1 We have an opportunity to review the work formally with the supplier department. | 1 2 3 4 | 5 6 7 8 | We have an opportunity to review the work formally with the customer. |
| | Comments: | | |
| 4.2 We provide comprehensive feedback to the supplier on problems and issues that have arisen. | 1 2 3 4 | 5 6 7 8 | 4.2 We receive comprehensive feedback from the customer on problems and issues that have arisen. |
| | Comments: | | |
| 4.3 The supplier is pretty good at applying lessons learned to the way they work next time. | 1 2 3 4 | 5 6 7 8 | We are pretty good at applying lessons learned to the way we work next time. |
| | Comments: | | |
| 4.4 We have got things 'just about right' in our relationship with the supplier. | 1 2 3 4 | 5 6 7 8 | We have got things 'just about right' in our relationship with the customer. |
| | Comments: | | |

## How does it work?

One way of using it is to ask each side to complete it first and then to bring them together to compare the answers and identify what actions need to be taken to meet expectations.

# DECISION TREE

## What is it?

A decision tree identifies the probability of an event occurring as a result of looking at the probability of each constituent choice being made.

## How does it work?

An analysis of the event is undertaken and the probabilities derived, which are usually based on the actual proportions of people making these choices in the past.

Figure A7 shows the result of a study of women returning to work. You will see that 14 per cent returned to the same job, so we could say that on the basis of this data, there would be a 14 in a 100 chance that women returnees will end up in the same job *all other things being equal*.

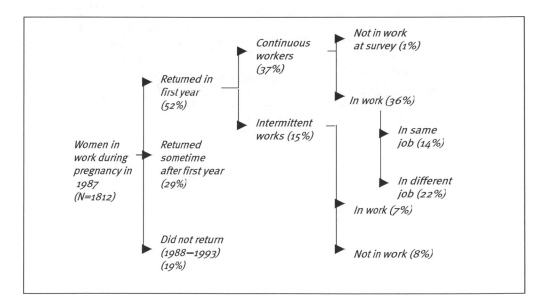

*Figure A7 / **Decision tree: mothers returning to work (1988–1993)***
Source: Policy Study Institute, 1996.

# FISHBONE ANALYSIS

## What is it?

A fishbone diagram is an example of a *cognitive map* (as are mind maps), which is a way of graphically displaying the connections between a collection of ideas, concepts and words. Fishbone analysis (also known as cause-and-effect analysis, or Ishikawa analysis, after Kaoru Ishikawa who invented it) is a structured way of getting at the real causes of a problem or situation. It provides a method of breaking a problem down into more manageable elements. Ishikawa described the process as 'looking for patterns between seemingly unconnected events, testing possible chains of causation to explain an event and finding a metaphor or a theory to help in looking forward'.

## How does it work?

Figure A8 is an example of a map designed to identify the root causes of late invoices.

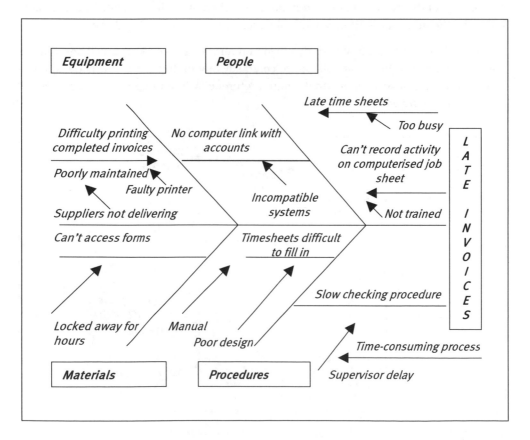

*Figure A8 /* **Fishbone analysis**

To produce a fishbone diagram, proceed as follows:

- Agree the problem statement with a team of informed and interested participants and put it in the box (see example of 'Late invoices').

- Choose four to six categories likely to have a bearing on the problem. The ones most frequently used are:

  - people
  - procedures
  - materials
  - equipment.

  In certain instances, you may want to use others, eg policies, processes and machinery.

- Don't worry too much about choosing the 'right' categories, they are only to help organise the suggestions from the team.

- Next, ask the team to spend five minutes individually writing down all the causes of the problem they can think of, bearing in mind the categories and referring to the process map if they have created one. Ask them to offer their ideas one at a time. Each suggestion is put on the chart as a line with an arrow pointing to the next cause up, and then the question 'why' is asked until no further causes can be found. (These usually end up being things outside the team's scope such as 'no money' or 'not enough staff'.)

- When one cause has been exhausted, continue with the next until all the team's ideas have been expended.

- Another way of using the fishbone chart is to do a process map and then use the steps in the process as the major categories. Having done this, chase up the problems associated with each step.

- Finally examine each root cause and brainstorm possible solutions.

## GANTT/MILESTONE CHART

### What is it?

A Gantt chart (named after Henry Gantt) is a two-dimensional graphical display that identifies all the activities in a project. It shows those activities that can be conducted in parallel and those that require to be completed in a sequence. It also shows the time required for each activity.

## How does it work?

To create one, list all the steps required to finish the project and estimate the time required for each step. Then list the steps down the left side of the chart with dates shown along the bottom. Draw a line across the chart for each step, starting at the planned beginning date and ending on the completion date of that step. Once completed, you should be able to see the flow of the action steps and their sequence (including those that can be undertaken at the same time).

The usefulness of a Gantt or milestone chart will be improved by also charting actual progress. This is usually done by drawing a line in a different colour under the original line to show actual beginning and completion dates of each step. When updated with the actual times taken for each activity, the chart clearly shows any variances to the plan and helps establish a more realistic forecast of time required for later activities. A number of software packages such as Microsoft Project automate the calculations and produce displays of progress against plan.

Figure A9 shows a typical chart.

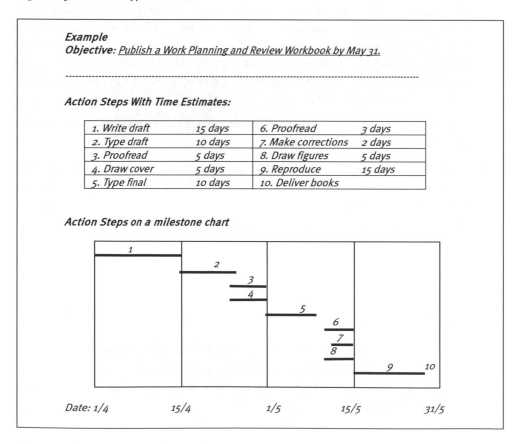

*Example*
*Objective: Publish a Work Planning and Review Workbook by May 31.*

------------------------------------------------------------------------------------------

*Action Steps With Time Estimates:*

| 1. Write draft | 15 days | 6. Proofread | 3 days |
| 2. Type draft | 10 days | 7. Make corrections | 2 days |
| 3. Proofread | 5 days | 8. Draw figures | 5 days |
| 4. Draw cover | 5 days | 9. Reproduce | 15 days |
| 5. Type final | 10 days | 10. Deliver books | |

*Action Steps on a milestone chart*

Date: 1/4    15/4    1/5    15/5    31/5

*Figure A9 / Sample Gantt chart*

Figure A10 is a different example that shows several features that would indicate problems to the experienced eye:

- It already forecasts an overrun on the first activity, but still expects to come in under the planned time.

- All the activities in future are sequential, allowing no opportunity for slippage.

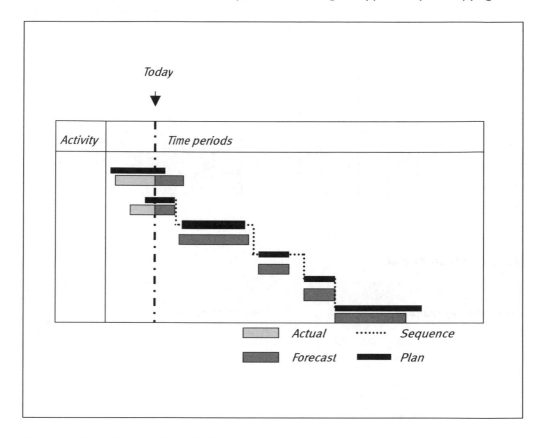

Figure A10 / **Another sample Gantt chart**

# HUMAN RESOURCE PLANNING TEMPLATE

Outline the key critical success factors for HR (maximum six) which have been identified as essential to the achievement of the business strategy.

Next complete the human resource demand plan shown as Table A6, the sourcing plan (Table A7), skill development plan (Table A8), wastage assumptions (Table A9), future resource forecast (Table A10), critical assumptions (Table A11) and competency analysis (Table A12).

Table A6 / **Human resource demand plan**

| Staff category | Key driver | Change in driver | Change in staffing % | Current staffing | Projected staffing | | | | | |
|---|---|---|---|---|---|---|---|---|---|---|
| | | | | | Year 1 | | Year 2 | | Year 3 | |
| | | | | | Max | Min | Max | Min | Max | Min |
| | | | | | | | | | | |
| | | | | | | | | | | |
| | | | | | | | | | | |
| | | | | | | | | | | |
| | | | | | | | | | | |
| | | | | | | | | | | |
| | | | | | | | | | | |
| | | | | | | | | | | |
| | | | | | | | | | | |
| Total | | | | | | | | | | |
| Comments | | | | | | | | | | |

Table A7 / **Sourcing plan**

| Resource gap/surplus | Projected staffing |
|---|---|
| | |
| Total | |
| What longer-term strategies are required to fulfil these needs? | |

Table A8 / **Skill development plan**

| Skill profile gap/surplus | Strategies proposed to deal with gaps/ surplus |
|---|---|
| | |
| Total | |
| What longer-term strategies are required to fulfil these needs? | |

Table A9 / **Wastage assumptions**

| Factors affecting the rate of wastage gap/surplus | | | |
|---|---|---|---|
| Current wastage rate | | | |
| Function | % Turnover | Assumed % over next three years | Comment |
| | | | |
| | | | |
| | | | |
| | | | |
| Total | | | |

Table A10 / **Future resource forecast – all staff**

| Function | Current strength | Projected number required | | | Expected wastage | | | Resource gap/ surplus | | |
|---|---|---|---|---|---|---|---|---|---|---|
| | | Year 1 | Year 2 | Year 3 | Year 1 | Year 2 | Year 3 | Year 1 | Year 2 | Year 3 |
| | | | | | | | | | | |
| | | | | | | | | | | |
| | | | | | | | | | | |
| | | | | | | | | | | |
| | | | | | | | | | | |
| | | | | | | | | | | |
| Total | | | | | | | | | | |
| Comments and assumptions | | | | | | | | | | |

Table A11 / **Critical assumptions**

| Staff category | Demand forecast assumptions | Wastage assumptions | Recruitment assumptions | Competence development assumptions |
|---|---|---|---|---|
| | | | | |
| | | | | |
| | | | | |
| | | | | |
| | | | | |
| | | | | |
| | | | | |
| | | | | |

Table A12 / **Competency analysis**

| Staff category | Staff member | Competency assessment | | | | Competence development assumptions | | | | Gap analysis | | | |
|---|---|---|---|---|---|---|---|---|---|---|---|---|---|
| | | a | b | c | d | a | b | c | d | a | b | c | d |
| e.g. Assistant | A B Smith | 3 | 2 | 5 | 5 | 4 | 4 | 5 | 4 | 1 | 2 | 0 | +1 |
| | | | | | | | | | | | | | |
| | | | | | | | | | | | | | |
| | | | | | | | | | | | | | |
| | | | | | | | | | | | | | |
| | | | | | | | | | | | | | |
| | | | | | | | | | | | | | |

# INTEREST MAPPING

## What is it?

In determining where conflict and resistance to change might be, it is sometimes worth trying to identify who will be advantaged by the changes and who will be disadvantaged. This in essence is interest mapping.

## How does it work?

Table A13 sets out a checklist to help you assess whether people or teams will be helped or hindered and therefore might be positively disposed or the reverse.

Another way of categorising interest is by plotting individuals on an interests/influence matrix shown in Figure A11.

# LIFETIME COST ANALYSIS

## What is it?

Products, industries, and dare one say people, go through life cycles. Figure A12 shows the typical stages of a product or industry. During the lifetime of a product, costs are incurred of varying kinds which when accumulated result in the lifetime cost.

*Table A13 / **Change in personal outcomes arising from the introduction of change***

*Using the checklist:*

*To determine whether an individual will be positive or negative towards a change, assess for each item whether the individual will see any change that might occur, as either positive or negative. Annotate with – or – – or + or ++.*

*Review the list. On balance is it positive or negative?*

|  | | Pre | Post |
|---|---|---|---|
|  | | Implementation | |
| Number of direct subordinates | | | |
| Levels to the chief executive | | | |
| Levels below | | | |
| Number of colleagues | | | |
| Budget | (i) Staff | | |
|  | (ii) Other resources | | |
| Impact of errors | | | |
| Impact of decisions | | | |
| Perceived discretion over things that effect them | | | |
| Access to key information | | | |
| Perceived influence by customers, suppliers etc | | | |
| Perceived influence internally | | | |
| Patterns of interaction – contacts upwards | | | |
| Patterns of interaction – contacts downwards | | | |
| Change in personal benefits (ego impact) | | | |
| Change in material benefits (financial) | | | |
| Involvement in major decision-making | | | |
| **So, is the person amongst the winners or the losers?** | | | |

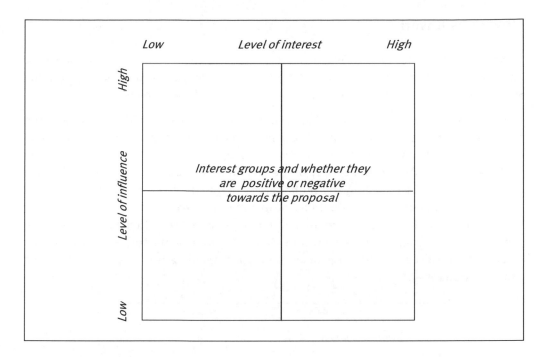

*Figure A11 / **Interests/influence matrix***

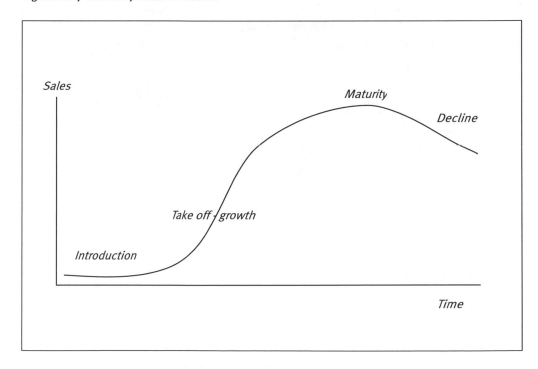

*Figure A12 / **Industry/product lifecycle***

## How does it work?

Consider a consumer product like a car. It is relatively cheap to buy but there are great costs in R&D and initial development, and increasingly it costs to dispose of it at the end of its life. The lifetime costs are the addition of all these elements.

Using the same concept, now consider a staff member. There are initial recruitment and induction costs, salary and overheads during employment, with maybe redundancy and pension costs at the end of service. The concept is helpful in considering differing staffing options. One must be wary of the assumptions about estimating the lifetime costs of employees based on the probabilities of length of service (though this is no different in estimating the probability of the life of a component in an oil refinery). Historically there has been shown to be a relationship between turnover and length of service (Silcock 1954). This is shown in Figure A13, and some studies show that the shape of this curve can be approximated by a mathematical expression comprising a mixed exponential.

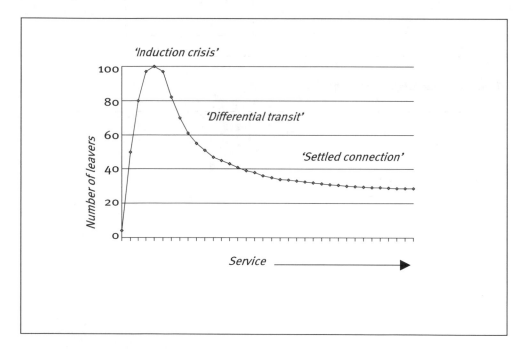

*Figure A13* / **Wastage curve**

Over long periods of time, the figures must be adjusted for inflation and purchasing power to make valid comparisons.

Lifetime costs are only one side of the cost–benefit equation: the other side is a figure representing the value added by the different categories of staff.

# METHODS OF FORECASTING

## What are they?

There are a variety of mostly statistical tools used to forecast future indices.

## How do they work?

'Forecasting', someone said, 'is always difficult, especially about the future'! Another writer was more disparaging: 'Five-year forecasts are very useful. They are useful for scrap paper, for making paper darts and for rolling into little balls to throw into the bin on dull days' (Finch 2001). Nevertheless, the audience for a plan will require forecasts, so below are some approaches. The important thing to bear in mind is to remind readers of the bases for the forecasts, the assumptions on which they rest, and to avoid misleading them by apparent spurious accuracy. If we have assumed a 10 per cent increase in sales and this comes to £53.9 million, it is wiser to leave the figure as 'around £54 million' or even '£50 to 55 million'. Place forecasts in the context of the present and recent history, so that readers can see for themselves whether the forecasted changes are reasonable from their perspective and knowledge.

> *We are forecasting a 10 per cent increase in sales, which is based on the assumption of similar market conditions as this year and is consistent with growth over the last four years, averaging 10.5 per cent.*

In tables, ensure that forecasted figures are in the same format as the historical set. Provide a commentary that explains the changes and particularly why historical trends will not be repeated in the future. Figure A14 gives an example.

## Correlation and regression

Figure A15 shows a scattergram of points plotting job performance against test score taken at an assessment centre. We can see that there seems to be a definite relationship – a correlation – between the two, though there are one or two points that do not fit the trend (high test score and low performance, and low test score and medium performance).

A statistic called the correlation coefficient expresses the strength of the relationship, and typically is presented as '$r = 0.5$'. The maximum score is 1. See a statistics textbook such as Owen and Jones (1994) for a fuller explanation. For our purposes it is sufficient to know that the correlation coefficient can easily be calculated in Excel or other spreadsheets. To show the relationship more precisely we could fit a line of best fit to the points and express this in an equation – the regression equation. A measure of how

|  | Last year | Current year | Forecasted next year |
|---|---|---|---|
|  | Q1 Q2 Q3 Q4 | Q1 Q2 Q3 Q4 | Q1 Q2 Q3 Q4 |
| *Labour turnover* | 3.4 4.5 5.6 7.5 | 7.5 6.9 5.5 6.1 | 6.0 5.5 5.0 4.5 |

*Labour turnover (historical, current and projected)*

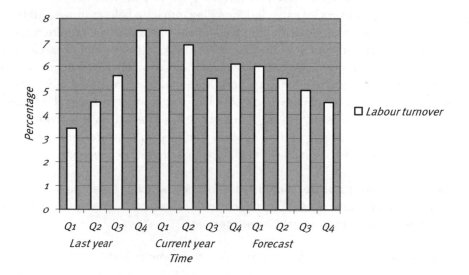

*(Voluntary leavers as a percentage of moving annual average of permanent employees)*

*Change in turnover comes from:*
- *Continuing roll out of supervisory training started in Q2 and showing good results where implemented. Roll out is assumed to be complete by end of Q1*
- *Labour Market assumed to be similar, with pressure on certain key skills easing due to economy*
- *Pay award this year assumed to be competitive as was the case this year, but was not in previous year.*

*Significant losses of staff last year as a result of new company located next door recruiting heavily, is not assumed to reoccur this year.*

Figure A14 / **Example of a forecast**

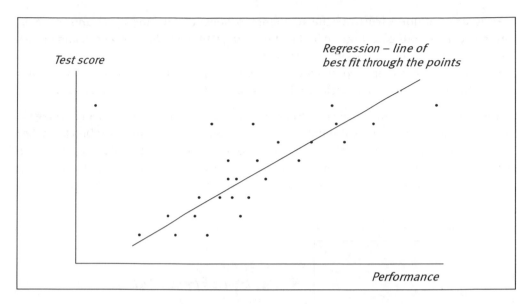

Figure A15 / **Scattergram of performance and test score**

Source: Assessment centre test and annual appraisal data.

well this line fits the points is known as the coefficient of variance, and in the above example is expressed as the square of the correlation coefficient expressed as a percentage (for example $5 \times 5 = 25$ per cent). We say therefore that a correlation coefficient r = 0.5 indicates that 25 per cent of the points in the scattergram lie directly on the line whose mathematical expression is the regression equation.

We must be clear that a correlation or regression equation is an expression merely of the statistical relationship and not necessarily of a causal relationship between the variables. Many examples in the literature are found where a statistical relationship has been assumed to be causal. During the 1960s the birth rate in Sweden month by month showed a high correlation with the number of storks sighted! So any statistical relationship must be supported by an explanation of *why* this relationship might occur, and any extraneous influence that might affect the relationship. Underlying relationships can affect results. In a travel agent, the number of days absent was related to the number of holidays booked. Later, it was realised that the company specialised in skiing holidays, and both the pattern of booking and the absence was related to the underlying variable of the winter season.

## Time series and trends analysis

The most common way in which we predict the future is to extrapolate the past, yet this is fraught with difficulty and ever more so in a changing world. While some historical trends are enduring, such as the relationship between housing costs and incomes, there is considerable fluctuation in the short term. Other trends are cyclical, and in such cases there is often a tendency to overshoot in the forecasts. When the economy is doing badly, the slump is predicted to be longer than actually occurs, and similarly when the economy is doing well, the boom is predicted to go on longer as well.

Forecasts can be improved by smoothing the data, such as through a moving average or by weighting the most recent data. In an 'age of discontinuity', as Peter Drucker called it, many of our enduring trends change rapidly and radically, and no amount of smoothing of the data can improve the forecasts. Nevertheless, an extrapolation of past trends can at least provide a base case to show what would happen if all the underlying factors stayed the same.

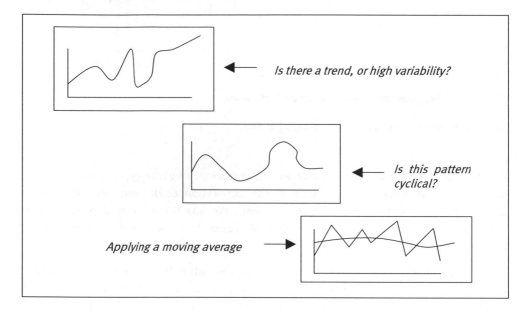

*Figure A16 / **Trends***

A more sophisticated approach than a straight-line extrapolation is to fit a curve to the data which can be represented by a mathematical expression. A classic example is the 'S' curve often seen in product life cycles (see Figure A12).

## Scenario planning and forecasting tools

Shell, the oil company, is widely credited with propounding scenario planning as a way of overcoming the over-emphasis on past extrapolation. The underlying assumption with many forecasting tools is that the future is lying there hidden waiting to be discovered, in the way that the natural sciences assume that nature is there to be discovered. This approach of looking at alternative scenarios is based on a different philosophical view.

In essence, scenario planning assumes that the future is not out there waiting to be discovered, but rather is the product of the myriad of decisions we and others round the world make today. If we examine these different ways the future might unfold, so we can begin to determine actions that will move towards a more desirable future and away from a less desirable one.

The key steps are:

- Determine the scope and timeframe of the project.

- Identify the current assumptions and mindset of the decision-makers. Clearly if you come up with scenarios that go against current thinking, they will need to be more convincingly argued.

- Create alternative, plausible scenarios of how the future may evolve, identifying key assumptions, signposts that might indicate which scenarios are more likely to emerge and critical decision points. There are some generic scenarios which are worth considering as part of a scenario plan: doing the same in a changing world, the best possible case, the worst possible case, catastrophe, and technological breakthrough which gives us a new way of working.

- Making decisions, such as which technology to back or location to move to, are fraught with dilemmas. The longer that options can be kept open, the greater the chance of getting the decision right, but the greater the chance also of missing some competitive advantage.

- In examining the assumptions, consider what PESTEL (see Chapter 3) factors are driving which scenario. You may wish to focus particularly on those factors that have high impact and are confidently predicted.

- Test the impact of key assumptions and other variables on the different scenarios.

- Develop action plans based upon:
  - The most robust solutions across all scenarios.
  - Strategies that leave options open until the most likely/desirable scenario is clear without foregoing competitive advantage.
  - Critical actions that promote the chance of the most desirable outcome.

Figure A17 shows scenario planning graphically.

## Validity and reliability of forecasts and estimates

Once, a forecast was presented in the following form:

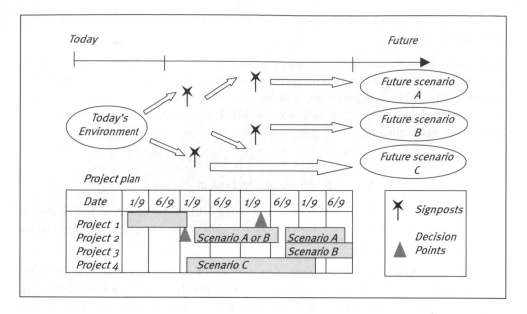

*Figure A17 / **Scenario planning***

> **We wish to invest £10,000 in a leadership programme and we estimate that as a result, next month we will be voted as a good place to work by our staff.**

This poses several problems and arouses at best scepticism:

- Is the outcome really a consequence of leadership training?

- What is the evidence that this level of investment will yield the result?

- Why do we think the effect will be as quick as next month?

If the following could be said:

> **We wish to invest £10,000 to improve retention. We have researched the reasons for turnover and find that the major cause is a lack of confidence in the leadership of the division. Our proposal is based on a leadership programme that has had good results elsewhere. An early test will be the staff opinion survey next month. This will give an opportunity to refine the programme or review whether it continues.**

The estimates are no less speculative, but at least they are supported by a clear argument.

In making statistical forecasts, errors are likely to be compounded and the effect can be dramatic quite quickly. In Figure A18, a forecast is made of labour turnover declining by 10 per cent per annum. The graph shows the effect of a 5 per cent and a 15 per cent reduction.

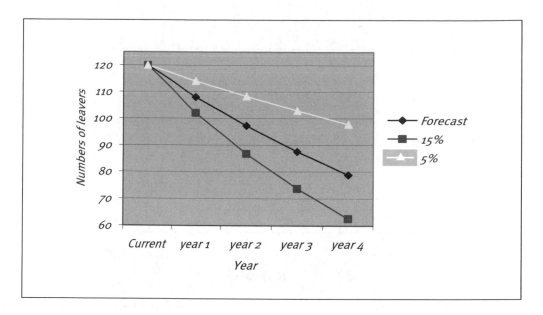

Figure A18 / *Labour turnover over time*

There is a 20.4 per cent variance by year four between highest and lowest estimates.

Whenever change from the current position is forecast, we need to describe what is driving that change. Sales rise because customers buy, costs rise because the organisation spends – why?

## Dealing with uncertainty

In a complex and uncertain world, no technique is going to be perfect. There are, however, statistical approaches that in some circumstances can help. See Figure A19.

### Point estimates

These relate to low complexity and low uncertainty. Where the variables are clearly known and the relationships explicit, an accurate forecast can be made.

*Example*

The forecast of school leavers in 2010 can be accurately forecast because those who will leave then are already in the school system. However even point estimates are based on assumptions that should be articulated clearly, such as the definition of 'school leaving age', actual school leaving age, immigration/emigration, mortality.

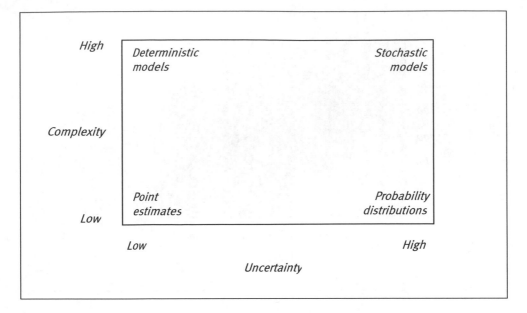

*Figure A19 / **Dealing with complexity and uncertainty***

## Deterministic model

These are used for situations of high complexity and low uncertainty. Where most of the variables are known, a model can be constructed that links all the parts together so that the implications of change in one part can be seen on the end result.

*Examples*

A model to identify the organisation's funding requirements for next year.

The staff planning system that links the railway timetable to the maintenance schedule for locomotives.

## Probability distributions

These are used in situations of high uncertainty and low complexity. Where incidents are of a random unpredictable nature, each event is impossible to predict, but with observation of these events over time a picture can be built of the probability of these events occurring.

*Examples*

News coverage teams work on probabilities of natural or artificially made disasters occurring in different parts of the world.

Market research organisations use probabilities of house moves occurring based on time of year and demographic factors ('baby boomers' and 'empty nesters').

### Stochastic models

Finally, these are used for a situation with high uncertainty and high complexity, where a series of events can be modelled by linking interconnecting probabilities. A statistical technique known as Markov chains is used as the basis for many of these models of social processes (Bartholomew 1967).

*Examples*

Predicting the spread of AIDS or new variant CJD

The media industry has explored different scenarios for its future using models based on probability estimates covering a wide range of elements (such as technology, competition and political factors).

### Delphi

This is an approach to harness the collective wisdom of many. Each individual is first asked for his or her opinion, and this is then given to others. They critique it and return it, encouraging the original individual to sharpen his/her argument. This process goes on until a consensus is reached of a set of clearly articulated positions, with the rationale of each laid out.

In its generic form, as Surowiecki (2005) has highlighted, collective intelligence brought to bear on a problem even when the participants have little or no knowledge of the subject in hand can dramatically improve the results.

## MEASURING CHANGE

## What is it?

These are techniques for identifying what has changed as a way of evaluating the benefit of interventions.

## How does it work?

The aim is to look for ways of detecting change by finding visible indicators. The experience curve, as the learning curve is sometimes called, can be used as an indicator and can be measured in several ways, such as the time taken to do a task, errors made or effort expended. For example, if the strategy calls for improvements in performance of key staff to be achieved by improved training, then a way of measuring the effectiveness of the training might be a comparison of the expected learning curve with the pay progression (see Figure A20).

Another approach might be to look at the breakeven between training and recruiting ready trained staff (see Figure A21).

The change might be measured by the variation in the trend of labour turnover over time, as in Figure A22.

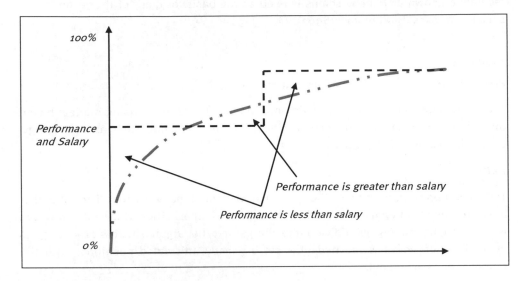

Figure A20 / **Evaluating training – method 1**

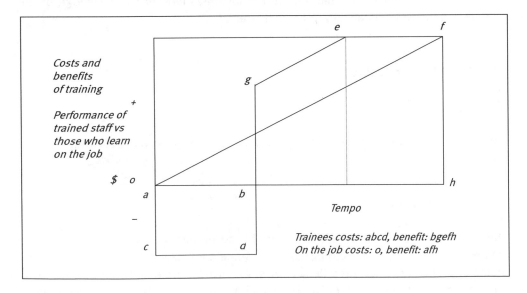

Figure A21 / **Evaluating training – method 2. Where is the breakeven point?**

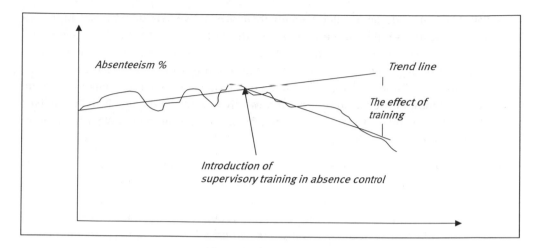

Figure A22 / **Evaluating training – method 3**

*Caution!*

We should not get so caught up in the need for measurement that we lose sight of the aim – to demonstrate whether we are achieving the requirements of the business plan for the organisation to be successful. If measures are not possible, seek indicators of whether the strategy is being delivered, possibly in the form of anecdotal cases.

## MILESTONE CHART

See **GANTT/milestone chart**, page 219.

## MODELLING

### What is it?

A model is a representation of reality. In business planning, a model seeks to represent the key features of a plan, usually in a computer, to allow sufficient experimentation and flexing to go on, and so avoid mistakes in the real world.

### How does it work?

The linking of human resource activity to subsequent business performance is a complex process, and requires a specific set of parameters to be derived for that business. Modelling essentially consists of three processes:

- *'What if'* analysis, also called 'sensitivity analysis', is where different scenarios are examined to see the consequences on the bottom line. 'What if the pay round costs 5 per cent instead of 4 per cent; what is the effect on the bottom line?' 'What if demand for the product is 80 per cent of the forecast what effect does that have on staffing numbers?' They can also be descriptive to encourage thinking in to the future. 'Imagine we had opened our new office, what would a typical day be like? Walk (in your mind) through the new office. Who do you meet? What is different from your current day?'

- *Probability analysis*, where the probability of different events occurring is examined. 'If the probability of getting approval for each of these pharmaceutical products is 0.5, 0.4 and 0.3, what is our best estimate of the number of staff we will need next year?' Complex statistical models using 'Monte Carlo' techniques can be used to establish a range of probabilities.[29] Another version of this approach to modelling emerges as a **decision tree**.

- *Combination analysis*, where the systematic array of all the permutations of a set of factors is examined to find the best set of circumstances. 'We have three teams, four projects, five sites and two methodologies. What gives us the best performance?'

There appears to be, so far, no universal organisational model, which will apply to all situations. Mercer HR consulting developed an organisational performance model, based on hundreds of studies in over 1,000 organisations where they identified six interconnected factors (CIPD 2005).

- **People** – *who is in the organisation; people's skills and competences, before and during their employment and the extent to which they apply firm-specific or generalised human capital.*

- **Work processes** – *how work gets done; the degrees of teamwork and interdependence among organisational units; and the role of technology.*

- **Managerial structure** – *the degree of employee discretion, management direction and control; spans of control, performance management and work procedures.*

- **Information and knowledge** – *how information is shared and exchanged among employees and with suppliers and customers through formal or informal means.*

- **Decision-making** – *how important decisions are made and who makes them; the degrees of decentralisation, participation and timeliness of decisions.*

- **Rewards** – *how monetary and non-monetary incentives are used; how much pay is at risk; individual versus group rewards; current versus longer-term career rewards.*

The aim of this model and others is to apply statistical, probabilistic equations linking changes in the above list to business outcomes, thereby allowing a business to see the impact of changes on the outcomes. Of course the success of any such model rests on the ability of the statistical relationships, often identified from historical data, to predict future patterns.

## 'NICILING'

### What is it?

'Niciling' is a tool for conflict resolution and is particularly useful in mediation. The mnemonic stands for:

- *N*eeds of each party.
- *I*mpact of each party's position on the other.
- *C*larify the source(s) of the conflict.
- *I*dentify and quantify the options and resources for resolution.
- *L*isten and learn to seek:
  - room to move
  - middle ground
  - win–win solutions.

### How does it work?

With the mediator between the two parties, each party is invited to express their needs. The mediator protects them from interruptions, so that they can vent their feelings as well as articulate their position. It is important to give them both equal airtime.

The next step is to get each side to listen to the impact it has on the other, again with each having an equal say. The mediator has to be careful to ensure even-handedness and to be showing no favour to either side.

After these two steps, some of the emotion in the conflict should have abated and the parties are beginning to understand the other viewpoint. The third step is to get them to agree on why they disagree. If there is agreement about something, then a bridge has been built that can be used for further progress.

The final step is to generate options for resolution, with the aim of looking for win–win solutions, or least those where neither side loses face.

## PROBLEM-SOLVING PROCESS

### What is it?

A set of steps that are designed to facilitate a group solving a problem.

### How does it work?

Below is a process that is a variation on a basic facilitation model and can be used with a group of those who have both an understanding of the problem together with those who have a stake in solving the problem.

### *Step 1*

Name the problem. Discuss it in the group to build a shared understanding. What are the symptoms of the problem?

### *Step 2*

Probe to identify what might be the underlying causes. Use *fishbone,* 'the five whys' or *root cause analysis*. Identify causes and effects. If appropriate use process mapping or flow-charting.

Some useful phrases:

- 'Describe the problem in detail step by step.'
- 'Imagine I know nothing …'
- 'What are the signs of this problem?'
- 'Under what conditions does this occur?'
- 'Who does it affect?'
- 'What are the consequences and particularly the unintended consequences?'
- 'What is stopping solving this problem?'

### *Step 3*

Identify the goal of your problem-solving. What does success look like? What is the ideal solution?

*Pause*

Insight often does not come instantly, but rather after some reflection and indeed relaxation (Archimedes was in his bath and Kekule was dozing in front of the fire).[30] Therefore allow the team time to stand back and reflect before moving on.

## Step 4

Identify possible solutions. Use brainstorming with flips or post-its.

Encourage broad thinking:

- 'What if money were no object?'

- 'What if you owned the company?'

- 'What would customers/suppliers/competitors suggest?'

- 'What would happen if we did the opposite of our current approach?'

## Step 5

Evaluate solutions. Use either multi-voting, selection grid or impact analysis.

## Step 6

Create an action plan that is:

- specific

- verifiable (how will we know if we have been successful?)

- time-bound

- where accountabilities are defined and discretions identified especially in respect of money to be spent.

## Step 7

Troubleshoot the plan to anticipate any obstacles. Use the *force field* or *contingency diagram*.

## Step 8

Establish a mechanism for monitoring and evaluating the plan. A variation of this goes under the mnemonic SCORE:

- *s*ymptoms

- *c*auses

- *o*utcomes desired

- resolution possibilities

- evaluation of effect.

## RISK ANALYSIS

### What is it?

Any business development is inherently risky, because of the unforeseen events that will occur. Risk analysis seeks to identify the risks, assess their importance and determine what can be done to manage risk appropriately. Risk assessment and control is briefly discussed in Chapter 6.

### How does it work?

No risk analysis is perfect; nevertheless, an analysis of some of the possible causes of variation is a useful exercise.

The degree of risk is a function of several factors:

- The impact of failure on the rest of the enterprise – financially, goodwill amongst customers or staff morale. Failure incurs costs from not achieving expected benefits as well as close-out costs such as redundancy costs of staff recruited.

- The opportunity costs associated with other projects that were foregone.

- The projected time before benefits accrue.

1. The first step in a risk analysis is the identification of the possible risks and their degree of severity. Use **SWOT** and PESTEL (see Chapter 3) to help. Look at external factors in the industrial or political arena, and internal human, financial and operational factors. Do not ignore the vulnerability that many projects have by relying on one or two key individuals.

2. Build a consensus about the possible scale of these risks and the impacts they may have. Consider using a *Delphi* technique (see **dealing with uncertainty** in the section on **methods of forecasting**).

3. Model the variables to see the impact on the bottom line of variation in each of these variables.

4. Where there are vulnerabilities, build as much flexibility as you can, by for example hiring staff on temporary or contract terms, renting space on short-term leases or buying currency forward to avoid exchange rate fluctuations. Flexibility of course comes at a cost, and a **cost–benefit analysis** will be necessary to see which options are worth doing.

5. Finally identify the worst-case scenario from **scenario planning**, plan how you would minimise the damage if this were to occur, and seek to ensure that the signposts for this possibility are closely monitored.

## ROOT CAUSE ANALYSIS

### What is it?

Problems can be manifested in many ways. If we react to what we find we may miss the real underlying cause. Root cause analysis seeks to get behind what is presented and get to the root.

### How does it work?

It was Albert Einstein who remarked, 'We will never be able to solve our problems at the same order of complexity we used to create our problems.' He was highlighting the problem of being locked into a mindset where it is difficult to step outside it and get a different perspective. One simple approach to root cause analysis is by asking a series of questions as in the box. Other more sophisticated approaches include Taproot[31] and cognitive mapping.[32]

---

### Root cause analysis

- *What* are the variances to plan? – the facts.

- *Why* have they occurred? – causes rather than apportioning blame (fishbone analysis).

- *When* did events happen/not happen?

- *How* has the problem occurred? – circumstances (force field analysis).

- *Where?*

- *Who* did/did not do what.

---

Solving problems is a process, and we engage different thinking processes at different stages of the process. Figure A23 describes the stages and suggests that when facilitating such a process, we need to signpost deliberately the mode of thinking we need participants to be in. See also **problem-solving**.

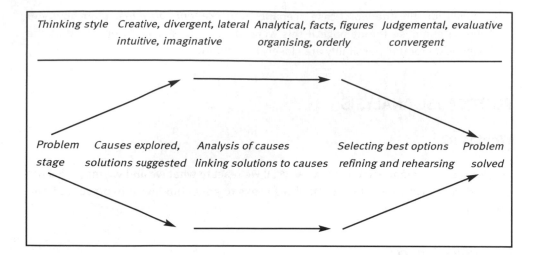

| Thinking style | Creative, divergent, lateral intuitive, imaginative | Analytical, facts, figures organising, orderly | Judgemental, evaluative convergent |
|---|---|---|---|

| Problem stage | Causes explored, solutions suggested | Analysis of causes linking solutions to causes | Selecting best options refining and rehearsing | Problem solved |

Figure A23 / **Problem exploration and resolution**

## SENSITIVITY ANALYSIS

See **modelling** and **risk analysis.**

## STAKEHOLDER ANALYSIS (SEE ALSO **INTEREST MAPPING**)

### What is it?

In any project there will be those who have some stake in its success or failure. There are inevitably winners and losers when change happens. Such losses and gains might be perceptual in nature, but no less real to the individuals concerned. Stakeholder analysis identifies those individuals and groupings that in some way are affected by the project, particularly those whom the project depends on for success. These people in turn may be dependent on the project for income, power or prestige, and so may seek to exercise some influence over the project's purpose, strategies and accomplishments.

### How does it work?

- *Step 1.* Identify the stakeholders

  At its simplest these can be identified by considering who stands to gain or lose from the project by using *interest mapping.*

- *Step 2.* Survey their views by interview or questionnaire on the following key themes:
  - Where does the proposed project impact you?
  - What do you expect the impacts to be?
  - If there are negative impacts, what are they? Can they be valued and how would you like the project to address them?
  - If there are positive impacts, what are they? Can they be valued and what could you do to support the project and its implementation?
  - What are the critical success factors?
- *Step 3.* Report the views by interest group.

Some views might be universal while others might be clustered across different lines than just 'supporters' or 'opponents'. In a project in Sarajevo to restore public broadcasting in Bosnia Herzegovina to a position of confidence amongst all the different factions to the conflict there, one group expressed the need for improved quality in the way everything was done. This group believed that only by improving each and every aspect of work could change be encouraged. They were disinterested in the project per se; rather they needed to see that their views of quality were incorporated in the outputs of the project.

These views might be presented in the form of a force field analysis.

## Force field analysis

A force field is an analysis of sustaining and restraining forces acting on an issue. For example, 'What are the things that are driving us toward solving this problem (sustaining forces)? Now, what is preventing us from solving this problem (restraining forces)?' See Figure A24.

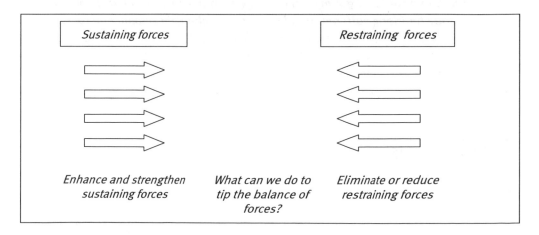

*Figure A24 / **Force field analysis***

Following identification of the forces, the next stage is to identify what can be done to tip the balance in favour of implementation, either by reinforcing the sustaining forces or by reducing the effect of the restraining forces. The aim is to build greater momentum and force for change.

Finally, one might consider ways of influencing these different groups. Cummings and Worley (1993) suggest three approaches: 'playing it straight, using social networks and going around the formal system'.

- Playing it straight involves identifying the needs of each group of stakeholders and presenting logic and information to show why they would benefit. Where they do not directly benefit, show why their acquiescence might benefit the whole company and so might limit their hostility or at least encourage their forbearance. Winning the respect of their superiors because of their altruism can be a powerful incentive.

- Social networks involve building alliances and coalitions to create sufficient support in the decision-making forums.

- Going round the formal system involves using the charisma and personality of the individuals involved to persuade others. However, the unintended consequences of such a strategy, such as a general flouting of the procedures, may be more serious.

In the case in the box all three were deployed:

> *I really believed in this new project to move towards a broad banding pay system, so I first made sure that all the senior managers had the facts and figures to show the impact on their people. I arrayed the benefits that would accrue in terms of more flexibility and replayed some familiar cases to show what would have happened. In addition, I got my old colleagues in the commercial division on my side as they had long suffered in failing to recruit the right people due to our old rigid pay system and they lobbied the commercial director on my behalf. At the board meeting I really pulled all the stops out to charm them and show my enthusiasm for the project.*

## SWOT ANALYSIS

### What is it?

Initial questions that many may ask of a business case are: 'Why this proposal? Where does it come from and how is related to the needs of the business?' As we have seen already, one answer is in relation to the vision, mission, strategy and goals of the organisation. One tool that helps to focus on where effort should be placed is a SWOT analysis – strengths, weaknesses, opportunities and threats. It helps to summarise and focus attention on the key issues. It is also convenient shorthand in talking about plans within an organisation.

## How does it work?

*Table A14 / SWOT analysis*

| Where the issues mostly arise | (What we plan to do) | |
|---|---|---|
| Internal | **Strengths**<br>(Build on them) | **Weaknesses**<br>(Fix them) |
| External | **Opportunities**<br>(Watch out for them and seize where you can) | **Threats**<br>(Be vigilant<br>Build defences) |

It is a good deal easier to build on strengths, and therefore they should be leveraged as much as possible in any plan. After all, those strengths probably have arisen as a result of a combination of skills, efforts and good luck built up over the years, and represent a facet of your organisation that may well differentiate you favourably from your competitors. Strengths can lie in a strong brand, cost advantages, skilled workforce, flexible culture, intellectual property or location.

Clearly weaknesses have to be addressed. However, even if they are not explicitly addressed they need to be allowed for in any implementation planning.

## Example

A department was implementing a new IT system. It had had a history of always being late in introducing new systems, and on this occasion recognised the weakness and put more effort into careful planning. A more disciplined process of change management kept the department on track, and ensured that variations to the original specification, which had hampered it in the past, were kept to a minimum. To be on the safe side, the project manager in putting forward the business case for the project had allowed considerable time for testing and implementation and incorporated some generous allowances for slippage.

Weaknesses can come in many forms, for example: low skill levels, limited distribution, slowness to adapt to change, blame culture, management that disempowers the workforce and does not get the best from them.

Strengths and weaknesses invariably are associated with internal factors. Externally there are threats and opportunities. Threats are always present for any organisation.

A charity that dealt with the rehabilitation of drug addicts believed that the need for rehabilitation was such that their work would always be required. However changes in government funding, coupled with a change in the pattern of individuals' charitable giving, resulted in a severe loss of income and subsequent closure.

The most dangerous time for any business is when it is successful and believes that there is nothing threatening it. Changes in markets, consumer habits, currencies, not to speak of world events such as disasters both human-made and natural, occur to every organisation. Each one of these has the potential to threaten the very existence of a business. New entrants to markets are often discounted at first, leaving them to become established. In the beginning of the Internet, online shopping was largely ignored by the major retailers, who saw this as a fringe activity for a specialised niche of customers. None would do so now.

Threats can come in many forms, and with markets being global, from many places. The consequence of the events of 9/11 had many unforeseen consequences in business. A manufacturer of penknives used to sell them successfully through duty free shops in airports. Overnight the business collapsed.

Opportunities similarly can be everywhere. A good start is to scan the environment (see analysing the environment in Chapter 2) where one is looking for:

- New technologies that you are currently not exploiting.

- New markets – geographical as well as new products or services that might be provided. 'Man's wants are unlimited' as one famous marketing maxim went.

- New skills or under-utilised skills and talents.

- New political shifts such as enlargement of the EU or changes in government policy.

- Changing market structure amongst competitors. Particularly, consideration needs to be given to the new entrants into the market place and analysis of what they are doing that you are not.

An opportunity like 'improving customer service' really is indicating a weakness – poor customer service – so a clear analysis of why it is a weakness in the first place needs to occur before the opportunity is a realistic prospect.

## Limitations

While it is a widely used tool, SWOT analysis does have several disadvantages. Hussey and Jenster (2003) argue that those who are asked for their SWOTs invariably have only a limited perception of the issues. Indeed if you asked people externally to the department or business, they may come up with very different lists. In addition, the closer you are to an issue, the less you can see it dispassionately. You may easily overlook something of great significance to others. It is also easy to confuse what *was*, what *should be*, what *might* be, what *could* be with what *is*.

Bob Empson (2003) urges users of a SWOT to be specific. 'Our people' is not specific enough to know what gives competitive advantage. Strengths such as these can easily disappear overnight if they are not nurtured and maintained, so it is important to understand clearly what characteristic is the strength so it cannot be lost. He also suggests that long lists can inhibit clarity and prevent focus on the issues that are really important. As he says: 'Its very simplicity can also lead to mistakes in its development and use, with consequently flawed strategic decisions.'

Clearly some of the ways to deal with these problems is by way of ensuring that one compares and contrasts the views of several people, that long lists need to be prioritised and not forgotten when the action plans are formulated, and that headline statements are underpinned with more thorough analysis. It may also help to have an external facilitator who can ask some of the hard questions of the group.

# TIMELINES

## What is it?

A timeline is a simple technique for identifying the sequence of activities. This might be the first rough introduction to a more sophisticated approach of project management such as *Gantt charts* or network diagrams.

## How does it work?

It consists of a line marked by relevant time intervals with key milestones on it. Figure A25 shows an example of a project team installing some new equipment.

# VALUE CHAIN ANALYSIS

See **cost analysis tools,** pages 208–209.

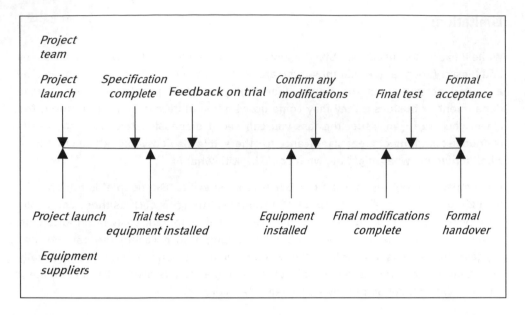

Figure A25 / **Timeline analysis – an example**

# Notes

## Chapter 1

1    *People Management*, 8 November 2001.

## Chapter 2

2    This principle was first propounded by Aristotle and articulated in the nineteenth century by the German philosopher Hegel, with a process of 'thesis, antithesis and synthesis'. It is known as the 'Hegelian dialectic' and is the foundation of the scientific method.

3    Myers-Briggs Type Indicator and FIRO B are psychometric instruments. See www.CAPT.org for details of MBTI. FIRO B is available for licensed users from OPP at www.opp.co.uk

## Chapter 3

4    Triangulation is an approach towards social enquiry where more than one method is used to verify the findings. See Flick (1998).

5    An earlier version of this mnemonic was PEST, but modern concerns about the environment and the complex legal structure in which business has to operate have lead to PESTEL.

6    The rate of return hurdle is the interest rate on capital, often expressed in the payback period that new investment must achieve if it is to be approved. It could be argued that it should be the rate at which a business can borrow money on the open market. However, most businesses will set a much higher rate than this, as the market will expect the performance of the business in terms of return on capital to be significantly higher than borrowing rates.

7    Ethical trading Initiative at www.ethicaltrade.org

8    Sarbanes-Oxley refers to US legislation on corporate governance and reporting introduced after the Enron and World Com scandals.

9    An employee assistance programme (EAP) provides staff with the opportunity to talk confidentiality to a counsellor, often by telephone, and in some cases face to face, about any problem they may have. The company pays a premium per head of the staff population and receives a general report about the use of the service, but no individual details about what was discussed. The suggested benefits lie in happier staff, less absenteeism and so on.

10   The Hawthorne effect is so called after a famous early experiment in increasing productivity. Whatever the researchers did, productivity went up, until they realised that it had little to do with the new work methods, but rather it was as a result of the motivational effect of being observed.

## Chapter 4

11   The comment was made in the newsletter of the Manpower Society in 2005.

12   See a text like *Guide to business planning* by Friend and Zehle (2004) for further details on accounting conventions. They have produced a business planning model that can be downloaded from www.guidetobusinessplanning.com

## Chapter 5

13   Psychologists call this process 'cognitive dissonance', first suggested by Festinger in 1957.

14   Based on template at:www.ogc.gov.uk

15   TUPE – provisions relating to employment rights on the transfer of an undertaking are contained in the Transfer of Undertakings (Protection of Employment) Regulations 1981 (SI 1794), as amended by the Transfer of Undertakings (Protection of Employment) (Amendment) Regulations 1987 (SI 442), the Trade Union Reform and Employment Rights Act 1993, the Collective Redundancies and Transfer of Undertakings (Protection of Employment) (Amendment) Regulations 1995 (SI 1995 No. 2587) and the Collective Redundancies and Transfer of Undertakings (Protection of Employment) (Amendment) Regulations 1999 (SI 1925).

16   IIP – Investors in People. ISO 9000 is the international quality standard.

## Chapter 6

17   St Francis of Assisi is sometimes credited with a famous prayer which sums up this

principle: 'God give me courage to change the things that can be changed, humility to leave alone those things that cannot, and wisdom to know the difference.'

18  Private conversation with Roger Niven, The Management Coach House. www. tmch.org

19  Reported in the *International Herald Tribune*.

20  Myers-Briggs – see note 3.

21  Pecuniary spillover occurs when a cost or benefit arises without any changes in the input or output of the situation. For example, a factory that finds that demand for its products doubling because of a fire at its competitors is not creating new wealth. It is not using its plant or capital in a novel way to gain advantage. The extra demand is entirely fortuitous and the total demand in the market is the same. Pecuniary spillover is continually affecting organisational performance, making the measurement of the net effect of any improvement to the organisation's productive capacity hazardous.

22  Balaam's ass: in the fable the donkey starved because it could not decide between two equally attractive bales of straw.

23  Occam's razor is named after the fourteenth-century logician and Franciscan friar, William of Occam, who stated that entities should not be multiplied unnecessarily (it was originally stated in Latin). This has since become a principle in scientific enquiry, stated as 'When you have two competing theories which make exactly the same predictions, the one that is simpler is the better.'

24  The Abilene paradox is named after a story of a father who took his children to the ice cream parlour in Abilene because he thought he should be a good father. The children were happy playing but they felt they should go to respect their father. Their mother who had been busy doing something felt she should not be absent at a family outing, so she went along too. On reflection none of them had actually wanted to go to Abilene.

## Chapter 7

25  These points are suggested by David Clutterbuck in his course for the CIPD on marketing the HR function.

26  See a text book on organisation development such as *Organisation development* by French and Bell (1999) for further information on appreciative enquiry.

## Appendix

27  www.saratogainstitute.com

28  Industry data often in the form of key ratios can be found from companies like Dun

and Bradstreet, ValuationResources.com or BizMiner.com. See *Perfect financial ratios* by Gasking (1993) for a helpful text on ratio analysis. See also DTI United Kingdom Benchmarking Index. www.dti.gov.uk/support/ukbi.htm

29  See the *Economist guide to business modelling* (Tennant and Friend 2005) for a fuller treatment.

30  Kekule first discovered the structure of benzene as a ring of carbon atoms, when he was on holiday in the Hertz Mountains.

31  www.taproot.com

32  See Decision Explorer from Banxia software.

# References

ARMSTRONG, M. (1992) *HRM – strategic action*. London: CIPD.

BAKAN, D. (1966) *The duality of human existence*. Boston: Beacon.

BARNEY, J.B. (1991) Firm resources and sustained competitive advantage. *Journal of Management,* Vol. 17, No. 1.

BARTHOLOMEW, D.J. (1967) *Stochastic models for social processes*. Chichester: Wiley.

BECKER, B.E., HUSELID, M.A. and ULRICH, D. (2001) *The HR scorecard – linking people, strategy and performance*. Boston: Harvard Business School Press.

BOWMAN, C. (2004) *Talk at the Cabinet War Rooms*, 20 September.

BURKE, W. and LITWIN, G.H. (1992) A causal model of organisational performance and change. *Journal of Management*, Vol. 18, No. 3, pp523–545.

CALAS, M.B. and SMICICH, L. (1999) Post modernism? Reflections and tentative directions. *Academy of Management Review*, Vol. 24, No. 4, pp649–671.

CANNON, J.A. (1979) *Cost effective personnel decisions*. London: IPM.

CANNON, J.A. (2004) Moving into self-employment. Unpublished PhD thesis, London University.

CAPALDO, G. and ZOLLO, G. (1994) Modelling individual knowledge in the personnel evaluation process. In: J.R. Meindl, J.F. Porac and C. Stubbart (eds), *Advances in managerial cognition and organisational information processing*. Vol. 5, pp275–313, London: Elsevier.

CIPD (2003) *Human capital: external reporting framework*. London: CIPD.

CIPD (2005) *Human capital: an internal perspective*. London: CIPD.

COFFEY, A. and ATKINSON, P. (1996) *Making sense of qualitative data: complementary research strategies*. London: Sage.

CUMMINGS, T.G. and WORLEY, C.G. (1993) *Organisation development and change*. Cincinnati: West Publishing.

CZARNIAWSKA, B. (1998) Who is afraid of incommensurability? *Organisation*, Vol. 5, pp273–275.

EISENHARDT, K.M. (1999) Strategy as strategic decision-making. *Sloan Management Review*, Spring.

EMPSON, R. (2003) *SWOT revision: the review*. London: White Maple consulting. www.whitemaple.net

FINCH, B. (2001) *How to write a business plan*. London: Kogan Page.

FISCHOFF, B. (1975) Hindsight and foresight: the effect of outcome knowledge on judgement under uncertainty. *Journal of Experimental Psychology: Human Perception and Performance*, Vol. 1, pp288–299.

FLICK, U. (1998) *An introduction to qualitative research*. London: Sage.

FRENCH, W.L. and BELL, C.H. (1999) *Organisation development*. New Jersey: Prentice Hall.

FRIEND, G. and ZEHLE, S. (2004) *Guide to business planning*. London: Economist.

GAMBLING, T. (1974) *Human resource accounting and manpower planning*. Research paper. Birmingham: University of Birmingham.

GASKING, T. (1993) *Perfect financial ratios*. London: Century.

GILES, W.J. and ROBINSON, D.F. (1972) *Human asset accounting*. Report by the IPM/ICMA working party. London: IPM.

GIOIA, D.A. and PITRE, E. (1990) Multi-paradigm perspectives on theory building. *Academy of Management Review*, Vol. 15, pp584–602.

GUBA, E.G. and LINCOLN, Y.S. (1994) Competing paradigms in qualitative research. In: N.K. Denzin and Y.S. Lincoln (eds), *Handbook of qualitative research*, pp105–117. Thousand Oaks, CA: Sage.

GUEST, D. (2000) *Effective people management*. London: CIPD.

HAMMERSLEY, M. (1996) The relationship between qualitative and quantitative research: paradigm loyalty versus methodological eclecticism. In: J.T.E. Richardson (ed), *Handbook of qualitative research methods for psychology and the social sciences*. Leicester: British Psychological Society.

HAMMOND, J.S., KEENEY, R.L. and RAIFFA, H. (1998) The hidden traps in decision making. *Harvard Business Review*, September/October.

HARTIGAN, J.A. and WIGDOR, A.K. (1989) *Fairness in employment testing: validity generalisation, minority issues, and the general aptitude tests battery*. Washington: National Academy Press.

HEKIMIAN, J.S. and JONES, G.H. (1967) Put people on your balance sheet. *Harvard Business Review*, Vol. 5, No. 1.

HEMPEL, G. (1966) *Philosophy of natural science*. New Jersey: Prentice Hall.

HENWOOD, K.L. (1996) Qualitative inquiry: perspectives, methods and psychology. In: J. Richardson (ed), *Handbook of qualitative research methods for psychology and the social sciences*. London: British Psychological Society.

HUFF, D. (1991) *How to lie with statistics*. London: Penguin.

HUSSEY, D. and JENSTER, P. (2003) *Turning intelligence into success*. CBI series in practical strategy. Chichester: Wiley.

ICMA and IPM (1974) *Human asset accounting*. Report of the joint ICMA and IPM working party. London.

*Investment appraisal* (1967) London: HMSO.

JICK, T. (1983) Mixing qualitative and quantitative methods: triangulation in action. In: V. Maanen (ed), *Qualitative methodology*, pp135–148. London: Sage.

JOHNSON, G. and SCHOLES, K. (2001) *Exploring corporate strategy*. New York: Prentice Hall.

KAPLAN, R.S. and NORTON, D.P. (1996) *The balanced scorecard: translating strategy into action*. Boston: Harvard Business School Press.

KEARNS, P.T. (2005) *Evaluating the ROI from learning*. London: CIPD.

KEMP, V. (2001) *To whose profit*. Godalming: WWF.

KINGSMILL REPORT (2003) *Accounting for people*. London: DTI.

KOTLER, P. (1999) *How to create, win and dominate markets*. New York: Free Press.

KUBLER-ROSS, E. (1969) *On death and dying*. New York: Macmillan.

KUHN, T.S. (1996) *The structure of scientific revolutions*. Chicago: University of Chicago Press.

LEONARD-BARTON, D. (1992) Core capabilities and core rigidities: a paradox in managing new product development. *Strategic Management Journal*, Vol.13.

MACHIAVELLI, N. (2005) *The Prince*, translated by Peter Bondanella. First published 1514. Oxford: Oxford World Classics.

MANPOWER SOCIETY (2005) *HR benchmarking handbook*. London: Manpower Society.

McCLELLAND, D. (1987) Characteristics of successful entrepreneurs. *Journal of Creative Behaviour*, Vol. 21, No. 3, pp219–233.

MINTZBERG, H. (1993) *The rise and fall of strategic planning*. New York: Free Press.

NATHAN, R. (2005) *Career counselling*. London: Sage.

NUTT, C. (2005) Communication to Manpower Society members.

OECH, R. von (1992) *A whack on the side of the head: how you can be more creative*. Menlo Park: Creative Thinking.

OWEN, F. and JONES, R. (1994) *Statistics*. London: Pitman.

OXTOBY, D. (2005) *Effective business planning.* Presentation at the Grange Holborn Hotel, London, 11 May.

PEARN, M. and KANDOLA, R. (1993) *Job analysis.* London, IPM.

PETERS, T. (1991) *Thriving on chaos – handbook for a management revolution.* SOS Free stock.

PHELPS, M. (2002) *Human resources benchmarking.* London: Gee.

PONTEROTTO, J.G. and GRIEGER, I. (1999) Merging qualitative and quantitative perspectives in a research identity. In: M. Kopala and L. Suzuki (eds), *Using qualitative methods in psychology.* Thousand Oaks: Sage.

PORTER, M.E. (1980) *Competitive advantage.* New York: Free Press.

PORTER, M.E. (1996) What is strategy? *Harvard Business Review,* November/December.

RICH, S.R. and GUMPERT, D.E. (1985) How to write a winning business plan. *Harvard Business Review,* May/June.

ROBBINS, S. (2003) *Decide and conquer: make winning decisions to take control of your life.* London: FT Prentice Hall.

RUCCI, A.J., KIRN, S.P. and QUINN, R.T. (1998) The employee-customer-profit chain at Sears. *Harvard Business Review,* Vol. 76, No. 1, p90.

SCARBROUGH, H. (2003) *Human capital external reporting framework: the change agenda.* London: CIPD.

SILCOCK, H. (1954) The phenomena of labour turnover. *Journal of the Royal Statistical Society.*

SILF, M. (2004) *On making choices.* Oxford: Lion.

SILVERMAN, D. (1993) *Interpreting qualitative data.* London: Sage.

SPENDOLINI, M.J. (1992) *The benchmarking book.* New York: AMACOM.

STUTELEY, R. (2002) *The definitive business plan.* London: Prentice Hall.

SUROWIECKI, J. (2005) *The wisdom of crowds.* London: Abacus.

TENNANT, J. and FRIEND, G. (2005) *The Economist guide to business modelling.* London: Profile.

TROMPENAARS, F. (1999 ) *Riding the waves of culture.* London: Nicholas Brealey.

ULRICH, D. (1996) *Human resource champions: the next agenda for adding value and delivery results.* Boston: HBR Press.

VROOM, V.H. AND YETTON, P.W. (1973) *Leadership and decision-making.* Pittsburgh: University of Pittsburgh Press.

WEICK, K. E. (1995) *Sensemaking in organizations.* London: Sage.

WHEATLEY, M.J. (1999) *Leadership and the new science.* San Francisco: Berret-Koehler.

# Index